ZAMBIA

PROFILES • NATIONS OF CONTEMPORARY AFRICA
Larry W. Bowman, Series Editor

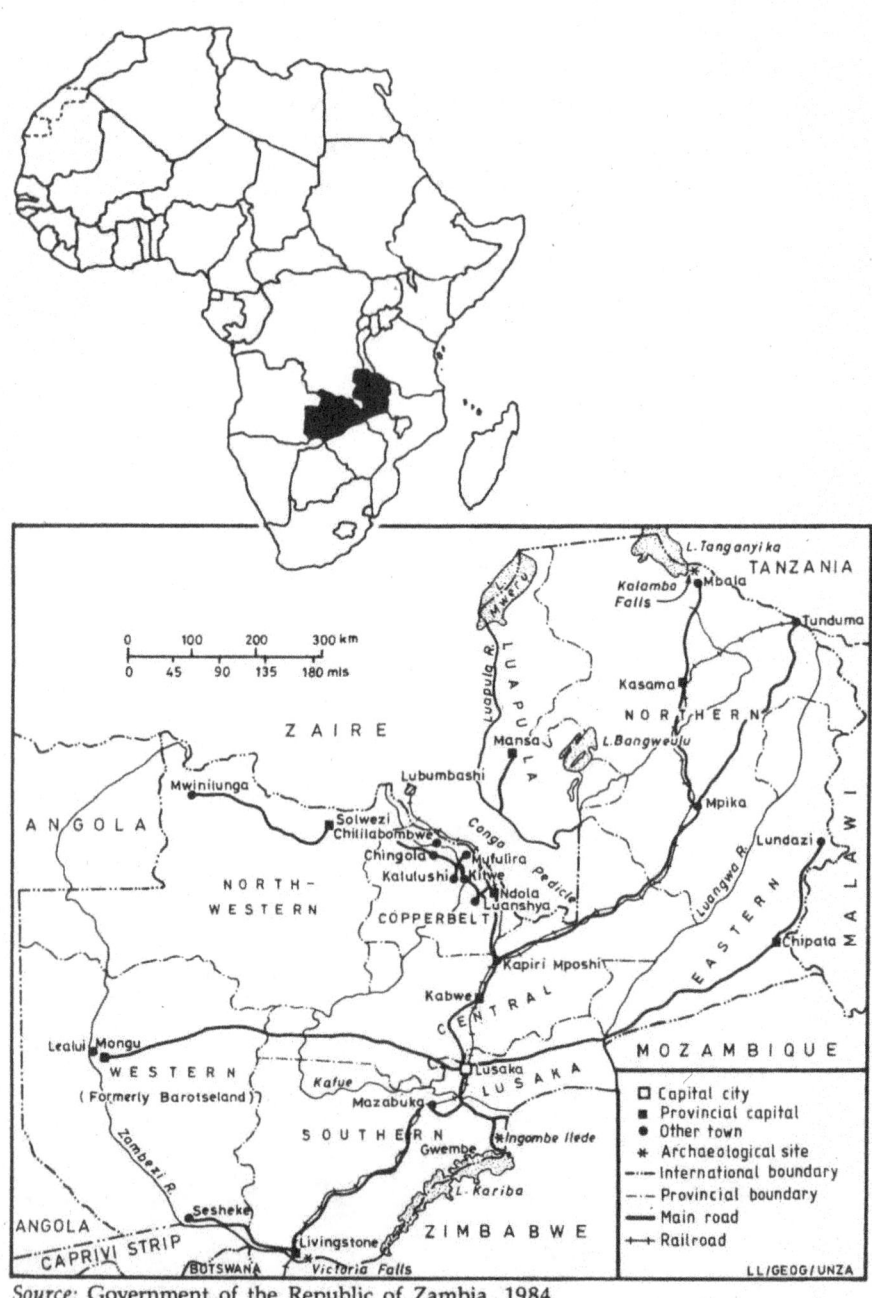

Source: Government of the Republic of Zambia, 1984

The Republic of Zambia

ZAMBIA

Between Two Worlds

Marcia M. Burdette

First published 1988 by Westview Press, Inc.

Published 2021 by Routledge
605 Third Avenue, New York, NY 10017
2 Park Square, Milton Park, Abingdon, Oxon OX14 4RN

Routledge is an imprint of the Taylor & Francis Group, an informa business

Copyright © 1988 by Taylor & Francis

All rights reserved. No part of this book may be reprinted or reproduced or utilised in any form or by any electronic, mechanical, or other means, now known or hereafter invented, including photocopying and recording, or in any information storage or retrieval system, without permission in writing from the publishers.

Notice:
Product or corporate names may be trademarks or registered trademarks, and are used only for identification and explanation without intent to infringe.

Library of Congress Cataloging-in-Publication Data
Burdette, Marcia M. (Marcia Muldrow)
  Zambia: between two worlds/Marcia M. Burdette.
    p. cm.—(Profiles. Nations of contemporary Africa)
  Bibliography: p.
  Includes index.
  ISBN 0-86531-617-1
  1. Zambia. I. Title. II. Series.
DT963.B87 1988
968.94'04—dc19   87-27957
                                                                                                                        CIP

British Library Cataloguing in Publication Data
Burdette, Marcia M.
  Zambia: between two worlds.—(Profiles:
nations of contemporary Africa).
  1. Zambia—Social conditions
  I. Title II. Series
  968.9'404   HN800.Z3
ISBN 0-566-00770-3

ISBN 13: 978-0-3672-1390-9 (hbk)
ISBN 13: 978-0-3672-1671-9 (pbk)

To John and our son, David

Contents

List of Illustrations and Tables xi
Preface xiii

1   Introduction   1

2   The Historical Context   5
    Geography, 5
    Human Settlement and Precolonial History, 6
    European Penetration and Domination, 11
    Toward Independence, 27
    Conclusion, 32

3   Society and Culture   34
    Village to Town, 35
    Cultural and Social Transformation, 37
    Urban Geography, 52
    Transformation of the Extended Family, 55
    The Role of Women, 56
    Religion and Traditional Medicine, 59
    Conclusion, 62

4   The Political Economy of the First Republic, 1964-1972   64
    Restructuring the Political System, 65
    Presidentialism, 75
    Humanism and Socialism, 77
    Restructuring the Economy, 78
    The Changing Social Bases of Society, 92
    Conclusion, 94

| 5 | **The Political Economy in Decline, 1973–1985** | 95 |

1973 to Early 1975: The Downturn Begins, 96
Politics in a One-Party State, 104
Mid-1975 to 1980: The Mines Falter, 110
Intraclass Struggles, Corruption, and the
    Atrophy of UNIP, 114
From 1981 Through 1985: The Crisis Deepens, 117
Zambia's Waltz with International Lenders, 122
Sources and Signs of Opposition, 127
Conclusion, 131

| 6 | **Zambian Foreign Policy** | 133 |

Regional Geopolitics, 133
Zambia's Predicament and Policies, 1964 to
    Mid-1975, 134
Regional Foreign Policy, Late 1975 Through 1985, 139
Zambia and South Africa, 143
Zambia, the Frontline States, SADCC, and the PTA, 145
Zambia in Third World Affairs, 149
Zambia and the Superpowers: Nonalignment, 155
Conclusion, 159

| 7 | **Zambia's Future, Zambia's Choices** | 160 |

Appendix A: Glossary   171
Appendix B: Abbreviations and Acronyms   172
Notes   174
Selected Bibliography   191
Index   197

Illustrations and Tables

Photographs

2.1	Victoria Falls	6
2.2	Kariba Dam	7
2.3	*Litunga* entering canoe	10
2.4	Old mine on the Copperbelt	16
2.5	Old man playing bowed instrument	21
3.1	Musician outside traditional house	36
3.2	Young couple undergoing a traditional wedding ceremony	45
3.3	Bemba water jars and their maker	50
3.4	Lozi basket with lid	51
3.5	Picketing miners' wives, 1981	58
3.6	A seamstress	60
3.7	A bishop and pastors of an apostolic church	61
4.1	Anode casting plant	88
5.1	President Kaunda's official portrait	108
5.2	Worker pulling cobalt starting sheets	112

Figures

4.1	Copper prices, 1963–1972	79
5.1	Copper prices and terms of trade, 1973–1983	101

Maps

	The Republic of Zambia	*frontispiece*
2.1	Human migration and settlement	8

6.1	Road and rail routes	135

Tables

2.1	Group organization of the major mines in the mineral industry until December 31, 1969	18
3.1	Percentage distribution of population in provinces, 1963, 1969, and 1980	38
3.2	Population by nationality and citizenship, 1969 and 1980	39
3.3	Income distribution	43
4.1	Major events in the First Republic, 1964–1972	66
4.2	Student enrollments, 1964–1982	67
4.3	Medical facilities, 1964–1982	68
4.4	Chronology of John Mwanakatwe	72
4.5	Contribution of copper industry to GDP, revenue, and exports, 1963–1972	80
4.6	Growth of the manufacturing sector, 1954–1967	81
4.7	Important dates in the economic reforms of 1968–1972	86
5.1	Major events in the Second Republic, 1973–1986	97
5.2	Copper and cobalt prices, production, exports, and value of exports, 1973–1984	99
5.3	Contribution of copper industry to GDP, revenue, exports, and value of exports, 1970–1983	102
5.4	Chronology of an opposition national politician, Simon Kapwepwe	105
5.5	Chronology of the president, Kenneth D. Kaunda	109
5.6	Marketed production of some selected crops, 1979/80–1983/84	119
5.7	Central government expenditures by functional classification, 1980–1984	121
5.8	Zambia's transactions with the IMF, 1971–1983	123
6.1	Zambia's trade with South Africa, 1970–1979	143
6.2	Zambia's creditors as of December 31, 1984	156
6.3	Zambia's trade with selected countries, 1982	157

Preface

When I undertook to write this general introduction to Zambia, two questions came to mind. Why should I, not a Zambian citizen, write this book? Second, how could I write a general study of Zambia when my own research has focused on mining, manufacturing, and foreign policy? Some self-justification always enters answers to such questions, but I will attempt here to review briefly my state of mind and intentions.

Certainly a Zambian scholar would bring particular depth and sensitivity to a study of his or her society. I hope that not many years will pass before such a person is able to find the time, space, and financial backing to write such a book. Until then, it is possible that a sympathetic outside observer can collect information and put forward impressions that are valuable to the ongoing discussion of why Zambia is in the predicament it is and where Zambia is bound. I have attempted to write this book in such a way as to aid the average North American or European reader (not the specialist) to understand Zambia and the dilemmas faced by that society and its leaders. As my writing concluded in late 1985 many new events, such as auctioning of the country's foreign exchange, were just in the process of unfolding, so I could only touch on those circumstances in this book. Studies to follow will tell the tale of their effects.

How should I tackle complex questions about culture, women, and peasant agriculture when what I really know best are aspects of urban political economy, specifically the mines and manufacturing industries? I drew liberally on published and unpublished materials available mostly in Zambia, which the reader will find cited in the notes to the chapters. To interpret this mass of material, I benefited from discussions with researchers and staff of the University of Zambia and the Institute for African Studies. Intellectually, I found this a most satisfying and stimulating exercise, as it helped me place my knowledge of the industrial sector in its complex social setting. Studies of agriculture and local politics were particularly helpful in avoiding the myopia that comes from focusing only on the modern industrial sector and the current market imbroglio. I followed up this interest with trips to some far-distant villages where I gained a better sense of life beyond the urban one. The new insights I gained there infused some optimism into my overall rather bleak vision of the political economy now and in the near future. The enthusiasm, creativity, and generosity of the "common man and woman" permit me to hope that Zambians will find a way out of the current economic doldrums other than simply "muddling through" tied to the visions of the foreign aid donors.

In the five years that it has taken me to write and revise this book, I have received great help and support from many friends and colleagues. Foremost is my husband, John Saxby, whose kind words were often matched with a keen eye for detail and a sharp editor's pencil. Many a weekend he took care of our energetic son, David, so that I could write in peace. The editor of the series, Larry Bowman, has been a constant support, and the staff of Westview Press has been understanding of the particular problems facing an author completing a manuscript in a Third World setting. Thanks are due to the Institute for African Studies, which kindly allowed me to be a "squatter" in their offices while the vital early chapters were churned out. Many friends helped me at various stages and with a variety of skills. Special mention should be made of Bonnie Keller, Kaye Turner, and Stephen Chan who took time from their busy schedules to listen to me talk about various topics, to read drafts, and to comment critically on them. Ilse Mwanza and Susan Antkiewicz added their thoughtful remarks as they typed drafts of the chapters. An old friend, Mwesa Mapoma, enlightened me on various nuances of Zambian music, art, language, and popular culture, while other colleagues at the University of Zambia—Owen Sichone, John Chileshe, Gilbert Mudenda, and Axon Kanduza—introduced me to many complex topics. The cartographers of the university's Geography Department, Liomba Liomba and Aleck Musitini, demonstrated that given a minimum of foreign imported items, they can produce good quality maps and charts. Patrice Communal and Gisela Geisler were most generous with their photographs, as was the professional artist Tom Hill. The Zambia Information Services' photographic library provided many historical and modern black-and-white prints that I have used in this book. Finally, my students at the university were a source of ideas and encouragement. Especially helpful were the students in my course on industrialization and development. Always good-natured about my experimenting with ideas and readings, these young scholars also critically posed questions and complexities to some oversimplistic assumptions. To all the above I owe a debt of gratitude. Of course, any and all mistakes and misinterpretations are this author's sole responsibility.

Marcia M. Burdette
Harare, Zimbabwe

1
Introduction

To the visitor new to Central Africa, Zambia and its peoples present a set of confusing and intriguing impressions. After stepping off the airplane, train, car, or bus, one is immediately confronted with a country that seems to mix together European and African realities. In the rural areas, roofs are of thatch, roads are dirt paths, and the way of life is pastoral and rather slow. As one approaches the urban centers and the mining towns, the houses are brick with tin or shingled roofs, roads are tarred, and the pace of life approximates any medium-sized Western city. In the capital itself, Lusaka, visitors are often heard to exclaim, "this doesn't seem like Africa at all!"

These two realities exist side by side in modern Zambia and sometimes give the observer the false impression that there really are two separate worlds in Zambia. Yet the people in the rural and urban settings are not distinct—their histories and their families are intertwined. And the future of the country is bound up in the balance to be struck between the countryside and the city, between mining and agriculture.

Zambia has some of the richest deposits of copper and cobalt in the world. Gigantic industrial mines have until recently been premier exporters of high-grade copper to industrial economies of the West as well as Japan and China. To add to that great resource advantage, Zambia has the reputation of being one of the most stable countries in Africa. As of 1987 it boasted the same chief executive since independence in 1964, Dr. Kenneth D. Kaunda. Zambia has had regular elections, a civilian government, and no successful coup d'états to date. The first decade of independence was a period of prosperity and hope. The new government proclaimed its commitment to a brand of socialism and then invested heavily in social welfare programs, which improved the lives of many Zambians. The copper price was high and money was available for an ambitious national development plan as well as for comfortable living by the new black elite. A tumultuous period of multiparty politics (1964–1972) was followed by apparent internal stability with the promulgation of one-party rule in 1972.

In the mid-1970s this calm and prosperity began to give way to growing economic difficulties, greater social inequalities, and dislocation. Although potentially one of the strongest economies in the region, by 1985 when this study concluded, Zambia was experiencing a serious economic decline from which recovery is not at all assured. From 1974 to 1980 the gross domestic product (GDP) per capita declined by 52 percent.[1] Private consumption shrank by 21 percent from 1975 to 1979. The mines, which had provided much of the state's revenues until 1974, now contributed little to the nation's treasury.[2] Yet in the midst of this economic crisis, the rich grew richer. According to an International Labor Organization (ILO) study the richest 5 percent of the population by 1976 controlled 35 percent of total incomes;[3] by 1985 the accumulation of wealth in the hands of a few was even more extreme. What happened to the mineral-based economy that caused such a rapid decline? How in the face of the rhetoric of socialism and the reality of many social welfare programs had Zambian society fragmented into such extremes of wealth and poverty?

Signs of political discontent surfaced in the 1980s, starting with an attempted coup d'état in 1980 and marked by constant murmuring against the regime. The electoral system continues to be plagued by growing apathy among voters, indicated by a declining party membership though masked by enforced voter registration campaigns. Within government, the executive steadily accumulates power, the focal point of rule is more and exclusively the president, his advisers, and personal office. Despite these political signs of stress and the overall economic crisis, the country remains stable. Why is this so? What does the future hold in a system where there is no well-defined successor to the president or opening for legal opposition? In the 1980s several prominent Zambians became involved in the international drug trade; former members of the government were investigated and detained for their involvement. What within the Zambian elite encourages such activities? Why, in light of their considerable personal wealth, do they become involved in this illegal and dangerous form of international commerce?

At independence Zambia followed the development orthodoxy of the day and attempted to industrialize using an import-substitution strategy. This strategy is based on the notion of limiting imports by supplying those needs internally, thus constructing factories to supply intermediate and final consumer goods to the population and other industries. This seemingly logical strategy has left Zambia in the 1980s with a desperately under-productive network of state-owned companies, many of which are permanent lossmakers, with most operating way below capacity. What went wrong with this approach? Do the prescriptions of the "Aid Doctors" (the World Bank and International Monetary Fund (IMF) primarily) hold much hope for the ailing manufacturing sector of Zambia?

In 1975 Zambia was one of the few non–oil exporting nations with a substantial balance-of-payments surplus.[4] By 1985 the country was deeply in debt and behind in repayment of interest on the external loans. Foreign suppliers were threatening to cut the country off and politicians were forced to invoke some rigorous and unpopular policies in order to try to keep the economy afloat on IMF loans. What happened in this decade to drive Zambia from a comfortable international trading position into international debt peonage? Why do international banks think it worthwhile to keep Zambia afloat?

Although Zambia is known to have great agricultural potential, tsetse infestation, unreliable rainfall in certain areas, and high internal production costs have slowed down the development of commercial agriculture. Beginning in 1975 President Kaunda and other political leaders began proposing a "back to the land" policy, arguing that Zambia's future is in agriculture. Given that this is supposed to have been the government policy for over a decade, why has so little development taken place in agriculture? As of 1985 a few hundred large commercial farmers (many of them expatriates) still provide most of the food for the towns, while the bulk of the peasant producers only service the familial and local markets. Between 1979 and 1981 over 30 percent of the annual marketed maize (the staple food) needs for Zambia were supplied by imports.[5] What lies behind this inability or lack of desire to reorient the economy toward agriculture, especially with the pressures in that direction from external aid agencies? How likely is it that Zambia's leaders can successfully encourage people to turn to peasant farming?

Much of the discussion of Zambia's achievements and problems centers on the personality of President Kaunda. Not only has he dominated domestic politics since 1964 but he is also the symbol of Zambia's complex and contentious foreign policies. President Kaunda has become an important Third World spokesperson, but he has great difficulties in diplomacy close to home. With the nation located in the cauldron of racial and regional wars in southern Africa, Zambia's leader has attempted to maintain a fragile balance between warring parties and also act in accordance with Zambia's own economic needs. Of prime importance have been trade and transport links; a constant factor has been ambiguous relations with the regional giant South Africa. Officially, the government has always taken a strong stance against the immoral apartheid policies of the Afrikaner leaders. More quietly, Zambia has traded extensively with the Republic of South Africa. In the early 1980s, when certain of the economic restraints connected to the struggle for Zimbabwe had been removed, the Zambians seemed to be drawing closer still to their announced enemies. In late 1985 the shops in Lusaka were filled with goods made in the Republic of South Africa. What is the nature of Zambia's relations with South Africa? Do the new regional pacts, such as the Southern African Development Coordination Conference (SADCC) or the Preferential Trade Agreement (PTA) offer Zambia greater flexibility in developing economic alternatives to ties with Pretoria?

This book attempts to answer some of these questions by tracing details of policies and allocations of funds in some cases and in others by discussing battles over policies. To answer the more interesting questions, I turn to the key features of the political economy and the nature of the class that runs Zambia, whom I call the "governing class" to distinguish it from an external "ruling class."[6] In such new societies, the full outline of a class configuration is as yet quite hazy, but the nature of the local dominant class already affects the making of policy and also helps explain the intractability of some of the problems Zambia faces. The social basis of the unions in Zambia is explored to understand the evolution of early politics and the reasons for the fragmentation of the nationalist alliance. Finally, the plight of the peasants and the urban poor is discussed as a sad outcome of policies since independence. I begin with a review of Zambia's precolonial and colonial history to set the context of the complex social fabric of the nation and the uneven and distorted development of the economy.

2
The Historical Context

The different peoples of modern Zambia have long and important, though separate, histories. Zambia was not a "nation" as defined by common language, kinship, political authority, or geographical distinctiveness until it was pieced together by British mercantile interests in the late nineteenth century. In the prior four centuries, the economic life of the region had been gradually reoriented to external markets. Yet the nation's ethnic groups lived in relative isolation, one from another. In the eighteenth century, those who controlled the external markets drained the region's wealth in the form of minerals, capital, and labor. Initially the foreign powers were Arab, Swahili, and Portuguese; later the British brought the area under direct colonial rule. The bulk of this chapter explores the era of British rule, broken into three separate periods extending from 1890 to 1963. A review of modern Zambian society, however, requires a brief survey first of the geography of the country and then of the precolonial histories of the peoples found within its modern territorial delimitations. Finally, the period of European penetration is examined in which to varying degrees, through different economic mechanisms and under different political dispositions, the modern Zambian political economy was oriented toward the external markets of the Western industrial states and South Africa.

GEOGRAPHY

The resolution of European disputes over colonial boundaries in the late nineteenth century left Zambia with its modern butterfly shape, which encompasses two distinct wings of the country: the northwest, west, and south in one wing and the northeast and central areas in the other (see *frontispiece*). Despite this arbitrary division, most of the outlines of the country follow the geographical lay of the land. The Zambezi and Luapula rivers and lakes Mweru, Kariba, and Tanganyika all form international boundaries. Situated high on the great central African plateau, most of the land undulates at 4,000 feet above sea level. Beautiful waterfalls and river valleys cut into this plateau but are hidden far away from the main roads. The country is most famous for the spectacular Victoria Falls and the man-

PHOTO 2.1 Victoria Falls.

made Lake Kariba that divide present day Zambia and Zimbabwe (see Photos 2.1 and 2.2).

A large wedge is sliced out of central Zambia. This is the Congo or Katanga Pedicle, product of an agreement struck among British and Belgian colonialists and private commercial speculators in the early years of the twentieth century. As a result, Zambia shares with Shaba Province of Zaire (formerly Katanga of the Congo) some of the richest copper- and cobalt-bearing ores in the world. Zambia's peculiar shape also means that the country has eight immediate neighbors—Zaire, Angola, Namibia (South-West Africa), Botswana, Zimbabwe, Mozambique, and Malawi. The peoples of central Africa have been arbitrarily assigned to these different countries, and their long migrations have diminished, although not totally ended.[1]

HUMAN SETTLEMENT AND PRECOLONIAL HISTORY

Humans and their ancestors lived in central Africa close to half a million years ago. Archaeological digs at Kalambo Falls in the extreme northeast and Victoria Falls region in the south are rich with evidence of humans in the Early Stone Age as well as the Middle and Late Stone ages. The remains of the famous Broken Hill Man were found in 1921 at a mine site in Kabwe on the central plateau. This almost complete human skull

THE HISTORICAL CONTEXT

PHOTO 2.2 Kariba Dam connecting Zambia and Zimbabwe, with Kariba Lake to the right, and a section of the power station on the hill on the Zimbabwean side.

may be over 125,000 years old. According to archaeologist Brian Fagan, however, agriculture, cattle, and metal tools were common only in the past two thousand years.[2] He has suggested that a combination of tsetse fly (antithetical to cattle rearing), shortages of good grass during the long dry season (April to November), and problems of clearing tropical hardwood forests kept the land relatively underpopulated and hindered much prehistoric migration to Zambia.

Iron Age cultures were fairly widespread in Zambia by about A.D. 500.[3] The pottery record suggests that some of the present cultures of northeast, central, and southern Zambia, and the present inhabitants, are at least partly descended from people who established themselves in the region nearly a thousand years ago.[4] A "Tonga Diaspora" early in the second millennium brought the ancestors of the modern Ila and Tonga into the southern lands (see Map 2.1[a]). A grave site discovered at Ingombe Ilede in the south that included objects of gold, as well as copper, iron, and ivory, indicated the emergence of groups distinguished by wealth and social status and provided the first clear sign of long-distance trade between central and southern Africa and the east coast in the fourteenth or fifteenth century. These Iron Age societies were later overrun by intruders.

Today's six million Zambians are, for the most part, descendants of relatively recent migrants to the area. Between 1500 and 1800 the northern, eastern, and western parts of Zambia were settled by Lunda and Luba

MAP 2.1 Human Migration and Settlement, A.D. 1500–1900

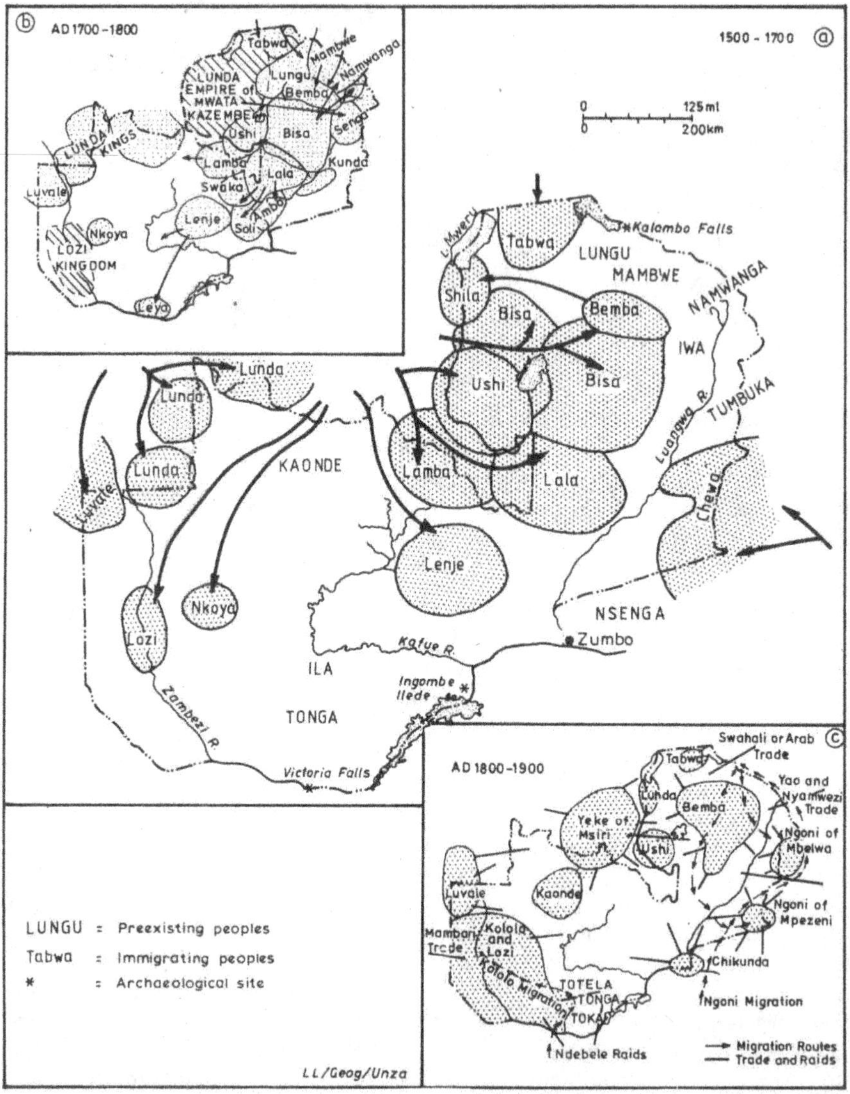

Source: Adapted from H. W. Langworthy, *Zambia in Maps*, ed. by D. Hywel Davies (London: University of London Press, 1971), p. 33. Reprinted with permission of Edward Arnold Ltd. and D. H. Davies.

[Luvale] peoples of Congolese origin who introduced traditions of chieftainship and established several important kingdoms.[5] The Lunda Empire of the powerful Mwata Kazembe appeared in the Luapula Valley in the early eighteenth century. The chief's control of the transcontinental trade made Kazembe well known to Arab and Portuguese traders. By the end of the eighteenth century, however, Kazembe faced a contending power to the east, the Crocodile Clan led by Chitimukulu.[6] This ritual warrior chief shaped the people now known as the Bemba into a thriving confederation. Bemba warriors raided their neighbors and participated in the long distance and regional trade between the Luangwa River and Lake Mweru[7] (see Map 2.1[b]).

The two kingdoms developed a complex pattern of alliances and control of diverse economic activities. Kazembe, for example, encouraged clans to mine and smelt copper and iron ore, making ingots for sale to other tribes or traders. Others engaged in commercial trade in salt, ivory, and slaves in return for beads, cloth, and guns, trading with Portuguese and mestizo merchants who sold to Saudi Arabia and Europe copper, gold, and ivory mined and sometimes processed in the interior.[8] Later, Kazembe's dynasty established a profitable trade in slaves and ivory with Arab and Swahili traders from Zanzibar and the coast, and with the Nyamwezi and Yao of western Tanzania. Although the Bemba also traded in salt and ivory, they were more famous as slave raiders. By the 1870s or early 1880s they had brought much of the Bisa, Lungu, and Tabwa territory (formerly Kazembe's tributaries) under their control (see Map 2.1[c]).

Eventually competing claims over trade and tribute brought the Bemba and Lunda political organizations into conflict. Wars between them contributed to the devastation wrought by the slave trade. Throughout the 1800s the peoples of the region fell prey to raiders and slavers—the Arabs and Swahili from present-day Tanzania and Malawi, and the allies of the Portuguese on the coasts. By 1870 Kazembe's kingdom was in serious decline, but the looser Bemba confederation preserved much of its power until the late nineteenth century.[9]

Compounding the effects of the slavers' depredations were the incursions of warrior nations from the south. For much of the nineteenth century, central and southern Africa was buffeted by an outpouring of peoples from South Africa, fleeing the conflicts of Boer and Zulu over land and cattle (*mfecane*). The northern march of the Ngoni, forced out of Natal, brought them across the Luangwa River valley to the edge of the Bemba confederacy. After a series of battles with the Bemba between 1850 and 1870, the Ngoni settled in the country of the Chewa- , Nsenga- , and Tumbuka-speaking peoples of the east and south.

The history of the west is dominated by the Lozi, whose ancestors also appear to have come from the Congo.[10] Peoples claiming common Lozi heritage migrated into the area and imposed their rule over the preexisting population around the late seventeenth century. Their economic and political systems were more sophisticated than those of the earlier peoples. Using

PHOTO 2.3 The *Litunga* of the Lozi people entering canoe as part of the *Kuomboka* ceremony, Western Province.

labor-intensive cultivation of the Bulozi floodplain of the upper Zambezi River, they drained and cultivated much of the land. When the floodplains were inundated, the people migrated en masse to higher ground in a ceremony called the *Kuomboka* (see Photo 2.3). Their comparatively sophisticated feudal political structure was based upon a centralized kingship (the *litunga*) with close tributary relations to minor chiefs and a bureaucracy made up of commoners. The political unity of the Lozi proved quite fragile, however. It shattered under the pressures of a second warrior nation, the Kololo (or Makololo), coming up from the south.

Led by Sebitwane, the Kololo conquered the Lozi in stages from 1840 to 1850 and left a linguistic imprint of the Sotho language of South Africa on Silozi. In 1864, however, the Lozi dynasty was restored under a new *litunga*, Lewanika. No sooner had Lewanika consolidated his position than he had to contend with both a fierce intrusion from the south by the Ndebele and harassment by Portuguese and mestizo agents from Angola.

By the final decade of the nineteenth century, major migrations had transformed the human geography of the area and left a complex and heterogeneous society, economic links with the transcontinental trade, and new forms of political organization. Perhaps the most important political innovation was the institution of chieftaincy. Here too there was considerable diversity. Some chiefs—called paramounts—were major political actors and ruled large kingdoms. Other chiefs were minor officials, little more than village headmen. According to Elizabeth Colson, the Tonga had no chiefs or other forms of authority before the advent of colonial rule.[11] Although most people lived under the rule of a chief at the start of the twentieth century, the power and significance of that political form varied greatly. One heritage of this diversity is that the peoples who compose modern-day Zambia have historically distinct concepts of political authority and legitimacy.

The lack of a common political and social history and shared institutions did not mean economic isolation or backwardness. Rather, as we have seen, precolonial Zambia combined the fact of social diversity with varying degrees of incorporation into continental and even world trade. The very processes that created that diversity, however—the upheavals of migrations, wars, and the slave trade—rendered those societies vulnerable to another intruder.

EUROPEAN PENETRATION AND DOMINATION

Indigenous economic and political structures could not repel the concerted efforts of white adventurers, missionaries, traders, and mercenaries who closed in on central and southern Africa at the end of the nineteenth century. Portuguese explorers had penetrated the region as far back as the late sixteenth century. By the late nineteenth century missionaries had established missions, big game hunters were visiting, and itinerant traders like George Westbeech were active in Barotseland in the 1870s. The most famous early European, David Livingstone, crisscrossed most of modern Zambia between 1854 and 1873. His lurid descriptions of the slave trade set off a wave of missionary fervor in Britain. The effects of these early whites, however, were limited in comparison to those of European agents obtaining land and mineral rights.

By the 1880s, an imperialist "scramble for Africa" was in full force. Portuguese agents hoped to link together their colonies of Mozambique and Angola through the lands of the upper Zambezi. King Leopold II of Belgium, personal ruler of the Congo Free State, looked southward from his colony for more territory. The Germans established a colony in Tanganyika (now Tanzania); in 1884 they annexed South-West Africa (now Namibia). The European powers met in Berlin in 1884-1885 to set the ground rules for dividing the continent. In the scramble for colonies that followed, little or no consideration was shown for the African peoples' sensibilities or their rights to the land, except insofar as the European agents could claim title to these lands from the marks of local chiefs on pieces of paper.

For the British, the interests of the other European powers in the central African plateau threatened their own imperial designs for the southern portion of the continent. British imperialists, eager to control the presumed mineral wealth of central Africa, demanded sovereignty over the area north of the Boer republics (the Transvaal and the Orange Free State) in South Africa. In addition, they sought to forestall possible Boer-German hegemony over the central part of the subcontinent. Gladstone's Liberal government, however, would not pay for the extension of British power. So the challenge was picked up by the millionaire Cecil John Rhodes.

Rhodes had come to South Africa at the age of sixteen for health reasons. He made his fortune from the diamond mines of Kimberley. By 1887 Rhodes and his partners in De Beers controlled much of the world's diamonds and began to expand into gold mining. Rhodes dreamed of establishing British dominion over the lands from the southernmost tip of the continent to the Mediterranean through a "Cape to Cairo Railroad." He was particularly interested in gold reefs reported to lie north in Katanga (now Shaba Province of Zaire).[12] Zambia lay between. Thus began the era of white domination that lasted for sixty-five years, the consequences of which Zambia lives with today.

Company Rule, 1899–1924

Rhodes and his partners used dubious treaties and force to establish their claims over the region north of the Limpopo. In 1888 Charles Rudd, acting on commission from Rhodes, obtained the signature of the Ndebele paramount, Lobengula, granting the British merchants rights to all the minerals in Matabeleland, the southwest of modern Zimbabwe. On the basis of the Rudd Concession, the British Crown gave the newly formed British South Africa Company (BSAC) a charter to develop all the lands "north of the Transvaal and west of the Portuguese possessions." The imperial government appeared to be prepared to subcontract the business of establishing British control if it could save money by so doing. With the backing of the British Crown, representatives of the BSAC fanned out over the region seeking the marks of local chiefs or headmen, granting the company concessions over the lands and the minerals that lay beneath.

The BSAC acted in the worst tradition of chartered companies of the Crown in the nineteenth century. Diplomacy, trickery, trade, and force were all used to obtain concessions. Local political leaders were led to think that the company men were direct emissaries of the British queen. Often they made what they considered military alliances against their enemies. Frequently, they signed away land rights believing that the newcomers would simply settle locally as so many peoples had done before only to find that the BSAC claimed exclusive ownership of the land. The spurious legality of the Lochner, Thomas, Sharpe, and Wiese treaties was the vehicle for British imperial interests in the race to control the lands between the Zambezi and Katanga. These treaties paved the way for later colonization and claims over the minerals, which lasted into the 1960s.

Treaties between the contending European powers defined Zambia's modern borders. An Anglo-German accord in 1890 gave Germany access to the Zambezi River via the Caprivi Strip in the extreme southwest and established the northeastern border with Tanganyika. King Leopold II and the British government delimited the Congo/Rhodesia frontiers in 1894, giving the Belgians the Katanga lands "whose 'pedicle' nearly cuts Northern

Rhodesia in half."[13] Arbitration in 1905 of the Anglo-Portuguese Convention of 1891 finalized the western border, which excluded parts of Lewanika's kingdom and granted these lands to Portugal's colony of Angola. This area later became Northern Rhodesia in homage to the individual whose driving will (not to say megalomania) was instrumental in the land's incorporation into British and South African spheres of influence.

Although these treaties and concessions accorded the BSAC considerable formal authority over the lands that became Zambia, resistance to company rule by African peoples and their leaders made the reality quite different. For example, the Bemba paramount refused to sign any treaties and rejected the whole notion of foreign control. Not until 1899 did the company succeed in extending its authority over Bembaland by force. Large-scale resistance was also mounted by the Ngoni in 1898 and culminated in their defeat and the loss of vital cattle herds. More generally, company rule ended the regional systems of trade in ivory, slaves, guns, salt, and copper. This, and the company's forceful subjection of peoples like the Ngoni, effectively ended the economic bases of existing kingdoms.

BSAC administration, once the company armies and police forces had established its supremacy, was characterized by neglect. As the real objects of Rhodes had been to exploit Katanga and the gold reefs of Mashonaland (in today's Zimbabwe) and to forestall other European powers, administering the vast territory was a low priority. "The British South Africa Company's territory north of the Zambezi was very much an appendage to its real seat of power in Southern Rhodesia. Seen from that vantage point, Northern Rhodesia was simply an awkwardly shaped piece of debris resulting from Rhodes's failure to obtain Katanga."[14] In 1891 Harry Johnston was appointed by the British Crown to oversee the lands, although he was in fact British commissioner and consul-general based in Nyasaland (now Malawi) and had his hands full fighting the Yao slave dealers. Not until 1895 did the company strengthen its administrative structures. True company rule began with the practical decision in 1899 to split the huge and sprawling territory into North-Eastern Rhodesia and Barotseland-North-Western Rhodesia. The Kafue River was the dividing line between the territories; the country was united and named Northern Rhodesia in 1911.

Initially Northern Rhodesia appeared to be a bad investment for the BSAC. The copper deposits, made up of deep-lying sulphide ores, could not be mined profitably at that time.[15] A lead mine began operation at Broken Hill (now Kabwe) in 1902 but did not offset the administrative expenses to control the vast territories. These inauspicious early indicators proved correct: For the period of company rule, the BSAC paid no dividends to its shareholders. In his study of the BSAC, Peter Slinn suggested that the company directors wanted to find a way to make the lands pay for themselves, while retaining the company administrative powers and consolidating its mineral rights.[16] The directors resolved first to turn Northern Rhodesia into a reserve of cheap labor serving the white-owned mines and farms of the region. Second, Northern Rhodesia was to be opened up to a limited amount of white settler farming. Last, the territory would be administered as cheaply as possible with a minimal administrative framework made up of a handful of whites, relying on African chiefs to enforce decisions. Barotseland was to have a special status that gave the *litunga* and the chiefs some political autonomy and economic rewards.

During the company's rule, its officials put an end to formal slavery (by 1912), but recruiting agents from Southern Rhodesia and Katanga scoured the land looking for able-bodied young men to work under conditions only slightly above forced servitude. To gain income and generate labor, the BSAC administrators levied a "hut tax" on the local people. This meant that each family had to pay a tax each year. Adult men had to work for wages in the few white-owned businesses or farms in the territory or find employment outside in order to pay their taxes. Others willingly migrated in search of adventure and new opportunities.

The company also sold land to a few white farmers, both to offset costs and to encourage European or South African settlement. From 1903 onward, good farming lands were alienated from the Plateau Tonga in the south and the Ngoni in the east. Other areas were affected indirectly. Although Barotseland proper was immune from land seizure because of its special treaty status, the Lozi economy was undermined nonetheless as recruiting agents and chiefs struggled over available labor. The delicate floodplain agricultural system declined with the loss of male labor. When epidemics of anthrax and pleuropneumonia decimated Lozi herds of cattle, the other mainstay of the economy contracted rapidly too.

Slowly the lands were incorporated into South African and European economic systems. In 1904 the railroad from Southern Rhodesia was extended across the Zambezi River just below Victoria Falls into the north. Built through the central strip in the north, by 1910 it connected Livingstone to Elizabethville (now Lubumbashi), the capital of Katanga. Robert Williams, another of Rhodes' associates, both backed this railroad extension and launched Tanganyika Concessions Ltd. (TANKS) whose prospectors pegged Kansanshi mine on Zambia's Copperbelt. As Williams also held a share in the Katanga mining company, Union Minière de Haut Katanga (UMHK), he promoted the extension of the rail line to tap those flourishing copper mines in order to obtain revenues for the BSAC was well as to supply the Congo mines with cheap coal and coke from Wankie Colliery in Southern Rhodesia. Almost as a sideline, this railroad linked Northern Rhodesia to the south. No one knew at this time the full degree of the mineral wealth on the southern side of the Katanga syncline. Nonetheless, the railroad began the process of economic incorporation of the lands north of the Zambezi into the South African and British economies. The following year, 1911, the new capital for a united Northern Rhodesia was placed at the southernmost town, Livingstone, near Victoria Falls and the railroad bridge. A more typical colony was forming with white administrators and settlers arriving. Not surprisingly, these changes held implications for the political life of the territory.

The white population was never more than a handful in company days. In 1921 the 3,634 resident whites[17] included administrators, missionaries, settler farmers, and a tiny sprinkling of businessmen. The settlers' politics revolved around their relationship with the largest white population to the south (Southern Rhodesia and South Africa) on the one hand, and with the company on the other. For the former, the principal question was whether or not to join a union or to form a closer association with the southern territories. For the latter, settlers questioned their limited representation within the administration (as the "unofficials") and the company's monopoly over land rights.[18] BSAC directors were not receptive to any requests that lessened their power or cost them money. As it was, the company directors were eager to avoid their existing financial commitments for administering Northern Rhodesia because the territory was still not making money for them.

In 1922 the settlers in Southern Rhodesia held a plebiscite and voted for "responsible (self) government," opening the way for the transfer of Northern Rhodesia to the British Colonial Office two years later. In the transition, the company wisely held on to its mineral rights to the northwest and thus to further claims over the lands that became the fabulously rich Copperbelt. Promises to African chiefs and headmen were lost in the shuffle of papers on European desks.

British Colonial Rule, 1924–1952

The British government administered Northern Rhodesia from 1924 to 1952, aiding the establishment of a large-scale copper industry that by the 1940s was exporting sizable amounts of raw materials and capital. The "Cinderella" colony more than paid for itself by 1952. In the early days, however, colonial officials had to decide how to control the vast territory and preferably how to make it pay for itself. Despite the marked increase in white population (from 3,634 in 1921 to 13,846 in 1931),[19] to rule the expansive lands directly with so few white officers and settlers must have appeared both expensive and impractical. In 1931 the colonial authorities adopted the doctrine of "paramountcy of native interests," which by definition was never honored, but which gave an ideological cover to a modified system of indirect rule. Under this system the protectorate of Northern Rhodesia was to be governed by a combination of British colonial civil servants and "Native Authorities," consisting of chiefs, headmen, and their advisers. In many ways, indirect rule was simply a recognition of the limitations of British authority and was based on traditions of obedience and respect for the existing local political leaders. Furthermore, it helped the colonial authorities preserve the rural areas as reservoirs of labor and saved money by having the existing political authorities collect taxes and extract that labor. For the tiny white population, an executive council (made up of colonial officials) and a legislative council (partly elected) were introduced. Both lines of administration (African and white) were headed by the governor appointed by the British Crown. Barotseland continued under its own unique semiautonomous administration.[20]

PHOTO 2.4 Old mine on the Copperbelt of Zambia.

The first governor of the protectorate, Sir Herbert Stanley, wanted to promote as much white immigration as possible. Despite the supposed paramountcy of native interests, more land was alienated from the Africans and reserved for exclusive European (white) use. As we shall see, this land alienation involved around 60,000 Africans and made for serious hardships for the Lamba and the Plateau Tonga (along the line of rail) as well as the Ngoni and Chewa of the east. Their suffering proved unnecessary as most of the whites who came to the protectorate during the Crown's rule went to the burgeoning Copperbelt.

The Development of the Copperbelt. Freebooting exploration at the headwaters of the Kafue River and the Kafue "Hook" by rather small-scale speculators and prospectors in the first quarter of the twentieth century had left the country with a multitude of small claims (see Photo 2.4). A few individuals stood out for their endurance and farsightedness. Edmund Davis (later Sir Edmund), an Australian by birth, was at the center of six separate exploration companies. An associate of Rhodes and later a director of the BSAC, Davis was chairman of Bwana Mkubwa Mine, the first copper mine in Northern Rhodesia (located near modern-day Ndola). He helped open the first lead and zinc mine at Broken Hill (modern-day Kabwe) in 1902. Perhaps his most significant contribution, however, was to encourage the BSAC directors in 1923 to allow exclusive mineral prospecting rights to new large-scale syndicates with the capital and technical expertise necessary to develop the minerals of the Copperbelt.

The transfer of administrative authority from the company to the colonial office coincided with a technical breakthrough that made the mining of Northern Rhodesia's copper enormously profitable. By the late 1920s new financiers and speculators had created a maze of companies to prospect for Northern Rhodesia's minerals, especially its "red gold," copper. They introduced a flotation process[21] that made the area's sulphide ores exploitable; then technological change led to a financial consolidation of the industry and profoundly affected the economic life of Northern Rhodesia, the British Treasury, and the BSAC.

By 1928 the early mining concerns were consolidated into the hands of a few individuals. Two groups of companies became paramount in the copper industry of Northern Rhodesia, although it was not until the 1940s that they truly monopolized the area. One company in particular, the Anglo American Corporation of South Africa Ltd. (AAC or Anglo), controlled by the Oppenheimer family, was vital in the development of the Copperbelt mines and hence the linkage between Northern Rhodesia and South Africa.

Ernest Oppenheimer (later Sir Ernest) seemingly inherited the mantle of Cecil Rhodes as a diamond and gold king.[22] Arriving in South Africa as the twenty-one year old representative of a diamond concern, he launched the AAC in 1917 to develop new gold mines. Later he gained the chairmanship of De Beers as well as a seat on the board of Barclays Bank. In 1923 he looked northward to the Rhodesias for more investment opportunities. His companies purchased interests in the new mining ventures forming there. Subsequently, these shares were transferred to a new company, the Rhodesian Anglo American Corporation Ltd. (Rhoanglo), incorporated in Britain in 1928. Through complex and sometimes devious share swapping, Anglo became the largest individual shareholder in the BSAC, which in turn held a sizable stake in Rhoanglo. Sir Ernest and his partners played their cards and capital very skillfully. By the 1930s Anglo had a double claim on revenues from Northern Rhodesia from dividends on profits made by Rhoanglo mines at Broken Hill, Rhokana, Nchanga, Bancroft (now Chililabombwe) and Bwana Mkubwa (see Table 2.1) and indirectly from royalties paid by the mines to the BSAC and then dispersed among its shareholders, one of which was Anglo.[23]

The only real competitor to Davis and Oppenheimer was Alfred Chester Beatty. An engineer by trade and U.S. citizen by birth, Beatty drew together British and U.S. venture capital in 1914 and incorporated Selection Trust in Britain in order to develop various mineral companies overseas. Selection Trust bought into the promising Bwana Mkubwa mine, and in the early 1920s Beatty cooperated with Oppenheimer to float another company. Between themselves they convinced the BSAC directors to subdivide Northern Rhodesia (outside Barotseland) "into six vast [concession] areas, each bigger than a European principality."[24] This brief period of cooperation, however, was followed by a longer era of intense competition.

TABLE 2.1
Group Organization of the Major Mines in the Mineral Industry until December 31, 1969*

Anglo American Corporation of South Africa Ltd. (AAC or Anglo) founded in 1917 in South Africa

    Rhodesian Anglo American Corporation Ltd. (Rhoanglo; founded in 1928; renamed Zamanglo)
        Bancroft Mines Ltd. (opened 1957; now Chililabombwe)
        Nchanga Consolidated Copper Mines Ltd. (opened 1939; now Chingola Division)
        Konkola Mine (opened 1957; part of Nchanga in 1986)
        Rhokana Corporation Ltd. (opened 1932; now Nkana Mine)
        Broken Hill Mine (opened 1902; 1940 for underground processing; now Kabwe)
        Bwana Mkubwa Mine (opened 1913; closed, reopened 1970)
        Kansanshi Mine (opened 1952; flooded in 1957; reopened)

Selection Trust Ltd. founded in 1914 in U.K.

    Rhodesian Selection Trust (RST; founded in 1928, renamed Roan Selection Trust)
        Mufulira Copper Mines Ltd.
            Mufulira Division (opened 1933)
            Chibuluma Division (opened 1956)
            Chambishi Division (opened 1965)
        Baluba Mines Ltd. (opened 1966)
        Roan Antelope Mines Ltd. (opened 1931; now Luanshya Mine)
        Mwinilunga Mines Ltd.
        Kalengwa Mine Ltd. (opened 1970)

---

* Name changes since 1969 included.

Source: AAC and RST organization charts, December 1969; M. Bostock and C. Harvey (eds.) Economic Independence and Zambian Copper: A Case Study of Foreign Investment (New York: Praeger, 1972), Appendix A, "The Terms of the Takeover," p. 220; D. Hywel Davies, Zambia in Maps (London: University of London Press, 1975), p. 92; and Simon Cunningham, The Copper Industry in Zambia: Foreign Mining Companies in a Developing Country (New York: Praeger, 1981).

In 1926 Beatty reconstituted Selection Trust and in 1928 established a subsidiary company, the Rhodesian Selection Trust (RST), exclusively to develop and control mines in the Rhodesias. Through more complicated exchanges of mining stock and concession rights, RST gained control over Mufulira and Roan Antelope (now Luanshya) mines and held the concession rights to the areas that later became the Chibuluma, Baluba, Kalengwa, and Chambishi mines. Mufulira proved a spectacular investment. Its extensive veins of high-grade copper ore underwrote the profits of the RST group for almost forty years. The American Metals Company of New York (now AMAX, Inc.) became an important shareholder in RST in the 1930s, as U.S. capital proved vital to the development of several of the RST mines. However, management remained primarily in British and secondarily in South African hands until the late 1960s by which time the name had been changed to Roan Selection Trust.

Anglo and RST had driven out the smaller firms and prospectors and began to raise the capital necessary to construct large-scale copper mines and a refinery plant using the expensive flotation process when the Great Depression undercut world demand for copper and the availability of capital. Several mines closed down before they had begun full-scale production. The future of the industry looked bleak. Then the stimulus of new war industries in Europe increased worldwide demand for copper and other base metals. The Copperbelt began one of its greatest booms, first of construction and then of mineral production.

> Mufulira [mine] began producing in 1933 and in 1934 a refinery was opened at Nkana. The growth of the Copperbelt transformed the foreign trade of Northern Rhodesia; the value of exports increased five-fold between 1930 and 1933, and the contribution of copper rose from 30 per cent to 90 per cent. Further advances were assured by the rearmament programmes of both Britain and Germany and in 1939 Nchanga was brought into production. During the Second World War the Allies made heavy demands on the Copperbelt mines, and by 1945 Northern Rhodesia was firmly established as one of the world's major copper producers, contributing about one-eighth of the non-communist world's total product. The war also enabled Broken Hill to take on a new lease on life; the payable surface deposits were exhausted by 1940 but underground mines had been developed which yielded rich new supplies of lead as well as zinc and vanadium.[25]

From the start the industry exemplified a system of externally directed development: The war and expansions and recessions of the industrial states, rather than local realities or needs, have been the decisive factors in the industry's strength.

The Establishment of the Colonial Political Economy. An intricate corporate mating dance in the 1920s and 1930s left Northern Rhodesia with an industry dominated by an interconnected corporate oligopoly. The mines proved profitable for the British Treasury as well as the BSAC and the actual mining groups. Despite growing mineral exports, however, the tax and revenue situation of the colony was not strong. For one thing, the Northern Rhodesian government could not tax the concession-holding company directly. On the basis of its treaty rights, the BSAC received royalties from the mines whether RST or Rhoanglo made a profit or not. Further, under a special arrangement the BSAC was taxed only by the British government. The Crown in turn paid only half of this revenue back to Northern Rhodesia. Moreover, the mining groups paid a tax to the Northern Rhodesia government if and when they made a profit. Of the total amount of money taken in taxes and royalties in 1936-1937, only 12.5 percent went to the Northern Rhodesian government.[26] Through these tax arrangements, both the original concession holder and the imperial power gained from Zambia's mineral wealth without investing in the mines. From "1930 to 1940 Britain had kept for itself £2,400,000 in taxes from the Copperbelt, while Northern Rhodesia received from Britain only £136,000 in grants for development."[27] As Stewart Gore-Browne, the settler politician, put it, the Imperial "Trustee" was receiving funds from its "Ward" rather than the other way around.[28]

The predominance of the mines evoked tensions and reactions within the white community, which by the 1940s had been transformed from a small number of farmers and administrators to a relatively large urbanized population with an organized white working class of around 5,000.[29] These changes had political implications. Although all whites were united in racial privilege, there were distinct interests—colonial administrators, company representatives, farmers, and white mine workers—at variance with each other. These political interests played their role in the federation that was established between 1953 and 1963.

The changes wrought on the African people by patterns of white immigration, settlement, and politics, significant though they were, were minor in comparison with those caused by the copper industry. Forced migration, social dislocation, sometimes deep rural impoverishment, but also resistance led to the economic and political organization that in turn transformed colonialism.

African Migration and Social Dislocation. By the 1930s large-scale mining and land alienation had deeply affected the social fabric of the peoples of the region. Migration out of the territory, common during the first few decades of the twentieth century, was slowly transformed into a pattern of internal migration by the growth of the copper industry and the decline of the rural areas. Both "push" and "pull" factors acted on the African people, drawing them out of the villages. Able-bodied men from various parts of the protectorate and neighboring colonies were attracted to the Copperbelt, working on contracts up to two years in length. Others worked as farm laborers on white farms along the line of rail from Livingstone to the Copperbelt. Africans were discouraged from becoming long-term residents of the towns, because the whites on the Copperbelt felt threatened by the far larger number of Africans working in the mines, especially the militant Bemba and the more educated Nyasaland clerks. To protect their jobs, the white miners forced the companies to use a color bar excluding Africans from jobs above a certain level. Also colonial authorities enforced a series of regulations requiring African men to return to their home villages after completing a contract. Families were discouraged in the mining camps so "single" men lived in huts around the mine openings; later they were removed to barracks and small, tin-roofed houses in compounds. Miserable living conditions were complemented by racial abuse from the managers and immigrant white miners alike. Mining authorities presumed that miners would retire to the rural areas. Despite brutal and unstable conditions, by 1937, 18,000 African men worked on the mines in Northern Rhodesia. By 1943 nearly 33,000 were miners and many stayed for several contracts.[30] Slowly the foundations of an African working class were being established on the Copperbelt, recognized belatedly by the "stabilization" policies of the mines.[31]

PHOTO 2.5   Old man playing bowed instrument, watched by young boy.

In the face of this obvious social transformation, the colonial authorities clung to a belief that the village was the ultimate home for the African. Such a policy was meant to protect the rural economy—the reservoirs of labor—as well as to save money. Rural homesteads were expected to absorb the injured, elderly, and sick. Such thinking ignored the serious economic decline of the rural economy by the 1930s because of the loss of male labor at important times of the year such as planting. In the mid-1930s in addition to the 30,000 men away at the Copperbelt, absent from Northern Rhodesia altogether were 50,000 men working in Southern Rhodesia, 10,000 in southern Tanganyika, and untold others still at work in Katanga mines and the Transvaal.[32] In a total population of approximately 1.3 million, the loss of nearly 90,000 able-bodied men deprived the family of support and protection as well as labor. Where agrarian techniques required the kind of heavy physical work traditionally done by men, such as *chitemene* (Bemba word for "slash-and-burn" agriculture), shortage of manpower meant a decline in agricultural production. Audrey Richards, surveying Bembaland in the 1930s, found that in one year over 70 percent of the taxable males were away looking for wages.[33] Sometimes this loss of labor meant that basic food crops had to be changed (as from maize back to cassava or millet). Rural people, especially old people and children left behind (see Photo 2.5), suffered periods of malnutrition and starvation directly linked to the loss of labor.

It was not only the pull of the mines and the white-owned farms that altered the agriculturally based social structure of traditional societies. The other side of the coin was the push of the land alienation. Under the company, some lands had been alienated in the east and along the rail line. The displaced Africans, following the Southern Rhodesian model, were then placed on "reserves." The British colonial administration, eager to encourage more white immigration, established commissions between 1924 and 1946 to study the issues and advise the government on the "land question."

Generally, the government followed the recommendations of the commissions, reclassifying the land over time into four categories. The first category was land privately owned by the mines, concession holders, or settler farmers. By 1927 approximately 15,000 square miles were allocated to the BSAC and the North Charterland Exploration Company (NCECO) alone within an overall 12 million acres (or 6.5 percent of the whole country) reserved for whites. A second category was Native Reserves, where some displaced Africans were dumped. Because of severe ecological disasters and human misery caused by overpopulation and soil erosion on the reserves, new lands commissions sitting from 1938–1946 extended the size of these reserves. Crown lands, the third category, were originally set aside for whatever use the colonial authorities saw fit. In 1947 the majority of these lands became Native Lands, governed by African customary law and meant eventually to absorb the reserves. Finally, Barotseland Protectorate retained its own status because it already was "in essence a native reserve."[34]

Land alienation has deeply influenced rural underdevelopment in Zambia to the present day. The productive capacity of Zambia's best land has not been fully exploited, while the poorer lands that were once the reserves have suffered from overpopulation and overgrazing of cattle. It was from the choicest (because of features such as soil, availability of water) or most potentially profitable lands (because of proximity to the mines or access to the rail line) in Central and Southern provinces, around Mbala in the far north of Northern Province, and around Chipata in Eastern Province that the highest proportion of Africans were moved. These lands were reserved for whites. Ironically, the large influx of white farmers never materialized. Unexpectedly, too, some tracts of alienated land, cleared of people, attracted tsetse fly and became unhealthy for humans and cattle. In the reserve areas, primarily in Eastern Province and bordering white areas along the rail line, pressure on land became intense even though Northern Rhodesia as a whole had a low population density. The reserve's carrying capacity was insufficient for the numbers of people resettled on them.

A vicious cycle developed. The crowded reserve lands were overgrazed and overtilled. Their fertility declined and the effective population pressure thus increased still further. Systematic pressure on land pushed people to the urban areas and exposed families to the kind of social fragmentation more common in highly industrialized societies, a result shared with all southern African economies.

Natural and man-made disasters disrupted traditional life at the close of the nineteenth century when the area was hit by a series of plagues—rinderpest, locusts, and even smallpox—robbing people of cattle and crops and sometimes decimating whole populations. In the 1920s and 1930s the economic cycle of the industrial areas disrupted urban and rural patterns. A construction boom on the Copperbelt drew men to the towns and mines and then abruptly forced them away only to draw them again when the mines reopened.[35] The villages, whatever their capacities, had to absorb these shocks. Africans in the Protectorate of Northern Rhodesia were anything but "protected." They suffered deeply the effects of their connection to distant European markets and concerns and from events that had little relationship to domestic conditions.

Economic Underdevelopment. By the 1940s, the economy, now harnessed to the economies of North America and Europe as well as to the growing capitalist core in South Africa, was gradually incorporated into those systems. Profits extracted from the copper-bearing ores and generated by the labor of black and white miners flowed out of the protectorate. Payments abroad in the form of interest, dividends, and profits steadily mounted through the 1940s. By 1945, £1.5 million was externalized in this fashion; in 1949 the total had reached £9.5 million, which was 30 percent of the total export earnings of the territory.[36] The drain was noted by white and black inhabitants alike, but the effects were most severe on the African population.

Under colonial rule, very few services were introduced for a people undergoing rapid urbanization and dislocation because of the mining industry. Education and health services went primarily to the white residents. Industrial and mining infrastructure was confined to a narrow band along the line of rail and the Copperbelt. The colonial authorities did not build a self-centered industrial base. Rather, the peoples and minerals of the north were exploited for the advantage of the settlers in the south, the shareholders in South Africa, Europe, and North America and the British government. The railroad that forms the spine of the colony was meant simply to serve the mines of the Copperbelt and Katanga and did not reach out into the rural areas to help the African peasant enter cash farming. Moreover, government gave white settlers agricultural and marketing assistance to combat competition from those peasant farmers who had begun to produce for the growing urban market. Just over a thousand white commercial farms produced most of the food for the town and the mines. The mass of the indigenous people were marginalized from the growing cash economy in agriculture. The vast northeast and far west with their widespread villages were useful to the colonial authorities, white mine managers, and farmers primarily as a source of cheap labor for the centers of commerce and industry.

Consequently, Northern Rhodesia's inhabitants existed in an unequal society with a regionally unbalanced economy. Half a century of colonial rule produced almost no development away from the Copperbelt and rail line. Most major cities and towns are found there today. The road network connecting provincial capitals to this spine was quite underdeveloped as were most marketing and agricultural facilities outside the main corridor. The underdeveloped rural regions were linked by migrant labor to an enclave of advanced mining and capitalist agriculture to the disadvantage of the countryside. From the harsh world of the mines and rural impoverishment grew the nationalist movement to challenge and eventually overthrow colonial rule.

The Federation Period, 1953-1963

Within British colonial circles, the idea had long been current that Northern Rhodesia should be part of a larger entity, probably including Southern Rhodesia and possibly even extending to South Africa. As a counterweight to this "amalgamationist" stance were the policies invoked by British politicians such as Lord Passfield (formerly Sidney Webb) who, in his capacity as British colonial secretary, had been the originator of the memorandum on paramountcy of native interest. Yet the dominant voice of regional white politics was for amalgamation in some form or other. Antipathies between British and Afrikaner politicians, the coming of self-rule to Southern Rhodesia in 1923, and finally the victory of the Afrikaner-based Nationalist party in South Africa in 1948 interrupted any smooth consolidation of all the settler territories. By the late 1940s there reappeared the idea of federating Northern and Southern Rhodesia and including Nyasaland too. Politics over federation tended to divide the populations of all three territories along racial lines.

Many whites in Southern Rhodesia were strongly in favor of establishing permanent racial supremacy in the area, and they were joined by many whites in the north. Northern settler politicians pressured their government for some form of federation with the south where whites were greater in number and solidly in control of government. Two influential politicians of the time were Lt. Col. Sir Stewart Gore-Browne and Roy Welensky. Gore-Browne was a scion of a wealthy British family; he had a large estate (Shiwa Ng'andu) in Northern Rhodesia and behaved much as a country squire might have done. He also led the settlers in the legislative council from 1939-1946.[37] Welensky was born in Southern Rhodesia of an immigrant Lithuanian father and Afrikaner mother. After a brief stint as a boxer, Welensky joined the railroad and became a trade union leader,[38] only later to serve as a prime minister of the Federation of Rhodesia and Nyasaland and be knighted.

Vastly different in backgrounds and temperament, Gore-Browne and Welensky also differed over the form of federation they considered preferable. Along with Leopold Moore, a pharmacist and journalist from Livingstone, they took a dim view of the colonial office's administration of the territory and of the royalties paid to the BSAC and British Treasury from the copper mines. Under pressures from these local politicians, "in 1949 the British South Africa Company was induced to surrender its royalties in 1986, and meanwhile agreed to pay 20 percent of them to the Northern Rhodesian Government; after income tax had been levied, . . . [the Northern Rhodesian

Government] now received altogether half the value of the royalties each year."[39] In 1948 settler politicians, led by Welensky, obtained political permission from the colonial office to press for closer association with Southern Rhodesia. Initially the mining companies hesitated in fear that they might be "milked" to the advantage of the south. In general, however, the white community supported a form of federation with the Southern Rhodesians and Nyasalanders.

Talk of closer union with the south aroused both traditional African leaders and more urbanized and educated men and women. "In 1944 a senior Bemba chief raised his voice against amalgamation in the Northern Provincial Council and from 1950 several chiefs spoke out firmly against plans for federation. In 1953 a petition to Britain's Houses of Parliament against federation was signed by 120 chiefs, including the Bemba and Ngoni paramounts."[40] Most rural people feared a further loss of land, but the more educated and urbanized Africans feared that closer relations with a larger number of white settlers could mean heightened racism and exploitation and an even slower pace of African advancement. Despite opposition by African leaders and to a lesser degree by some colonial officials, in 1953 the British government inaugurated the Federation of Rhodesia and Nyasaland (also known as the Central African Federation).

Economically, the federation was supposed to be a common market. According to the preamble to the constitution of the federation, it also was meant to foster partnership and cooperation between their inhabitants. In reality, it was a political scheme that favored the whites most and provided the capital for the development of the industrial and service sectors of the Southern Rhodesian economy.

Superimposed over the three territories was a federal government whose executive and parliamentary branches were based in Salisbury, the capital of Southern Rhodesia. Local administration (including native affairs) were left to the settler governments, with Barotseland's autonomy protected. Foreign relations were handled by the British, presumably after some consultation with the federal government. The taxes on the mineral industry in the north were added to taxes from Southern Rhodesia and Nyasaland and sent to the federal coffers. Funding for all three territories was voted on in the federal parliament, an institution in which the south dominated. Between 1954 and 1960 the Northern Rhodesian government paid £176 million to the federal treasury, £133.2 million of which came from taxing the mines. Federal expenditures and federal income tax paid back to Northern Rhodesia was far less. From 1954-1960 the net loss to Northern Rhodesia was £56.1 million.[41]

Officially, "paramountcy of native interests" was now replaced by "partnership between the races." A remark has been attributed to the first federal prime minister: this "partnership of black and white is the partnership between a horse and its rider."[42] Bearing out this more realistic assessment, the majority of the population—the Africans—were marginalized politically. This held true despite later reforms. "The Federal franchise provided for a small African electorate and six African seats in the Federal legislature. In Northern Rhodesia approximately 7,000 Africans were enfranchised under the 1959 [Benson] Constitution which provided for eight African seats in a Legislative Council of twenty-six members."[43] Not surprisingly, this federation led to the organization of African resistance in all three territories. This resistance was affected by a rapidly expanding economy during the federal years and a jockeying for leadership among the newly educated and urbanized Africans.

The early years of federation were ones of unparalleled growth for the copper industry in Northern Rhodesia and for the economy of the federation as a whole. According to Hazlewood, the gross domestic product "of the federal economy was 54 percent greater in real terms at the end than in the first year of federation."[44] Yet growth was not steady nor were the benefits equally spread. A major reason was fluctuation in production connected to variance in foreign trade, especially for the copper industry. For a brief time, the Korean War sharply increased the world demand for copper. New investment flowed into the mines as refineries were built or expanded, and output increased commensurately. But in 1954 there was a mild recession, followed by another in 1957. Nonetheless by 1960 the Copperbelt accounted for almost 16 percent of the free world's supply of copper; more than 238,000 Africans were employed in industries throughout the colony.[45]

Growth occurred in those sectors directly linked to Western capital. Urbanization and industrialization were connected so that by 1963, "six towns held 69.6 percent of all urban dwellers, half of them in Lusaka and Kitwe."[46] Increasing numbers of people poured into the cities and towns. The Copperbelt boasted a population of 400,000 Africans and 40,000 whites by 1956. Wages and salaries for Africans between 1954 and 1963 rose an average of 205 percent compared with a rise for non-Africans of 25 percent.[47] Still economic expansion for Africans was not smooth, nor the benefits widespread. "In 1953 there were nealry 270,000 Africans in employment but there was a sharp fall in 1954 and the 1953 level was not reached again until 1957 when a prolonged decline set in. Yet the adult male population continued to grow as part of a long-term growth in the population made possible by improved famine relief measures, hygiene and medical care: by 1960 the total population was about three million."[48] Many new town dwellers swelled the ranks of the urban unemployed, as the growth in the economy as a whole and an accelerated urbanization were not paralleled by a growth in the job market. Individuals grew desperate in this situation and turned to crime. Others directed their antagonism against traditional authorities or the colonial and mine officials.

A constant source of complaint in the north was the drain of money to Southern Rhodesia under the federal tax system. Taxes built the industrial and governmental base in Salisbury; little returned to build infrastructure in the north. Roberts estimated that by 1963 (the final year of federation) Northern Rhodesia had sustained a net loss of £97 million to the rest of the federation.[49] Salisbury (now Harare) rose to be a dramatic and modern city, and the industries located there began to serve northern markets, undercutting competitors on the Copperbelt. When the building of a hydroelectric dam was under consideration (in the late 1950s), the choice of a site on the Kafue River in the north seemed obvious because it was close to the major consumer, the mines, and did not present many serious construction difficulties to the engineers. Yet the final decision was to build the major installation on the southern bank of the Zambezi River at Kariba, giving effective control over the power generators to the settlers in the south.[50] Finally, basic industries such as iron and steel, coal, and machine tooling were developed in the south, ignoring the north despite the mines' effective demand for these products. So the economy continued to be unevenly developed in the federation days both within the region and between its inhabitants. Under federation, moreover, the north became even more structurally dependent on the south despite the legal fiction of partnership.

Throughout the federation years, African opposition continued to grow, although the reasons varied with the different classes. Urban working class Africans felt the impact of direct taxation by the federal government more heavily than did white residents. The Africans also bore a growing burden of indirect taxes. Despite increases in black wages, large gaps between the income of the whites and blacks continued. This was particularly visible in the mining industry where in 1952 the average monthly wage for an African mine worker who worked on a surface was 83 shillings compared to the white man's £89.0. Underground rates were 101s. 7d. for the African and £101 for the white.[51] Finally, although the color bar was officially abolished with the multiracial federation, it still existed informally and benefits were constrained by a tight job market. Little investment went into agriculture to aid the peasant farmers. Education and social services to Africans were limited by the small share that the northern territorial government had of the federal wealth. As the last straw, when dissatisfied whites agitated for more control of their territorial governments and demanded a new constitution, Africans feared that new institutions might be even less favorable to them than the existing ones. Thus social, economic, and political factors combined to force African politics into its modern nationalist phase.

TOWARD INDEPENDENCE

As we have seen, African protest against European rule dates back as far as the imposition of company administration but was generally regionally limited and not militarily successful. Federation elicited opposition from both traditional leaders and from a new stratum of Africans, often urbanized and usually with some Western education. A new leadership forced itself to the fore, willing to oppose militantly the whites and able to transform older institutions and create new ones to embody their demands.

By the late 1940s a new generation of Africans had come to adulthood under colonial rule. Men who had served in the world wars, fighting for British survival, were awakened by their exposure to the irrationality of racism and the reality of "white man's weakness." A select few also managed to obtain postsecondary education abroad and were exposed to new ideologies such as Fabian socialism and Gandhian passive resistance. In their hands, African trade unions and welfare societies became the precursors of the political parties of the 1950s and the seedbed for nationalist politics. Later the cooperation between trade unions and the parties became the key to the death of the federation and the birth of an independent Zambia.

The Trade Union Movement. From 1935 to 1956 the Copperbelt was rocked by a series of militant strikes organized by the African mine workers fighting for better wages and living conditions and an end to the color bar, which blocked advancement into apprenticeships and more skilled jobs. Clerks, subforemen (called "bossboys"), and semiskilled mine workers spearheaded confrontations among the mining companies, white fellow mine workers, and colonial authorities. These were the first challenges to the colonial order in the modern idiom, that is, on its own terms.

Strikes and slowdowns forced the mine owners to reconsider their manner of dealing with the laborers and the effectiveness of the institutions that were supposed to "keep the Africans in line." In 1938 the mine managers and colonial officials introduced a new set of institutions, including urban advisory councils for residential areas surrounding the mines. Eight years later the colonial government set up a territorywide African Representative Council (ARC) to deal with all "native" problems as well as to advise government. In some cases, these semirepresentative bodies did act as conduits of African opinion to the colonial rulers. However, often the ARC was referred to as a "toy telephone" that in any case was not helpful in situations of hardheaded wage disputes as in the 1940 strike.

Labor discontent continued unabated until in 1947 the British Labour government sent the Scottish trade unionist William Comrie to the protectorate to advise the African workers how to form a trade union and conduct collective bargaining. In 1949 a national union for all African mine workers was created and called the Northern Rhodesian African Mineworkers Union (NRAMWU) to distinguish it from the white mine workers union that had been established twelve years earlier. The black union and others that followed were protected under government ordinance and quickly became powers to be dealt with in the territory. An African Trades Union Congress (TUC) was created in 1950 with the miners and railway men the strongest of the participating unions.

Henceforth, the African unions became major actors in nationalist politics. Lawrence Katilungu, Northern Rhodesia's leading trade unionist (he headed both the NRAMWU and the TUC) joined the fray against federation. Katilungu, who had begun as a missionary teacher, left and became a "spanner boy" on the Copperbelt, eventually rising to senior interpreter at Nkana Mine, was a powerful man. He spoke for other trade unionists who were greatly concerned with possible loss of their few hard fought for rights and benefits if Northern Rhodesian federated with the avowedly racist and settler-dominated Southern Rhodesia. Although their primary focus was economic bargaining, the trade unions became more and more involved in politics. Their leaders entered into uneasy relations with the newly forming African political parties.

The Welfare Societies and Early Political Parties. Welfare societies had existed since the 1920s as organizations of like-minded men and women who tried to help each other during times of stress, for example, in the unexpected death of a member. In 1922 schools' inspector Donald Siwale set up the first welfare association in Northern Rhodesia with the aid of missionary teacher David Kaunda, father of Zambia's first president. Between 1929 and 1931 welfare associations spread to towns along the rail line; in 1933 there was an unsuccessful attempt to federate these societies into a nationwide organization. In 1946 Dauti Yamba, a schoolmaster, and George Kaluwa, a trade unionist and farmer, spearheaded the drive for the Federation of African Societies, which endured.

Over the next years this association gave way to a more explicitly political organization led by a group of African clerks, lower-level civil servants, and teachers. The "new men" (and they were mostly men) came from different ethnic groups and parts of the country but found that in the towns they shared a growing awareness of themselves as part of a "nation" and as racially and economically exploited. They formed the nucleus of an African petite bourgeoisie, inserting a new stratum between the workers and peasants, on the one hand, and the traditional leaders within the African social system, on the other. This stratum or "protoclass" turned the welfare federation into a political party, the Northern Rhodesia African Congress, in 1948. As the momentum of political organization took over, the more compromising groups and leaders were overtaken by more militant bodies and spokesmen.

The colonial government resisted the idea that the town-based associations could speak for the majority of rural Africans. Despite the aid of some sympathetic whites, this early party was frustrated in its attempts to consolidate nationwide resistance to federation. Another former schoolmaster, Harry Nkumbula, joined the congress after returning from studies at the London School of Economics. While in the United Kingdom, Nkumbula had been caught up in antifederation politics (along with another firebrand of the time, Dr. Hastings Banda, now the archconservative president of Malawi). Upon his return to Northern Rhodesia in 1950, Nkumbula joined the fight against federation. Gaining the presidency in 1951, he reframed the old congress into the African National Congress (ANC). This new party had a strong base in Nkumbula's home territory of Southern Province and especially among the Ila and Tonga speakers but also had support in other regions.

The invigorated ANC quickly drew in more militant leaders, such as the young Kenneth Kaunda who had trained as a teacher after graduating from Munali secondary school in Lusaka. He became prominent in the Mufulira welfare society on the Copperbelt and later returned home to Chinsali in Northern Province and served on the local provincial council while he worked as a trader in used clothing to keep himself and his family alive. With the help of such able and energetic young politicians, congress established branches throughout the protectorate although with little success in North-Western Province and in Barotseland. A particularly active branch in Ndola, the main commercial town on the rail line, fostered politicians such as Justin Chimba (organizing secretary of the Northern Rhodesia General Workers' Trade Union) and Reuben Kamanga. Soon Simon Kapwepwe, a welfare assistant from Kitwe who had gone to India on scholarship returned to the federation filled with ideas of racial equality and passive resistance techniques that had served the Indians well in their struggle against British colonial rule. The ANC adopted many of the basic Gandhian principles and put forward demands for universal adult suffrage and an end to racial discrimination and segregation. The breakup of the federation was only part of the demands of the newly politicized African leaders.

The congress faced serious problems: an uninformed rural population and an ambivalent mine workers' union. Foremost was the disagreement over strategy between the miners' union and the congress. The mine workers were interested in short-term economic gains from wage disputes with the mine bosses. The union leaders followed these sentiments. Under the direction of Katilungu, moreover, their efforts were richly rewarded. Between 1947 and 1956, the mine workers at the highly paid end of the wage scale (the semiskilled) had their wages increased by 200 percent. Those at the bottom end had their wages increased by 400 percent.[52] Equally, employers often threatened to dismiss anyone taking an active part in antifederation politics, although the mine owners were more circumspect in their warnings.

On the other hand, the leaders of congress, such as Nkumbula and Kaunda, despite education and skills of the white-color level, had only a toehold on the lower ranks of the colonial state. They were not likely to gain by cooperation; rather they were threatened by federation and possible influx of more whites and probable increase in racist job discrimination. Pay disputes alone could not embody the concerns of this incipient class or serve as the adequate focus for political mobilization of the whole African population. Crucial to these leaders was entry into the formal political arena and, in fact, gaining some power within the state and the economy. To do so, they needed a mass-based party backed by the political muscle of the unions. Yet when the congress leaders required the support of the unions the most, they could not rely on it. For example, in 1952 Nkumbula organized the Supreme Action Council to draw together the trade unionists, the traditional leaders, and the congress politicians to oppose federation. Boycotts and demonstrations followed, but the key event, a two-day period of national prayer (with the intention that those praying stay home from work) was not supported by Katilungu's powerful mine workers' union. Neither did the congress gain the backing of the African members of the legislative council. When federation was voted in by the white population, for a brief period African political organization declined.[53] Yet the social disruptions and changes implicit in the economic dynamics of expanding copper production and increased urbanization continued unabated and led to new political activity.

In October 1958 a group of Young Turks, discontented with past failures of the ANC and in particular with Nkumbula's leadership, broke away and formed the Zambia African National Congress (ZANC). Katilungu hung onto the leadership of the NRAMWU until 1960, but his replacement, John Chisata, was more willing to cooperate with the politicians. The political current released by the insult of federation channeled itself into more militant nationalist politics and spawned new political parties.

The Emergence of UNIP. ZANC's leaders came from a particular stratum of a "new" petite bourgeoisie of a special kind.[54] They were more educated and younger men; most of them drew a salary from the mines, government, or the unions; the group could be termed a salariat. ZANC's president, Kenneth Kaunda, was a former teacher; the first deputy president, Dixon Konkola, was a railroad trade union official; the general treasurer Simon Kapwepwe, a former welfare worker on the mines; Munu Sipalo worked for a Copperbelt commercial firm. Their ranks were joined by an even smaller social category—independent professionals. Sikota Wina was a journalist and a member of the Lozi traditional hierarchy; Grey Zulu, the manager of a cooperative society; and Lewis Changufu, a Lusaka businessman.

Most ZANC politicians had gained experience in the welfare associations, unions, and African councils. They expressed the sentiments of people who were not so fortunate in education and employment but were equally disillusioned with the inability of the old congress to organize adequate opposition to federation. To make matters worse, Nkumbula seemed increasingly prone to compromise with the white politicians, as indicated by his willingness to participate in the upcoming elections under a compromise constitution (the Benson Constitution).

ZANC's formal platform was not very different from that of the ANC. Its leaders, however, were willing to boycott the elections and engage the state in potentially violent situations whereas the congress leaders were growing more conciliatory toward the settlers and federal authorities who governed the territory. The younger ZANC (later United National Independence Party—UNIP) men roused the countryside as in the serious disturbances on the Copperbelt and Northern Province in 1961. Late in 1959 the ANC split, with the young lawyer Mainza Chona leading the second ANC. This splinter party later merged with UNIP. Harry Nkumbula and Lawrence Katilungu were being overtaken by younger and more militant men.

Antagonisms between the African and white communities intensified in the last years of the Central African Federation. Frictions between the two competing African political parties eventually encouraged the federal authorities to repress the more militant movement. ZANC was banned in 1959. Its leaders were sent to jail or detained in remote rural areas. Rather than silencing dissent, imprisonment and enforced rustication tended to harden the resolve of the individuals and to spread their beliefs. The banning of ZANC also made a sham of the federal government's claim to be a multiparty and multiracial partnership.

The most articulate spokesmen for ZANC—Kaunda, Kapwepwe, and Sipalo—wanted to unite the African community behind two goals: an end to federation and the introduction of government by the majority. Antiracism, pan-Africanism and the principles of social and political equality were deeply imbedded in the platform of a new party they helped form in 1960, calling it the United National Independence Party (UNIP).

By the early 1960s the federal authorities accepted the failure of the Central African Federation and were seeking alternatives. It was not clear whether the ANC, UNIP, or the white settler parties (or a coalition among them) would assume the political kingdom. The dilemma for Whitehall was how to transfer governance to a new group of people without large-scale communal violence and without substantially altering the colonial economy. In order to effect such a transition the British needed to locate representatives of an incipient class linked to the current economy who would also be acceptable to the more militant African nationalists. A bitter struggle over constitutional change eventually decided the fate of the federation.

As the federation crumbled, the colonial office manufactured a compromise. Using a two-tiered electorate roll, the colonial authorities held an election in 1962 under the new constitution. The British hoped the election would legitimate the new government consisting of whites and Africans alike competing through the multiparty format. The new constitution, however, gave a distinct edge of power to the white settlers. The peculiar electoral regulations led to odd alliances such as that between the ANC and white settler party, the United Federal Party (UFP). Eventually Nkumbula and Kaunda patched over their disagreements and cooperated in November 1962 in by-elections that brought to power an African majority government. The first national assembly had a multiracial membership that was elected by several political parties and included a few independents. Kaunda became minister of local government and social welfare, Kapwepwe became minister of African affairs, and Nkumbula became minister for African education. The first African-led government was now in place, and it began to change the political and social structures of the former protectorate.

CONCLUSION

Most UNIP and ANC energies prior to self-government had been directed at wresting the state from settler hands. Now they had to run a government. They faced daunting challenges. The ANC/UNIP coalition needed to establish control over a territory in which the vast majority of the people had no sense of national identity and over an economy dominated by a mineral industry owned by powerful foreign corporations and structurally dependent on the south. The loyalties of the resident white population were in doubt. Moreover, the government, given the degree of underdevelopment of African manpower over the seventy-four years of foreign domination and the eventual departure of the colonial civil servants, was pitifully short of personnel to staff the state.

On the positive side, these new leaders had the support of the general population and much enthusiasm from UNIP and ANC ranks. The "Brave New World" for Zambia was an exciting place. Challenges were faced boldly, and only now, after twenty years, is it possible to assess the relative successes and failures and their causes. To understand the direction that the political economy of Zambia took, we need to turn and look more carefully at the cultural and social setting, which set constraints for government policies.

3
Society and Culture

Despite the national slogan "One Zambia, One Nation," modern Zambian society appears to be split into two distinct worlds. One world is urban or *peri-urban*,[1] characterized by big buildings, modern shops, automobiles, hotels, Western clothing, street crime, restaurants, discos, and dance contests. In another world are small villages spread out over the more sparsely populated rural areas. Villagers live in homes that have no electricity or running water, often with thatched roofs. An occasional grocery serves their basic needs for goods. Few visitors or vehicles pass by their homesteads, and daily life and work are determined by the sun rather than the clock.

Such seemingly separate worlds hide a more subtle reality. Within the urban communities are many subdivisions based on class, ethnicity, race, and language; the rural world is more homogeneous. But the whole society is in transition from a more rural life to a more urban one. Although the worlds themselves seem bewilderingly different, people circulate between them, making major adjustments in their behavior and expectations. Zambians are very mobile people, and the culture and societies of the towns and the villages are inextricably interlinked. Coming to town does not mean a total rejection of rural life or relatives left on the land. Nor does dwelling in the agricultural areas mean living as one's ancestors did, abandoning urban values and Western ideas. Colonial rule, schools, Christianity, wage labor, and cash crops have introduced changes in the villages as well as the cities.

Zambian society today reflects a mixture of the old and the new, indigenous and foreign cultures. Eventually a new culture with its own values and behaviors will emerge, but now people must reformulate roles and expectations and are often unsure of the future. The social and personal dislocation implicit in such a rapid cultural transformation is difficult for people at all socioeconomic levels. The confusion creates tensions for everyone and problems for the government. Equally, conflicting cultures allow exciting and energetic social innovations, especially by the young.

As the issues of Zambian society and culture are broad ones and have received considerable attention by specialists over the years, only a few topics are selected here to illustrate the twin themes of this chapter—the syncretic nature of modern culture and the evolution of an urban society with distinct class stratification.

VILLAGE TO TOWN

Over one hundred years ago, no cities existed in Zambia. Peoples of different ethnic groups had little contact with one another except through long-distance trade or warfare. By 1980, 43 percent of the total population lived in or around the towns.[2] In these urban settings, diverse peoples interact on a daily basis. Some subconsciously take on new norms and discard their old ways. Others consciously try to maintain communal identity. Yet all urbanites have to adapt to some degree. To explore this fascinating social evolution, let us first look at the cultural starting point—a Zambian village. Here people appear to be living much as their ancestors did before the colonialists turned their worlds upside down. Careful observation, however, shows how much rural life has adapted to the social and cultural changes of the past seventy years.

The village of Mutondo is located in Chief Chungu's area, northwest of Lake Bangweulu on the edge of the swamps in Northern Province. Mutondo is very poor indeed and isolated from the nearest towns of Luwingu, Mansa, and Kasama because of poor roads and an absence of public transport. The population of the Third Ward, of which Mutondo is one village, is approximately 6,000, more than half of which is female. The average age of the head of household is fifty years. The villagers of Mutondo earn very low incomes, mostly from selling some of their crops at the market. Average village income figures are distorted by the salaries of the few civil servants—including a medical assistant, an agricultural assistant, primary school teachers, and a headmaster. Many women have no cash income at all and never use money in their daily lives. They seem to subsist totally outside the market economy of the rest of the nation.[3]

A backward economy, poor agricultural conditions, the distance from towns and railroads, and lack of farmers who are particularly innovative all contribute to the poverty of Mutondo. The subsistence economy was deeply affected by the loss of males from the village to the Copperbelt and towns, a loss that began in the 1920s and continues today. The domination of urban centers in the national economy has meant that many villages such as Mutondo have been forgotten or policies meant to aid them have been ineffectual.

Although agriculture today is the basic economic activity, the Bisa people of the region did not derive sustenance primarily from agriculture before colonialism but from long-distance trade and hunting. Their land was an ecological borderline between the swamps around Lake Bangweulu and the woodlands of the Bemba plateau. Bisa had acted as intermediaries from both Kazembe and Bemba overrulers in precolonial days. In colonial times export of labor was the main source of income. Only recently have Bisa people turned from hunting to cultivation but without sufficient tools, labor, inputs, or extensive farming knowledge. As a consequence, food production has been very low. In the early 1960s, when President Kaunda visited Chungu's chieftaincy, he deemed it one of the poorest in Zambia.

PHOTO 3.1 Musician standing outside traditional house, Luwingu District, Northern Province.

Recent introduction of foreign aid has altered the bleakness of this economic picture. People have been encouraged to embark on rice production. This has potential, given the fortuitous availability of the underutilized swamps, which do not require much fertilizer to produce a good crop of rice. The introduction of oxen has been more problematic, but overall vegetable and maize production has shown a slow increase.[4] Whether these indicators of economic progress will be sustained when the foreign-aid agencies leave is uncertain.

Visually Mutondo is attractive, with houses following along a dirt road that loops at the end enclosing a large shade tree. Most houses are made with mud-and-wattle techniques and have thatched roofing (see Photo 3.1), no electricity or running water, and no formal sanitation system, but a few are of brick with metal window frames. The chief's house is outside the village, in keeping with tradition, and the primary school seems to occupy the center of the village. Modern urban living seems far away in the slow pace of Mutondo, but closer inspection reveals many urban influences. Roofs of galvanized iron sheets and metal window and door frames are purchased with men's wages from sojourns in the cities or on the mines. Wells are now found with cement bases, a manufactured bucket and chain. Bicycles are common and often one encounters an older man cycling along wearing his safety helmet from his days on the mines. Younger men work in the fields with heavy rubber boots, either from the Luwingu shops or from previous jobs. Many women wear *chitenge* (a locally printed cotton cloth) from the shops or cloth distinctively from Zaire. Everyday life in Mutondo demonstrates influences of the outside world.

The age and sex distribution in Northern and Luapula provinces[5] is borne out in Mutondo as well. The majority of the population is female, and a large percentage is young children. The males tend to be either elderly or quite young as in other parts of the rural Zambia. Declining employment in the towns is said to mean that more people who leave school now return to Mutondo after unsuccessful attempts at locating work in the towns. This is still a minor trend: Overall, there is a shortage of working-age men for heavy agricultural work.

Finally, the authority structure of the village reveals an active chief and elders. A parallel structure of elected or selected leaders staffs the Ward Development Committee[6] (a UNIP party organ) and other locally based organizations. Traditional power is strong enough that the "new men" will hesitate to oppose or undermine the view of the chief. Yet some decisions lie outside the chief's purview or experience. The villagers struggle to select people who can represent them well at ward-, district-, and provincial-level meetings where a good command of English is obligatory. Such differing needs sometimes draw traditional and elected leaders and their backers into conflict with one another. The general cultural bias however is toward decision making based on consensus, so many of these tensions are submerged in the politics of daily life in Mutondo.

Mutondo on the surface is truly isolated and very traditional: It has in fact internalized cultural, economic, and political influences from outside. In particular, Mutondo reflects both negative and positive aspects of migratory labor due to the incorporation of the area into an economy based on industrial mining. Although Mutondo is typical of Zambia in some ways, nonetheless the extensive ethnic pluralism and cultural distinctiveness of the regions of Zambia make generalizations about a "national rural life" dubious. To have an accurate picture of rural Zambia, one would have to travel to and live in many different parts of the country to observe the sets of behavior that exist in each community, noting elements that are common or distinct. Two experiences shared by all Zambia's villages, however, have been the steady exodus of men to the towns and the related stagnation of the rural economy.

CULTURAL AND SOCIAL TRANSFORMATION

Social Heterogeneity and Social Change in the Urban Context

In less than two generations nearly half of the people have relocated in and around the cities and towns. This pattern developed before independence despite official disapproval of African "detribalization" and ur-

TABLE 3.1
Percentage Distribution of Population in Provinces, 1963, 1969, and 1980

Province	1980 Census	1969 Census	1963 Census
Lusaka*	12.2[a]	8.7[a]	5.6[a]
Central*	9.0	8.9	8.9
Copperbelt*	22.0	20.1	15.6
Eastern	11.6	12.6	13.9
Luapula	7.3	8.3	10.7
Northern	11.9	13.4	16.2
North-Western	5.3	5.7	6.9
Southern*	12.1	12.2	13.4
Western	8.6	10.1	10.4
TOTAL ZAMBIA	100.0	100.0	100.0

* The old line - of - rail provinces.

[a] As Lusaka Province was created in 1971, population figures for this province were probably extracted from the district census tables and should be treated with caution.

Source: Figures from Preliminary Report, 1980 Census of Population and Housing (Lusaka: Central Statistical Office, January, 1981), Table 2, p. 2.

banization. The trend accelerated with independence and the removal of legal restraints to urban migration. After 1964 people flooded to town, especially those urban centers grouped along the line of rail but also to marketing centers and local government *bomas* (provincial and district headquarters). By 1980 the old rail line (Central, Copperbelt, Lusaka, and Southern) provinces shared among themselves slightly more than 55 percent of Zambia's population (see Table 3.1). This urban population is multiethnic and multilinguistic.

Ethnographers are fond of pointing out that seventy-two separate ethnic groups (locally called tribes) live in the nine provinces of Zambia. They speak a multitude of languages and dialects but the major ethnolinguistic groups are the Bemba (36.2 percent), Nyanja (17.6 percent), Tonga (15.1 percent), Barotse (8.2 percent), and the northwestern group (10 percent), which includes the Kaonde, Lunda, and Luvale speakers. Members of all the ethnic and linguistic groups now live in all the nine provinces, although concentrations of particular groups still can be found near ancestral villages (e.g., the Bemba in Northern and Luapula provinces).

Urban Zambians living in multiethnic settings often try to maintain separate customs and languages in order to distinguish themselves from others, consciously or unconsciously. Unfortunately these cultural differences often breed myths and stereotypes that can lead to serious tensions among the communities.

A new division, in which people distinguish themselves by their region rather than by ethnicity, seems to have surfaced since independence. Although

SOCIETY AND CULTURE 39

TABLE 3.2
Population of Zambia as Classified by Nationality and Citizenship, 1969 and 1980

Nationality and Citizenship at Birth[a]	1969 Census Data	1980 Census Data[b]	% of Change	% of Pop'n
AFRICAN	3,998,644	5,621,311	+40.67	99.30
Zambian born		5,416,937		
Foreign born		188,749		
Not stated		15,628		
EUROPEAN[c]	41,253[d]	15,584	-62.22	.27
Zambian born		3,667		
Foreign born		11,656		
Not stated		261		
ASIAN	10,785	17,955	+66.48	.32
Zambian born		4,739		
Foreign born		13,026		
Not stated		190		
COLOURED	4,176	5,912	+41.57	.11
Zambian born		4,379		
Foreign born		1,332		
Not stated		201		
TOTAL POPULATION	4,054,858	5,661,850	100.00	100.00

[a] The data do not indicate people who have taken Zambian citizenship since their residence in Zambia, so these figures are likely to be low estimates of current Zambian citizenry.
[b] These figures are drawn from the unpublished Census Tables D-1 and D-2, which provide citizenship data along with age and sex breakdowns by province and district.
[c] The term European is used to cover all whites, including those from distinctly non-European origins, for example Australia and North America.
[d] The figure varies from the 1969 Census based on the author's retabulation of the original data. The 1969 Census figure for Europeans is 43,390.

Source: Republic of Zambia, 1980 Census, Provincial and District Tables, D-1 and D-2, unpublished.

each of the nine provinces is multiethnic, it is quickly noted (and commented upon) when one province receives a particular benefit such as a local factory, secondary school, or commercial maize depot. Often one hears such comments as "ah, these Northerners always get more" or "these Easterners stick together." One might interpret these comments as disguised ethnic consciousness. Yet the reality of interethnic mixing may mean that such statements indicate a new social division based on region emerging within the already heterogeneous nation.

Complicating ethnic and regional diversity are cleavages based on what is locally interpreted as a separate "racial" groups, termed "nationality groups" by the officials of the census. The primary "nationalities" are African, European, Asian, and Coloured (people of mixed ancestry). Their numbers have fluctuated considerably between the 1969 and the 1980 censuses as Table 3.2 demonstrates.

The African nationality group includes both Zambian-born Africans and Africans born in other parts of the continent. The people from other parts of Africa are not always welcome residents as it is popularly believed they are the source of various crimes from auto theft to emerald smuggling. Still, Zambia offers refuge to some 100,000 people from neighboring countries. The most important factor is the rapid increase in the African population— a 40 percent increase in 1980 over 1969. At this rate (3.1 percent per annum) the local population will double again in 22.5 years.[7]

One effect of decolonization and the downturn in the local economy is the rapid decline in the European population (all whites are called Europeans in Zambia)—down 62 percent since 1969. It is curious that also included in the "European nationality group" are the whites born in Zambia, which reflects either the failure of these people to take citizenship or an ambiguity in the official nonracial policies of the government.

The number of Coloureds had increased by 41 percent in 1980, but this group still constitutes less than 1 percent of the total population. The Asian nationality group is not only experiencing an increase in overall numbers but also receiving new immigrants. Interpretations of these figures are obscured by the lumping together as "Asian" all Indians, Bangladeshis, Sri Lankans, Pakistanis, and Middle Easterners.

Despite serious reservations any social scientist or demographer would have with the grouping together of diverse peoples and calling them "nationalities," important features about modern Zambian society stand out in the forest of figures. Racial or nationality distinctions remain relevant in daily social interactions. Often people harbor antagonisms and suspicions about other races based on perceived differences and as we have seen, historical memories. Particularly intense are frictions between Asian merchants, who compose a traditional petite bourgeoisie in towns, and the African majority, who are subject to high prices and sometimes racial abuse. Yet intercommunal violence has been rare despite the social and economic gaps inherited from colonial days and disturbances in the struggle for independence. As problems posed by a stagnant economy multiply in the 1980s and as an upper class visibly enriches itself, pressures are likely to build within this otherwise tolerant society and exacerbate both ethnic and racial tensions among the six million or so people resident in Zambia.

One feature of postindependence Zambia is the rapid stratification of people into classes. Distinctions within the African community in colonial days were masked by the fact of a common subjection to racial discrimination. Equally, class differences within the European community were obscured by the racial privileges they all enjoyed. Rapid upward mobility by some Zambians after independence led to the myth of an egalitarian society based on hard work and merit. By the 1980s, however, this early social fluidity has been replaced by the solidification into distinct classes. A wealthy class has emerged and is consolidating its position. Although its nature is disputed,[8] the individuals are readily identified by the common man as belonging to the *apamwamba*, a Nyanja word for "those at the top." Equally, an African working class is distinct within Zambia, a divided and contradictory petite bourgeoisie is observable, and stratification of the rural population is taking place.

In today's urban setting almost the full socioeconomic spectrum (excluding the rural population), from the wealthy in their suburban homes surrounded by high fences or walls topped with broken glass—the architecture of fear—to the quarters euphemistically called "high-density areas," referring to overcrowded slums, is to be seen. The gap between the rich and poor can be illustrated by a brief description of life for an *apamwamba* family living in the Kabulonga suburb of Lusaka (a high-income, low-density area), in contrast with that of the average dweller in the neighboring township of Kalingalinga (a low-income, high-density location).

The male head of a household located in Kabulonga is most likely to be a lawyer, civil servant, banker, manager of a parastatal, or a politician; he could also be a successful businessman or merchant. The family lives in a spacious house, surrounded by gardens, with all their needs tended to by servants. The lawns are bordered by tall concrete walls and the house sports heavy burglar bars on every window. Sometimes the husband will employ a night guard to protect the house and his Mercedes or Peugeot car, vital for getting to work but also a de rigueur status symbol. He may also have a Isuzu or Datsun pickup truck for trips to farms he purchased with government-guaranteed loans or the chain of rural bars he owns. Often the wife does not work. She divides her time between provisioning the house, possibly from the nearby luxury-laden Kabulonga supermarket (partially owned by Greek merchants) and social occasions. In rare circumstances, she will make a shopping trip to London or Swaziland to obtain the newest fashions and appliances. More often her day is composed of visits to female friends and relatives or shopping in suburban shops, as the center of Lusaka has become too dangerous for those with obvious wealth. With her own car, she will ferry around the children from the private schools they attend or possibly from the better public schools (Kabulonga Boys or the Convent, for example) located in the suburbs. She must also deliver the children to activities or friends who also live in dog-guarded concrete "compounds" that cannot safely be approached on foot. Often this task is lessened when the children are sent off to boarding school in the United Kingdom or Zimbabwe.

Upon returning home, the husband changes into a leisure suit, turns on the TV or video and waits for the meal, served by his wife, though usually prepared by the kitchen help. In the course of a heavy dinner of Western-style meat and vegetables as well as the traditional *nshima* (local maize dish, approximating a cross between hominy grits and mashed potatoes), the prototypical husband will consume several beers. Afterward he may travel to elite bars or hotels to seek company. The rest of the family will remain grouped around the TV until bedtime, as many consider it too dangerous to travel at night. Within its luxurious home, then, the *apamwamba* family leads a life of considerable comfort designed on the Western model.

But members are also quite isolated in these homes from friends and relations and intimidated by the rising crime rate in Zambia.

Abutting the wealth and ostentation of Kabulonga are the shacks and small dwellings of Kalingalinga. The poorest area within a larger settlement, Kalingalinga backs on the slightly more prosperous Mutendere township and the wealthy Kabulonga plots. Poorly serviced for transport, water, sewage, and stores, this slum is also highly insecure. Those employed or with a few possessions are preyed upon by the ever-present *kabalala*, or thieves. Jobs for men and women from Kalingalinga range from manual labor (garbage collection, street sweeping, house servants, and security guards) to lower-level white-collar jobs such as clerks, shop attending, nursing, and school teaching. The people in the white-collar category stay in Kalingalinga because of the desperate housing shortage and their low, fixed salaries. In the end of the dry season (October or November), the local outside water taps dry up. The paths and roads from Kalingalinga toward Kabulonga or the university to the west and north are lined with women going for water for cooking or bathing, passing those carrying heavy containers homeward with a baby on the back and one or two small children tagging alongside. The narrow dirt streets are filled with petty traders and the unemployed, often youths still wearing school uniforms though now squeezed out of the school system and without jobs.

Local schools are overcrowded and shabby, but places in them are highly prized, as education offers one of the few hopes for people to get out of a locality like Kalingalinga. Taverns and shebeens do a booming business. Opaque beer is cheap, and for many who have given up hope, it is solace from a hard and bitter existence. Ironically, the closest large grocery for Kalingalinga residents is the Kabulonga Supermarket. The rich and poor of Lusaka patronize it for the same reason: fewer shortages. They rub elbows in the crowded aisles, the former seeking imported liquor and meat and the latter, bread, salt, detergents, and milk.

Between the city center of Lusaka and these outlying suburbs and slums are communities like Northmead and Kalundu. Here the homes of the middle-level government workers and other employees are grouped around small shopping centers and markets. These are the members of the new Zambian petite bourgeoisie; they struggle to keep their cars on the road with few spare parts, inadequate mechanical workshops, and little public transport. Such unreliable cars often are called *sunka mulamu*, which roughly translated from Nyanja means "push me, my brother-in-law." The rapidly increasing cost of living (consumer prices in urban areas were calculated by the ILO to have increased by 13.6 percent in 1981, 12.6 percent in 1982, and by at least 20 percent in 1984)[9] makes it difficult to maintain essentials as well as to keep up outward appearances (Western three-piece suits for the men, modish dress and high heels for the women, and leather shoes and good clothes for the children).

Harassment by small-scale and organized *kabalala* is a fact of life in Kalundu and Northmead as are declining civic services such as street lights,

TABLE 3.3
Income Distribution in Zambia

Income Distribution	Year	Rural	Urban	Total
Households with incomes (in cash or kind) below the minimum basic needs level				
% of households with incomes below K100 per month	1980	80	25	60
% share of income of the poorest 40% of population	1976	12	14	8[a]
% share of income of the richest 5% of population	1976	25	28	35[a]

[a] National averages sometimes lie outside the range of rural and urban averages because the rural areas are worse off than the urban.

Source: ILO/JASPA, Zambia: Basic Needs in an Economy Under Pressure (Geneva: International Labour Organization, 1981). Based on Table 0.1, p. xxi, "Zambia: A Basic Needs Profile."

clean water, and adequate schools. Wives in these communities are likely to work out of a mixture of necessity and choice. Children are pushed hard to succeed in examinations and thus continue in a public school system that uses rigorous examinations to narrow the number of entrants for a postprimary education.[10] Hard work and savings can provide an occasional luxury item such as a TV, but the limited family income is often drained by the large and small demands of the extended family for cash and commodities.

A more extensive and sophisticated material culture makes stratification in cities like Lusaka more obvious than that in villages like Mutondo. The gap between the rich and poor is widening, although Zambia is one of the wealthier nations in Africa.[11] Available statistics reinforce the observers' impressions (see Table 3.3). By 1976 the poorest 40 percent of the population shared 8 percent of the income while the richest 5 percent shared 35 percent of the income. An ILO study projected that by 1980, 60 percent of the population would have households with incomes (in cash and kind) below the minimum basic-needs level.[12] In 1985 one economist argued that 10 percent of the population controlled over four-fifths of the nation's income.[13]

Over time, urbanization and stratification affect people's ethnic identity. The fluidity of culture under urbanized conditions makes it difficult to maintain ethnic lines. Often people no longer know what is truly traditional and what is borrowed or imported. Perhaps this began with colonial urban policy excluding women and non-working-age males from the towns as it is these very people who often are the custodians of culture in most societies. Migrants came to the towns in the 1920s and 1940s with behavior based on unspoken rules and traditions of their villages. Soon they faced new circumstances for which the older customs did not prepare them. So people created new cultural forms—sometimes blending together traditional features, often borrowing from another culture, and occasionally inventing totally new cultural forms. By the 1980s, although the means to create these forms still varied with class position, a wide range of urban dwellers were deeply involved in the task of cultural innovation.

The blending together of two or more cultures is perhaps most visible in the negotiations that surround marriage and child care. Historically, marriage took place between individuals but reflected a larger compact between families or lineages. In traditional African societies *lobola*, "bridewealth," was paid not to buy a wife but rather to establish an exchange between the man's and the woman's families and to compensate her family for the loss of her labor power. Ceremonies celebrated the event and a series of expectations began for the wider, extended family. In the majority of Zambia's ethnic groups, the children belong to the mother's side of the family (matrilineal). In a few, children are considered the "property" of the father's family (patrilineal). As long as people take spouses who share the same customary beliefs, all is well—at least as far as family expectations are concerned. But when people marry across cultural lines, tensions arise that must be dealt with before the marriage begins. Because most cross-cultural marriages occur in the towns, it is to the urban setting that we must look for new customs or norms.

To date, no hard and fast rules have emerged, but patterns are appearing. Young people often try to find a way to suit both families. This may entail going through the ceremony twice, in different locations and with different audiences. Many young married couples choose to reside in town to avoid pulls from either side. People search for answers to these difficult situations where traditions are not helpful. They often return to their own cultures, picking some aspects and blending them together differently. A couple may choose to be married in a civil center, live in town, and draw up a will for the husband. Or they may undergo a traditional ceremony but in Western dress (see Photo 3.2). As these are innovations, they are not fully accepted by the older members of the families. So these cultural innovations are fragile indeed.

A death sets in motion a set of cultural demands and tensions too. In many Zambian ethnic groups, the death of a husband signals his relatives to descend on the bereaved widow's home and take all items of value, sometimes even the children. In precolonial days, the lack of material possessions by the average family limited the number of items to be seized. Also the removal of goods was counterbalanced by the custom of reincorporating the widow and children into the lineage through marriage with a male relative of the deceased. The widow, therefore, would lose the dead spouse's goods, but she and her children would not be left to fend for themselves.

Urbanization and Christianity deeply affect this custom as well. An urban widow today may choose not to be remarried in such a fashion. If

SOCIETY AND CULTURE	45

PHOTO 3.2 Young couple, dressed in Western clothes, undergoing a traditional wedding ceremony in village, Southern Province.

her deceased husband's relatives are all married and she is Christian, she cannot marry in this manner. Her wishes may be respected, but the husband's relatives are not constrained to hold back. So the sudden death of a husband can leave an urban housewife and her children destitute despite previous comfort. Occasionally, women who do not cooperate are threatened with violence by the husband's relatives.

In recognition of the social disruption and poverty this custom causes for a growing number of urbanized women, the Law Development Commission has tackled the thorny question of a common inheritance law. But what new custom should they choose? One option borrowed from the West is the last will and testament. A husband may make a will that specifies what happens to his goods upon his death and register the will with the civil authorities. Although his wishes may not be immediately respected by the extended family, the widow (often with the aid of an older male from her family) can lodge a legal order for the return of goods obtained in the traditional manner. This borrowing of a Western tradition has become more common and is an indicator of cultural synthesis. But the idea of legislating a common inheritance law is so sensitive and difficult that it has been "in committee" for many years and is likely to remain so.

When blending of local cultures and borrowing from other cultures have not produced an adequate set of rules or institutions to deal with problematic situations, then the search is on for totally new cultural forms. Such new ideas can be disguised as tradition, but one notes on closer examination that the inspiration and form are new. An example is the national dress competition held each year. Kafue Textiles of Zambia, a parastatal company producing *chitenge*, sponsors this contest for dressmakers (mostly women) in an effort to pick the best "national" dress, recognizing that no uniform dress exists already. The products often reflect Western or West African designs, but many ideas are Zambian, directed to creating something new that will then become part of national life. Anthropologists and others may be right to be cynical about the possibility for authority to "create culture." Nonetheless, some aspects of modern Zambian culture truly seem original. The impetus offered by outside authorities operates only as a catalyst to the enthusiasm and creativity of the individual citizen.

Another example of cultural creativity is a popular column of political satire that appears weekly in the *Times of Zambia* under the byline of Kapelwa Musonda. Articles openly criticize Zambian politicians and civil servants, avoiding slander charges by slight alteration of details or by putting words in the mouth of the Everyman character "Comrade Bonzo." The identity of Kapelwa Musonda is not publicly known and hence subject to much speculation. It is significant that this column is printed in English, which carries its own cachet.

Language and Literature

Language too has undergone changes under conditions of urbanization and stratification. In a multicultural and multilingual society, language is a potent factor in national identity and integration. Unfortunately, many local languages spoken in Zambia, although derived from Bantu linguistic roots, are not mutually intelligible. Thus one must learn another's language to be understood. Who is forced to learn the other's language is an indicator of power that can turn language into a cultural battlefield.

After independence, the government made the decision to have eight official languages (Bemba, Tonga, Lunda/Luvale, Nyanja [Ngoni and Chewa], Lozi, Kaonde, and English). English was to be the language for government documents, debates in the national assembly, press conferences and political addresses by the president, education in primary and secondary schools and at the university. The seven indigenous languages were to share the official status with English and be used to some degree and in some areas for document publication, in literacy campaigns, and on Radio Zambia.[14] Unofficially, certain languages have emerged as linguae francae for distinct urban areas. Bemba is widely spoken on the Copperbelt and in Kabwe, Nyanja in Lusaka and Chipata, and Lozi in Livingstone. Nonetheless the major newspapers, the *Times of Zambia* (circulation 50,000), the *Zambia Daily Mail* (circulation 20,000), the *Sunday Times of Zambia*, the *Mining Mirror*, and trade and government magazines are all published in English. A few church, party, and union groups regularly print in local languages, and biweekly government newspapers appear in the eight official languages. Yet the most important media coverage is in English.

Aside from the problems that multilingualism presents to publishing and broadcasting institutions, deeper questions plague academics, civil servants, and politicians. Primary is the question of whether English—an alien language identified with the colonial oppressor—should be an official language at all. Pragmatic issues having to do with education and technical skills are cited to justify the current policy on English. Furthermore, some linguists suggest that the indigenous languages are "closed systems," unable to expand to deal precisely with modern topics of science and technology.

Underneath these educational and pedagogical questions lurk political issues of how language affects national unity and identity. As an illustration, writers and playwrights who want to express themselves are faced with a Hobson's choice—to write in English and reach the educated few or to write in a local language, have a small audience, and totally abdicate the opportunity of having an international reputation. To express themselves widely, authors are forced to use the "colonial language." Further, since 1966 when English was introduced as a medium of instruction in formal schooling, hidden class barriers are being erected against children from rural or peri-urban homes where English is not regularly spoken. Local languages are used in primary schools to discuss cultural topics but not for science or core subjects. Thus children are left with the impression that English is the linguistic medium for the modern world, and local languages have only marginal relevance. Because children who gain entry to secondary school are already a privileged elite, language separates them even further from the others of their generation who after primary education revert to a world conducted in local languages.

There are many problems with the current language policy. An announced political purpose for having English is to encourage national unity. In reality, however, more Zambians speak Bemba or Nyanja than English, and therefore using these local languages as the official ones would be more commonsensical. Researchers note that the country is becoming more, rather than less, heterogeneous linguistically, as the average urban Zambian is trilingual while his or her rural cousin is usually bilingual.[15] Perhaps the government could accept this diversity and make a virtue of it. Policy could be to encourage more languages than the current eight. But this alternative is fraught with problems, not least of which are the costs of trying to offer schooling, broadcasting, and so on in many different languages. Which languages could be used without slighting those who speak the neglected tongues? Such sensitive issues keep English in its predominant place. Language remains a politicized topic only temporarily patched over by the resort to English, which in turn makes class divisions more visible through language stratification.

Another unexpected outcome of the use of English in formal education is the stunting of Zambian literature. Literature, poetry, and drama began to appear in local languages when the colonial government's Department of African Education encouraged authors to write in their mother tongues so their products could be used in the few regional primary schools. The independent government's decision to use English and the semimonopoly over publishing enjoyed by the government body, NECZAM Press (National Educational Corporation of Zambia Ltd.), mean that authors are discouraged from writing in local languages. Worse still, Zambian schools are not yet turning out pupils who have mastered English sufficiently to write in great depth and with proficiency. Instead stories and novels from Zambian authors are often reviewed as being "imitative and unsophisticated."[16]

However, all is not lost in the area of language and literature. Zambian innovativeness has found an outlet in the creation of a new variety of English called *ZamEnglish*, which is used in daily speech. Hence, to go by foot is to "Zamfoot"; most interrogative sentences are punctuated with "isn't it?," just as many North Americans resort to "you know." Prepositions are either left off phrases, as in, "I'll come to pick you at half eight" and "one gets used . . ." (for "one gets used to it"), or added on as in, "we have to learn to cope up with these problems" or "I'm fed up now," meaning "I am full now." Verbs are altered to take on new meaning: A person who is constantly on the move will be referred to as "movious." "Town Bemba" and "Town Nyanja" are introduced into ZamEnglish as well. Some linguists denounce this as language decadence and an indication of poor instruction in English in schools. Others argue that this "loosening up of the language" is part of the growth and adaptiveness of any culture when using a foreign tongue. A few Zambian authors are grasping the opportunity that this new linguistic medium offers them and are turning out stories written in ZamEnglish.[17]

Much humor surrounds ZamEnglish. Often phrases commonly used by government are subtly turned. An example might be when a child is trying to coax a few ngwees (pennies) from a passerby with the phrase "Ah, Madam, there is a 'shortage' of two ngwee here" (a reference to the constant government explanation of failures of projects because of shortages of foreign exchange or materials). Or a remark overheard in the market when a younger brother tried to obtain money from a reluctant older sister. When all other inducements failed, he resorted to "if you don't give me the Kwacha, the consequences are too ghastly to be contemplated!" (paraphrasing the famous threat from the South African prime minister to Zambia's leaders). Thus the reliance on English has not stifled oral creativity or all literature. Yet the usage of English in most written and formal settings is a feature slowly distinguishing the upper- and middle-income groups from the lower classes and urban from rural.

Crafts, Art, and Music

The ferment in modern Zambian arts, crafts, and music is not as palpable as in language. Since the urbanization and industrialization of an essentially rural people began in the 1920s, much creative energy has gone into establishing new cultural norms and coping with life-styles both capitalist and alien. Adaptation to a way of life dominated by the clock, wages, and the market was a necessity. This deeply affected traditional crafts, art, and music.

The younger men who flocked to the towns were often the innovators in their home villages. They brought home manufactured goods—iron hoes replaced traditional hoes; textiles supplanted bark cloth; plastic and tin bowls and containers soon supplanted the clay pots and baskets; and factory-made shoes gained over sandals and other footwear. Within a generation, locally produced items were pushed aside by imported goods or town goods, which were often more durable and as cheap. So traditional crafts, always dependent on the local market, dwindled. Status attached to having "store-bought goods" also undermined the livelihoods of indigenous craftspeople. Traditional blacksmiths, once thriving and honored professionals, were driven almost to extinction by competition posed by manufactured tools and agricultural implements. Only a few men and women survived to pass on their craft skills to their descendants and apprentices. The rural areas are the repository for some indigenous crafts; others have vanished altogether.

In the urban setting local crafts and art are faced with other problems. The streets of the cities are filled with vendors selling malachite ashtrays, ivory bracelets, banana-leaf print drawings, batik cloth, or oil paintings. Many of the artists are not Zambians at all! Often they are Zairians, Tanzanians, or Zimbabweans. Indigenous crafts do not figure prominently on the street markets except the cheap and functional Bemba pots and Nyanja or Lozi basketry (see Photos 3.3 and 3.4). This strange pattern leads many anthropologists and students of local arts and crafts to despair that Zambia is losing its traditional artifacts. This despair may be premature. Arts and crafts do exist in Zambia, but their major presence is in rural areas. In the urban centers there is an overwhelming bias against traditional goods and preference for Western and imported items. All classes in society demonstrate this marked preference, which inflates the import bill of the nation. Machine-produced cotton cloth (*chitenge*) made by Zambian companies long ago absorbed most local demand, but now synthetic clothing (which is imported or whose components are imported) is more popular. Whether this is the result of cultural imperialism is hotly debated, but the economic effects are clear.

The government is sensitive to some problems that revolve around questions of cultural life. Policies have been introduced, with a flourish of rhetoric, to preserve traditional values. Institutions have been created to support and encourage production of local crafts. Some promotion has been forthcoming for Zambian musicians, theater people, and writers. An example of such official support is Kabwata Cultural Village in Lusaka. Set in one of the oldest portions of the city, Kabwata consists of some fifty *rondavels* (round huts made of brick with grass-thatched roofs), which were preserved by the government in 1973 to "serve Zambian traditional values." Carvers and painters live there with some government sponsorship to work and share ideas with the other artisans. There is also supposed to be a program of teaching aspiring artists these crafts, and there are hopes of sales to either government purchasers, local people, or tourists. On Sunday afternoons the National Dance Troupe performs in the arena at the village.

PHOTO 3.3 Bemba water jars and their maker, Chipata Compound, Lusaka.

The problems attendant on such official sponsorship of the arts are visible in the very artificiality of the setting. Meant to appear as a traditional village, the *rondavels* are surrounded by modern apartments and semidetached houses. The artists have to cope with all the problems of modern urban life but with no income other than government subsidies and their sales. The local population does not often come to Kabwata to buy; most of the onlookers and customers are tourists. The problems of trying to encourage traditional crafts within an urbanized and Western city go far beyond the capacities of a scheme such as the Kabwata Cultural Village.

Still, private enterprise has sprung up around local crafts. Most of it is rather marginal—often the artisans have family members hawk their goods in the streets, competing with foreign nationals. Expansion is con-

SOCIETY AND CULTURE 51

PHOTO 3.4 Lozi basket made of roots, with lid.

strained by a limited local market for such goods. Such constraints have deep implications for the future health or expansion of indigenous crafts.

The story is not so bleak in the realm of music, dance, and drama. Perhaps this is because music both is vital in traditional life and has a particular cachet in youth culture of Zambia as elsewhere in the world. Local bands or entertainers sport such colorful names as "The Witch," "Dr. Footswitch," and "Mosi-oa-Tunya" (The Smoke that Thunders—in reference to the local name for Victoria Falls). A few local singers have gained international reputations, and there is a certain amount of circulation of musicians among Zaire, Zambia, Tanzania, and Zimbabwe. A popular column in the *Sunday Times of Zambia* discusses pop music and gossip with all the jargon of the deejay on Western radio. Youth music seems largely an offshoot of Western jazz and rock with an overlay of "highlife" from West Africa and Zaire, reggae from the Caribbean, as well as some distinctly South African influences such as the "click sound" of the Xhosa. To distinguish what percentage of this mix is Zambian is an impossible task. A few observers suggest that Zambian musicians are now returning to locally derived music and innovating with the text of rhythm and harmony.[18]

Indigenous music is still vital to rural ceremonies. Oral histories, praise songs, and various events in the life of the lineage or village require their own complicated and distinctive music. Traditional drummers and other court musicians are part of the retinues of many chiefs. The radio broadcasts both traditional and modern music. In the rural settings music is part of daily life. Researchers try to gather the music, instruments, dance, and costume ideas from the elders in order to preserve an accurate record of the "pure," older ways. The intrusions of the cities, however, are steadily bending even rural music making to new ways and meanings as is characteristic of the cultural evolution for the whole society.

Sadly, the cultural transition to modern Zambia has involved a loss of some artistic elements of the older cultures that gave cohesion and meaning to the average person. Yet to end the discussion on a note of apparent deculturation is to undervalue the creativity and initiative of those who are struggling to incorporate aspects of the old with the new.[19] The cultural fluidity works against the backdrop of some serious social cleavages that are new for the society. Already mentioned are those divisions based on language, region, ethnicity, or race. Age also divides society as does gender; of growing significance are the divisions based on class. The context in which these tensions are most visible is again the towns and peri-urban areas. Class distinctions are most obvious in the urban residential patterns where the segregation previously based on race has been replaced by distinctions of wealth and status.

URBAN GEOGRAPHY

Zambian cities are quite decentralized, with residential areas far distant from offices and stores. In a country with chronic shortages of transportation, this sprawl is not rational. These patterns of urban geography have their roots in colonial racial segregation and the unique "logic" of colonial administrators. The strange evolution of Lusaka, the capital city, provides an illustration. Originally no more than a siding along the line of rail, Lusaka slowly became an administrative and commercial center for the central portion of the protectorate. In the 1920s, the authorities decided to move the capital from Livingstone to Lusaka, and this was completed in 1931.

As noted by Karen Tranberg Hansen, "British town-planning ideas for a generous, gracious city were superimposed on a town segregated economically, socially and spatially by race."[20] New government buildings were to be placed at a distance from businesses and the railroad depot. When the protectorate ran out of money in the Great Depression, many of the plans for a new capital were scrapped altogether, leaving gaping holes in "downtown" Lusaka. Local people who were discouraged from legally building near commercial centers were drawn to empty patches of land to southwest of the first-, second-, and third-class residential areas. Others were forced to squat in the outlying regions, such as the aforementioned Kalingalinga, beyond the immediate concern of the city authorities. Meanwhile, whites built handsome homes with spacious gardens and servants' quarters in first-class residential areas such as Kabulonga, which were in what we would call today the suburbs. The occupants relied on personal, governmental, or company transport. After independence, the new African elite and embassy personnel took over these homes and continued the practice of residential segregation.

For the rest of the population, housing was far more difficult. Some Asians and Africans who managed to locate nearer the towns in second-class areas could walk to work. But the growing number of Africans who lived in the outlying squatter compounds had to rely on lifts, very irregular bus service, bicycling, or "Zamfooting." So Lusaka's transport patterns today bear a strange resemblance to a Midwestern U.S. city built around the automobile and faith in cheap gasoline—sadly inappropriate in modern Zambian conditions.

On the Copperbelt, another residential division persists. The mines, a law onto themselves since the 1920s, built and administered their own housing. In the 1940s, they constructed dwellings for their African work force in keeping with new "stabilization" policies. This housing was located in mining townships, separated from other residential areas both administratively and geographically. Within these townships, racial and hierarchical patterns were clear. The white managers lived upwind from the smelters in exclusive suburbs, the white overseers and technical personnel were located in middle-echelon housing, and the various gradations of African employees lived within the "high-density areas," usually downwind of the industrial pollution.

Residence in mining townships was (and is) connected to employment with the mines. Loss of a job meant eviction. Status distinctions are visible today, with the size and siting of the house indicating the seniority or importance of the occupant. These mining townships still bear a distinct resemblance to military posts in Western countries, with new managers and technicians occupying the upper- and middle-echelon dwellings.

The social character of these mining townships reflects regulations set by mine management. Some people prefer to live in district council housing or squatter compounds because certain money-making enterprises (such as the brewing of beer) are permitted there. On balance, most mine employees prefer the townships as the dwellings are well made, municipal taxes are lower, better services are provided, and people seem to experience lower crime rates. The Copperbelt towns thus remain spatially separated into mining townships, district council areas, and a sprawl of illegal squatter settlements in the interstices.

At independence, UNIP leaders faced the reality of an inadequate housing stock, racially segregated residential patterns, strangely spread out urban cores, and inadequate transportation services. These were hardly the conditions for balanced urban growth. The most immediate problem was the ballooning of squatter settlements. Migrants had flooded in from rural areas in the early 1960s when the vigilance of the authorities relaxed and wage employment grew. Because these squatter areas were illegal, residents were not supplied with any public services. Although the inhabitants tried to make their "squatments" as comfortable as possible, the lack of roads, sewers, lights, garbage disposal, and running water made the compounds unhealthy, overcrowded, peri-urban slums.[21] Popular opinion dismissed such compounds in the 1960s as "crime-ridden ghettos filled with the unemployed, lumpen elements and people just from the bush." If UNIP was to live up to election promises, these squatter areas should be removed as soon as government was able to relocate the people into better-standard housing.

The new salaried personnel also pressured the government. In recognition of the need for the skilled, trained, and vocal Zambians to have adequate housing, government sponsored a series of housing programs. For the petite and aspirant bourgeoisie, loans were made available through the government, private companies, or the National Building Society. The working poor and the unemployed and underemployed, unable to provide the necessary collateral to get and to repay such loans and mortgage plans, had to build with their own resources.[22] This meant more slum housing appeared. To deal with the housing needs of the urban lower classes, the Ministry of Local Government and Housing began "site-and-service" schemes, and city councils built flats based on the English model. The original compromise was that the central government would lend money to local councils to provide service areas. Further, the central authorities would lend to the councils to build apartments for rental to middle- and low-income groups. The tenants would, through their municipal taxes and fees, repay the councils, which would subsequently build more housing.

In the experience of Lusaka, these policies were an example of "too little, too late." The site-and-service schemes were situated far from downtown, and residents were reluctant to relocate there from their more convenient squatments. Councils were not able to build enough housing to keep up with the influx of new town dwellers. Also, they had not provided the administrators necessary to act as large-scale landlords. Equally, not all renters were able or willing to pay their rates regularly. Programs were small and expensive and did not meet the burgeoning needs for urban housing.

By the early 1970s, it had become obvious that the resettlement schemes were impossible both financially and politically. Officials hesitated, perhaps influenced by sociological studies done by staff and students from the University of Zambia concerning the squatters and their settlements. Researchers had found that (contrary to common belief) most inhabitants of these squatter compounds had regular employment; they were not the "loafers and lumpen elements" as they had been portrayed. They were people unable to procure decent housing or in some cases, residents who preferred the squatter areas surrounded by friends and relatives to the isolation of a council flat. Many "squatters" were most reluctant to relocate. They considered the squatments their homes and some had invested considerable sums into houses or stores. Others had commercial activities that flourished in the squatments and would be outlawed in council areas. In general, the inhabitants were not new migrants to towns; most were long-term residents or second-generation urbanites who selected the squatter areas out of need and choice. Further, many were active supporters of the governing party, UNIP. What was needed was not a massive relocation but legalization of their settlements and extension of services to them.[23]

From such insight sprang the new housing policy of "squatter upgrading," initially funded by external aid agencies such as the World Bank. Upgrading has gone a long way toward transforming the face of the peri-urban areas and legalizing a social fact. Upgrading of homes and site-and-service schemes have been assessed as a success for which officials are justifiably proud. New squatter areas, however, continue to spring up with the rural-to-urban exodus. In the 1980s, more pressures will be placed on the town councils and planning authorities, which will have fewer resources to deal with them than they had in the prosperous 1960s and early 1970s.

TRANSFORMATION OF THE EXTENDED FAMILY

Dislocation, anomie, breakdown of the rural family, and undermining of authority structures typify rapid urbanization throughout the world. These are also found in Zambia. Despite it all, however, the extended family is still important, although transformed in certain ways.

The values placed on strong obligations to kin are maintained despite the breakup of the large coresidential households of relatives characteristic of the extended family in the rural areas. For example, the size of the typical urban home in a medium- or high-density area (two–three rooms), limited wage incomes, and high cost of living have constrained the ability of the whole family to live together as a productive unit. Although relatives still come to visit (often for long periods), the limited physical space dictates how many relatives can stay. Again the creative cultural impulse is at work. Although most urban homes are not large enough to encompass the fifteen to twenty members of an extended family, one division of the larger family may select an area in which to settle and build homes near one another. The relatives then share access to each house as though they were living in a village. Additional income goes to add on an extra room.

Urban dwellers keep in touch with rural relatives through travel or sending money and gifts and taking in younger relatives so that they can attend urban schools. (These are considered better, especially in the teaching of English.) Urban dwellers in middle- and lower-income groups often tell interviewers that they plan to retire to the village one day. Thus it is important to keep "a good name in the village," and this requires certain expenses and inconveniences. They see themselves as purchasing a kind of "social security" which they may never actually draw on if they maintain their town residence. Cousins help each other, nephews and nieces receive school fees from older relatives, younger sisters and brothers are readily incorporated into older siblings' married homes as unpaid servants, and so on. It is a rare Zambian home that does not have at least one member outside the nuclear unit living there on a permanent basis. Contributions toward the family income are common but not obligatory as it is assumed that at one time the individual (or his or her family) will reciprocate. Such social arrangements soften the harshness of urban life where so many social interactions are determined by the cash nexus.

Visiting family and friends on Saturday afternoon and Sunday after church is the norm rather than the exception. Funerals, marriages, graduations, stays in hospitals all draw out the large extended Zambian family. People who live far from relatives feel a distinct loss in physical separation from "the family." Despite rapid urbanization some elements of Zambian social structure have managed to avoid dismemberment by capitalist culture. Gender and age gradation, also part of traditional life, have been more disrupted and distorted more fundamentally than has the extended family. Yet the rapid changes since independence in the ability of people to accumulate have introduced conflicts within the extended family. Now some richer relatives are reluctant to fulfill all obligations, and the poorer members have some unreasonable expectations. Despite its resilience, then, the extended family too is being transformed. The role of women in modern Zambia is also undergoing some painful and disorienting adjustments.

THE ROLE OF WOMEN

In traditional society the status of women was inferior to that of men, at least among commoners. Women were considered, however, as a vital part of society. They reproduced the family and took the major share of agricultural labor. Men and women did not always do the same work in the fields; rather their labor was complementary. Heavy work such as *chitemene* clearing among the Bemba and Lunda or digging of canals in Barotseland was male labor and was matched by longer-term jobs of weeding, tilling, carrying of water and firewood, and heavy harvesting work done by women. Then as now, "women supply the bulk of the labor on land whose rights are held by men."[24] Yet women in traditional Zambian culture were respected and acknowledged members of society, although most customs prevented them from taking a very individualistic or outspoken role.

With the advent of large-scale migration of men to town (1920s onward) the economic and social balance between the sexes was upset. In the early days of company and colonial rule, men returned to their villages and to their womenfolk at planting and harvest times, bringing money to pay taxes, items for the household, and gifts for relatives. The rural household, in turn, rebuilt the health of men who had often endured strenuous and unhealthy work conditions. The men would stay to recuperate, to impregnate their wives, and sometimes to help clear the fields and plant new crops. Then they would return to the towns, mines, and commercial farms to work for wages. Women would be left alone with older relatives and children. In his study of the Zambian peasant economy, Lionel Cliffe suggested that men became workers and women became peasant farmers.[25]

Over the years the returnee and remittance rates began to decline. Many women were left alone permanently in the rural areas, prevented from following their husbands by strict colonial rules and traditional mores. When the stabilization policies began in the 1940s, more women managed to go to town to find their husbands or simply to try to make a new life for themselves and their children. Removed from familial networks, these women were vulnerable in a society that still believed that women should not have an individual or independent role and that any woman alone in the city was a prostitute.

It was a no-win situation for such women. If a woman stayed in the rural areas without a husband, she was condemned to dire poverty, facing all the disadvantages and difficulties of small-scale farming without the requisite labor power. If the wife followed the husband, however, she might find him with a "town wife" and surely practicing a life-style quite foreign to her village ways. Finally, those few who established themselves as urban dwellers in their own right faced strong disapproval from both traditional and European authorities. Correspondence between local African rulers and various colonial representatives is replete with references to such women as "loose" and "a threat to the stability of towns." The introduction of European norms of womanly behavior did little to raise the social position of the woman, simply replacing the argument that she should stay in the village with the phrase that "her proper role is in the home."

After independence, women were freer to live in urban areas, either with or without husbands. Now in labor disputes the women stand by their husbands and even march against the employers (see Photo 3.5). Some residual cultural and ideological attitudes toward women persist, however. These add an element of strain between the sexes in Zambia today, especially among those with some education. Popular columns in the newspaper and radio programs refer to violence and cruelty directed against women. Rarely a week goes by without a reference in the national press to a wife who was badly beaten or killed by her husband in a marital dispute. One analyst has described the relations between the sexes in the urban setting as "pathological."[26] This is possibly going too far, but the minimal sentences received by men for wife killing and the commonness of complaints about husbands drinking up their paychecks leave a rather bleak impression of male-female relations, especially in urban Zambia.

In even more desperate straits are the women alone in the rural areas, trapped in a cycle of poverty. They are marginalized in much of the village social life because of the threat they pose to those women who do have husbands. Several such women alone in Mutondo remarked that they did not attend village festivities for fear of causing bitter wrangling with the married women. In 1980 it was estimated that one quarter of rural households were headed by women and the vast majority of them were impoverished.[27] Many did not possess even a hoe for gardening but had to rely on begging from relatives or neighbors. Alone, impoverished, ill- or uneducated, malnourished and overworked, the lot of many rural women is harsh and seemingly intractable to mild reformist measures.

Still, there are some encouraging developments. In the past ten years some women have taken on far more active and aggressive roles, especially

PHOTO 3.5 Miners' wives picketing in the Copperbelt strikes of 1981.

in informal trading. Government policy against discrimination based on sex has been a boon to younger women who have the necessary skills to make a job application. "Zambianization" programs in the private and public sectors have led to openings for a few. Some women have managed to reach the top of the occupation or job category in law, politics, business, and academia. Because of the shortage of these "showcase women," it is common to find that they often change careers in midstream and at a very high level, recycling their names throughout the bureaucracy. Although there may be a certain amount of resentment among male colleagues of these famous women, the upward mobility of the few does not yet seem to have been impeded by any unified male resistance. Probably this is because they often act as female "spokesmen" in support of policies and practices of the governing class that defend male dominance.

Women from lower classes try to improve their lives through trading in the informal sector. One lively group are the urban marketeers. Usually in their late 40s and early 50s (past their major childbearing years), these "market mamas" are tough and sharp businesswomen. They run stalls in the major markets or set up small trading activities from their own homes. To ensure that they have good produce (a necessity as prices are fixed and consumers will shop around for the best products), these women must meet the farmers who unload in the central market at daybreak. To add additional items to their stock (such as cooking oil, rice, salt, and flour), they stand for hours at the state-run shops, circling again and again in line because they are allowed to purchase only a certain amount per turn. Then they must find transport to carry their goods back to their stalls or homes. A political element enters the scene, as the license to run a stall seems connected to party membership. Often these market mamas faithfully turn out for state visits and various political events. Many employ younger relatives, and a few are quite successful entrepreneurs. For the majority, this trading life is quite demanding; the women often become toughened to the rigors of very competitive business.

Other women try to earn through small, home-based crafts such as knitting or sewing (see Photo 3.6). Many must feed themselves and their children from gardens and they also try to produce a little surplus. Life for these women is difficult, and they live very close to the margin. As most families are large and as many husbands are engaged in activities that consume their wages before the end of the month, struggles between poor women and men can be brutal. The ready availability of *chibuku* (cheap opaque beer) adds an explosive element to an already difficult situation. In times of stress, men and women often turn to sources of solace such as religion and traditional medicine.

RELIGION AND TRADITIONAL MEDICINE

Zambia is predominantly Christian, with most people tending to identify themselves with some variety of Protestantism or Catholicism. The president, Dr. Kaunda, the son of missionary parents, is a model churchgoer and family man. Church spokespersons are given considerable space in the press, and church programs are among the most popular in the mass media.

Christianity in Zambia encompasses a wide variety of religious doctrines with the common threads of belief in Jesus and in an afterlife. Anglicans, Baptists, Methodists, and Roman Catholics are well established. Syncretic churches have a long history in the region too and in recent years seem to have gained many new adherents.[28] Many of the creeds and practices of these fundamentalist churches have strong charismatic elements. It is common to find "speaking in tongues," faith healing, and spirit possession, which link many of these religions with traditional beliefs. Many religious personnel labor to explain to people the upheavals in current life and to help individuals make sense of the bewildering choices facing them. Preachers

PHOTO 3.6 A seamstress, Old Chilenje, Lusaka.

and ministers emphasize practices such as adult baptism to draw in members who might have fallen away from prior religious beliefs under the lures of the city. Sometimes the proselytizing of fundamentalist churches brings their personnel into conflict with mainstream churches. Equally, some formal churches such as the Roman Catholics have incorporated a strong element of fundamentalist practices. The Lusaka archdiocese was rocked by a recent struggle between the local archbishop, Milingo, who practices faith healing, and the Vatican, which calls this "witchcraft" or at least "heresy."[29]

A growing number of Zambians are followers of millenarian sects such as the Watchtower Bible and Tract Society and the Seventh-Day Adventists. Often locally based missionaries receive personal and monetary aid from the mother organizations in Europe or North America. As in other parts of the world, these religious movements preach that "Christ is arriving soon" and have strict codes of personal behavior. To cite an illustration, the Watchtower society preaches strict asceticism and discipline along with the promise that there is a "better world hereafter." Jehovah's Witnesses see God as black and all whites as excluded from the Kingdom of God, a certain settling of the score that must have strong psychological appeal.

PHOTO 3.7 A bishop and pastors of an apostolic church, Old Chilenje, Lusaka.

Some analysts attribute the current popularity of these fundamentalist and charismatic churches and sects (see Photo 3.7) to the need to fill the gap in culture with the decline of traditional mores and the inappropriateness of imported norms to daily life. Others argue that these religious movements, with their internally consistent sets of rules and expectations and insistence on economic self-reliance, bind together members of the congregation in a way that bears a distinct resemblance to village life.[30]

One religious movement that was unique to Zambia was the Lumpa Church of Alice Lenshina. This church grew in Chinsali District in Northern Province—also the home of the president and the former vice president of the First Republic and an early UNIP stronghold. A charismatic preacher, Lenshina converted thousands to the dual belief that the faithful could not be injured by earthly weapons and that there should be a *total* separation of church and state. Members of this sect, therefore, refused to swear allegiance to the government. They were largely ignored in colonial and federation times, perhaps because they were far distant from the cities or the rail line. But when the nationalist leaders took power in 1964, UNIP came into conflict with the Lumpa church. A small but ugly war ensued. In the end, Lenshina was imprisoned, many people died, others fled to Zaire, and the church was suppressed. The emotional power of such syncretic religions continues however.

Another social institution that meets with widespread popular support is the practice of traditional medicine by an *ng'anga*. Some *bang'anga* (plural of *ng'anga*) are experienced herbalists and many function as folk healers.[31] It is not these relatively innocuous activities that draw the ire of the established churches and government, however. Some *bang'anga* are accused of practicing witchcraft. In Zambia, such a term covers a wide range of activities from the production of charms so that a person can pass an examination, to potions to hold a lover, to poisons to dispatch an enemy.[32] The average person seems to believe in the power of "witches," and consequently, they are both feared and respected. The *ng'anga* usually surrounds himself or herself with rituals and charms that are meant to impress the clientele and perhaps to justify the fee. Spirit possession is common; especially afflicted are women—which may reveal a reaction of women against their helplessness. Notwithstanding the skepticism outsiders have about these practices, witchcraft is widely believed by Zambians to make sense of otherwise puzzling events. Frequently claims and counterclaims of witchcraft end in violence. The people directly involved, therefore, lead a precarious life balanced between social status and personal liability.

Despite official disapproval of such practices, the traditional spiritualists and *bang'anga* ply their trades openly. In recognition of this reality, the government has tried to develop some programs that could incorporate the less controversial aspects of traditional medicine into wider health care. For example, an effort has been made to bring herbalists under the Ministry of Health, providing them with services and subjecting their potions and practices to some scrutiny. As one might expect, this plan has faced great opposition from the traditional healers *and* the medical profession. It is unclear whether the philosophies and interests of these two kinds of "doctors" could ever permit them to work cooperatively. Whatever the government position, traditional medicine is thriving in Zambia, although altered by the experiences of colonialism, Christianity, and urbanization.

CONCLUSION

In summary, Zambian society is a fascinating mix of traditional and modern cultures and behaviors. Rapid urbanization had led to deep social instabilities. The cities and towns, where just under half the population live, dominate the countryside. Exposure to Western cultures and ideology has left many Zambians with a taste for urban, middle-class life, rejecting African arts, crafts, and music. A stagnant economy seems likely to disappoint many who hold these expectations, especially the growing ranks of the unemployed who have attended secondary school.

Cultural heterogeneity continues to grow apace as languages and gender roles change. Even the most isolated villages are touched by the market and hence by the economic problems of today. Gaps in economic position between black and white in the colonial days are replicated today between rich and poor Zambians. Although the persistence of the extended family and continued availability of land lessen social tensions, a rapid population growth rate[33] means that interclass battles over limited resources are likely to become more blatant and more violent.

These cultural and class developments so visible in the 1980s were not predetermined in the 1960s. When the nationalist leadership took over in 1964, the rhetoric was replete with promises of greater democracy, preserving traditional culture, narrowing the gap between the urban and rural peoples, and extending services to all. How the group that came to power coped with the social time bomb that it inherited, how new classes evolved, and especially how a local upper class has consolidated itself in relation to other Zambians will be dealt with next.

4
The Political Economy of the First Republic, 1964-1972

This chapter sketches the key events in the evolution of the Zambian political economy during the early years and traces the rise to power of a particular grouping or fraction of national politicians within the new local governing class.[1] The terrain for this process was the state and the party (UNIP), and the prize was posts and privileges associated with office, as the new rulers did not have an independent economic base. An important factor underlying the policies and actions of the First Republic was the buoyant national economy: The value of mineral exports rose from K 239 million in 1963 to a high of K 729 million in 1969.[2] Initially the income and rents from the minerals were shared out among the new government, the foreign mining companies, and the international banks that held the loans. Plentiful financial resources allowed the government to introduce populist programs of health and education services to much of the population. Strong copper prices and high productivity on the mines also fed the egos and pockets of the new leaders, permitting a few to begin to accumulate considerable personal wealth. Most attention, however, went to the battle to control state and party as these were the foci of politics in the early years.

Despite such fiscal advantages, the path of the new governing group was not smooth. The language of politics was replete with ethnoregionalism because those traits were the resources that the different contenders brought to the struggle within UNIP and between the political parties. Ethnic rivalries demanded much attention of the leaders and tested the skills of the president to balance the contending sides. Also the persistence of foreign domination of the economy led to confrontations between the external "rulers" and the local "governors" that culminated in nationalization of most foreign-owned properties. Finally, under many pressures, the interclass alliances of the nationalist era, especially the one between the local petite bourgeoisie and the working class, began to disintegrate.

The substantive themes for discussion here are four: (1) the processes of takeover of the state and the introduction of welfare services; (2) the bitter ethnoregional conflicts that culminated in the introduction of one-party rule; (3) the growing accumulation of power in the hands of the executive—presidentialism; and (4) a struggle for control over the economy between domestic and foreign interests. It should be noted that these themes are surface indicators of the underlying process of class formation in Zambian society that took place in the years of the First Republic. More overt was the struggle by the national politicians to gain control over the state itself and then to restructure the political system to suit their needs and aspirations.

RESTRUCTURING THE POLITICAL SYSTEM

Promises and Politics: Political Takeover and Welfare Programs

The nationalist leaders who came to power in the 1962 elections were deeply dissatisfied with the semiindependent status conferred on the country by Britain. They demanded (and received) the right to hold in January 1964 another election, which brought full independence to the nation as the Republic of Zambia (see Table 4.1). The new government, which took office in October 1964, was a hybrid of a Westminster system with a prime minister and responsible cabinet and an executive system with strong powers located in a president. The two-tiered electoral system (with a main and a reserved roll) was maintained for the 1964 vote, yet universal adult suffrage made the outcome an African majority government a foregone conclusion. What was not clear was which African party—the ANC or UNIP—would dominate or whether the new republic would start as an alliance.

Three major parties contested the 1964 election.[3] UNIP gained fifty-five out of sixty-five seats on the main roll, sufficient to control parliament. The ANC rebuffed offers to merge with UNIP and instead became the loyal opposition with ten seats. The National Progress Party (NPP—formerly the settler UFP) gained the ten reserved seats.[4] Soon after the 1964 election, the NPP began to disintegrate, dissolving itself in 1966, and thus ending the era of white settler politics. With its majority in parliament, UNIP's leaders had a clear course to begin to transform the political and economic system and in so doing they altered the social framework of the nation as well.

Administrative reorganization and localization of posts had high priority for the members of the new Government of the Republic of Zambia (GRZ), as these changes were vital for delivering on campaign promises made by UNIP and also for offering rewards to party faithfuls. An early leadership decision was to consolidate the functions of government, which had been fragmented in the federal period. Diverse and formerly autonomous departments were placed under one central authority in some cases; in others, separate but connected ministries such as the Ministry of African Education

TABLE 4.1
Major Events in the Period of the First Republic, 1964-1972

October 1962	Elections brought ANC/UNIP coalition to government.
January 1964	New elections; universal adult suffrage; UNIP gained majority of seats.
October 24, 1964	1st Republic of Zambia, KK as President.
November 1965	Rhodesia's Unilateral Declaration of Independence; road and rail links to Zambia affected.
July 1966	United Party (UP) formed with following in the west.
February 1967	By-elections for Parliament; 2 seats--UNIP won.
March 1967	UNIP party elections; divisiveness surfaced.
February 1968	KK's temporary resignation; by-elections, 4 seats--ANC won.
April 1968	Mulungushi Reforms I announced at National Council of UNIP.
August 1968	UP (Lozi party) banned.
August 1968	National Assembly and Presidential elections; KK won.
August 11, 1969	Matero Reforms: 51 percent of mining shares were taken by GRZ.
August 25, 1969	Kapwepwe resigned temporarily.
November 1970	Mulungushi II--attempted takeover of banks.
August 1971	United Progressive Party (UPP) emerged, Kapwepwe left UNIP to head UPP with Chimba and Chisata.
December 1971	100 UPP members detained; by-election,12 seats--1 to UPP (Kapwepwe), 11 to UNIP.
February 1972	UPP banned, Kapwepwe and 122 followers detained; KK commissioned Mainza Chona to examine form for one-party state.
December 1972	Legislation passed introducing a "one-party participatory democracy."

and the Ministry of European Education were amalgamated. Staffing the middle and upper echelons of the bureaucracy was temporarily constrained by the shortage of qualified personnel. Many expatriates and white settlers stayed on in the Zambian civil service in the early years. In July 1966 the first black Zambians were appointed permanent secretaries to various ministries; in October of the same year the topmost civil service posts were Africanized.[5] Still as late as 1967 "whites held two out of three of the top 1,700 civil service posts, omitting vacancies."[6]

The civil service was rapidly expanded to provide more services to the nation (from 22,511 in 1963–1964 to 51,497 in 1967).[7] Black Zambians were promoted from lower-level positions. Despite the inevitable squabbles and inefficiencies from such a large number of new personnel, the civil servants made a mammoth effort to extend services to the African population, which had been so neglected under colonialism. The government spent heavily in the early years (from K 91 million in 1963–1964 to K 553 million in 1971),[8] and outstanding achievements were made in health and education.

Education. The rudimentary education facilities available to Africans during the colonial period were rapidly expanded and desegregated to offer

TABLE 4.2
Student Enrollments, 1964-1982

	1964	1974	1982
Primary	378,600	858,191	1,121,769
Secondary	13,900	65,764	104,859
Teacher training	1,500	2,900	3,343
Adult education	2,700	59,974	19,663
University of Zambia	-----	2,612	4,088
Technical & Trades Training Institutes	800	5,666	5,668
TOTAL	397,500	995,107	1,259,390

Source: Republic of Zambia, Central Statistical Office, Monthly Digest of Statistics 15, nos. 3-6 (March/June 1978), Table 63, p. 57; 18, nos. 4-6 (April/June 1982), Table 61, pp. 55, and 20, no. 12 (December 1984), Table 58, p. 53 (Lusaka: Central Statistical Office, 1978, 1982, 1984).

free primary education to a growing proportion of the children of the nation. At independence, less than 0.5 percent of the 3.5 million people had even full primary education,[9] so first priority had to go to building and staffing primary schools throughout the nation.[10] Then expansion of the narrow secondary school system had to be undertaken. Between 1964 and 1974 the enrollments in primary school more than doubled while the secondary school enrollments almost quintupled (see Table 4.2). Technical and trades schools, closed to Africans under federation as a concession to the white trade unionists, blossomed from an enrollment of a mere 800 in 1964 to 5,666 in 1974. The establishment of the University of Zambia in 1966 to provide tertiary education and to offer its own degrees required an enormous effort to recruit staff, build staff and student housing, and launch a university library. From a nation with only 109 university graduates at independence,[11] GRZ commitment of funds to the tertiary sector meant 2,612 students enrolled at university by 1974. This was to double again in the following decade. The opening up of the education system was very popular with Zambians and did much to sustain the popularity of the regime during the First Republic.

Health. In 1964, forty-eight hospitals served a population of more than three and a half million. Most of these institutions were located along the rail line, with ten run exclusively for mining personnel by the mining companies. The nineteen mission-sponsored ones were located outside the central corridor. As with so many other features of the imbalanced political economy of Northern Rhodesia, decent health care was restricted by race, class, and location.

The chief medical goals announced at independence were to "make health care more widely available, particularly in rural areas, at little or no direct cost to the people, and to institute preventive health measures."[12] By

TABLE 4.3
Medical Facilities in Zambia, 1964-1982

Number of Hospitals and Health Centers	1964	1968	1972	1976	1980	1982
Hospitals (total)	48	62	76	81	81	81
Government	19	27	36	42	42	42
Mission	19	12	12	11	11	11
Health Centers and Clinics	306	419	595	657	721	779*
Government	187	251	360	388	469	512
Mission	63	72	79	73	66	65
Urban/Dept/Industrial	39	68	106	138	120**	135
Mines/Other clinics	17	28	50	58	66	67
TOTAL	354	481	671	738	802	860

* Mobile clinics are excluded.

** In addition to the 120 urban/departmental/industrial clinics, there were twenty-seven mobile (government) clinics in operation in the urban areas and nine mobile (mission) clinics in operation in the rural areas.

Source: Central Statistical Office, Monthly Digest of Statistics 20, no. 12 (December 1984) (Lusaka: Central Statistical Office), Table 59, p. 54.

1972 the number of hospitals had increased by more than 50 percent; most of the new institutions were government hospitals and several were located outside the railway provinces. Health centers and clinics proliferated as the backbone of the prenatal and preventive health measures.[13] Government-run rural health centers nearly doubled in number (see Table 4.3). Again the UNIP government began to deliver on some of its promises in the independence struggle and electoral campaign. By the end of the first decade of self-rule, the legacy of a mere handful of public institutions with an urban bias and highly segregated facilities had been fundamentally transformed. Credit goes to the nationalist leadership, civil servants, and in particular the education and health personnel, who began to extend some of the fruits of independence to the people. But such a commitment had its direct and indirect costs to the new nation. Education and health services, free to the users, absorbed a considerable and growing amount of the national budget. Educational expenditures represented a healthy 16.8 percent of the national expenditures in 1972, while health services absorbed an additional 7.1 percent. Education, therefore, became the second largest category of government expenditure just behind Constitutional and Statutory,[14] while Health was the fifth largest item. Once established, these institutions required a continued commitment of funds; this became a steady drain on the budget.

An indirect cost of the welfare programs was the stultifying of any transformation of the bureaucracy. Perhaps because structural reorganization rarely occurs simultaneously with program initiation, after the early consolidation and localization efforts, administrative structures and procedures remained much the same through the First Republic. Despite changes in personnel, the traits of hierarchy and centralization of authority, so characteristic of colonial regimes, began to entrench themselves in the new government. Tordoff and Molteno, perceptive analysts of Zambian administration, argue that serious problems appeared in the extended civil service because of a lack of education and experience as well as sectoral (interethnic) disputes.[15] A survey of African civil servants at the senior executive officer and above posts in 1969 revealed that "at the time of joining the civil service, only 6 percent had university degrees, 22 percent a secondary school-leaving certificate at 'O' level, while 67 percent had less education (fully a quarter having completed only primary school)."[16] Lack of formal education was compounded by a dearth of in-service training, as "twenty-seven percent of the officers surveyed in 1969 had not attended any in-service course since joining the civil service."[17] The situation was worse at lower levels.

The civil service was also politicized. In theory, under the Westminster format a civil service is politically neutral, but in Zambia this was hardly adhered to. Political appointees at the top (the permanent secretaries and ministers especially), reflecting competing political interests at cabinet level, became enmeshed in personal and sectional disputes, which permeated the institutions and sometimes brought administration to a standstill. For dealing with such bureaucratic paralysis and ministrial infighting, Kaunda and his advisers devised a strategy that involved frequent changes at the senior levels of the party, the bureaucracy (the ministries), and the parastatal bodies (created after 1968). This tactic is called "reshuffling" and involves both officeholders' being shifted from one post to another and restructuring of the jobs themselves. A reshuffle could happen at any time without prior warning, simply announced at a presidential press conference.

In the First Republic, reshuffling meant that many ministries and departments went through a bewildering change of identity and personnel. Important functions were intermittently reallocated to different individuals and posts. For example, between September 1964 and June 1971, there were eighteen major shifts of ministries.[18] The national economic planning body, potentially key to the transformation of the economy, was shifted from the Ministry of Finance (as the Office of National Development Planning, ONDP) to the Office of the President in 1965, put under the guidance of the vice president until early 1969, after August 1969 reabsorbed in Finance and Development (renamed the Development Planning Division), then rehoused in the Ministry of Development Planning and National Guidance in late 1970, and then back to Finance.[19]

A strategy parallel to reshuffling was the steady increase in the number of cabinet-level posts. The first independent cabinet held sixteen individuals; by December of 1972 there were twenty-six members of cabinet, including the president, vice president, secretary-general of government, a minister heading each of the eight provinces, and fifteen in charge of central ministries.[20] This proliferation of posts added both to the cost of government and to the general confusion. Together, reshuffling and increasing the number of jobs achieved some of Kaunda's aims: Senior politicians and civil servants could not stop governmental action through building power bases within administration because they could not expect to serve for longer than eighteen months in any particular post.

The short-term gain of this tactic was to lessen bureaucratic paralysis. But in the long run there were serious drawbacks. First, rapid changes in personnel did not transform the bureaucracy. Rather it deflected attention away from the reshaping of government to suit the needs of the new state. Second, by the end of the First Republic (1972), the reshuffling of posts and holders became self-perpetuating, as no one influential person or ethnolinguistic group could be left out of power for too long. Third, because these reshuffles were organized or at least announced by the president,[21] appointees were (and are) aware of the debts they owe their patron rather than feeling that their promotions were based on meritorious service. Confusion and feelings of loyalty to the president helped undercut the tendency toward stasis among groups locked in warfare in the bureaucratic trenches. Yet the overall effect was that patron/client politics intruded into the operations of the civil service, affecting and infecting the other arenas of national politics—interparty politics and intra-UNIP politics, especially in the years 1967–1972.

"Tribalism," UNIP's Consolidation, and the Introduction of a One-Party State

Many interpreters of Zambian politics focus on the ethnoregional or ethnolinguistic conflicts,[22] generally termed *tribalism*, to explain the political upheavals of the First Republic that led to an end to the multiparty system. The lure of such an interpretation is strong, as much political discourse, especially in the local press, tends to analyze Zambian politics in the light of ethnolinguistic alliances and antagonisms. With the benefit of hindsight, however, a different understanding of Zambian politics reveals how national politicians and some civil servants used the language of tribalism to mask a more complex process of class consolidation and personal accumulation of power and prestige.

This brief discussion should begin with what is meant by tribe. Archie Mafeje persuasively argued back in 1971 that analysts should restrict the term *tribe* to specific forms of economic, political, and social organizations that can be fixed in space and time.

> A relatively undifferentiated society, practising a primitive subsistence economy and enjoying local autonomy, can legitimately be designated a tribe. When such a society strives to maintain its basic structure and local autonomy, even under changed economic and political conditions, perhaps it can be said to exhibit "tribalism." But to impose the same concept on societies that have

been effectively penetrated by European colonialism, that have been successfully drawn into a capitalist economy and a world market, is a serious transgression.[23]

These general observations hold true for Zambian society so disrupted and altered by urbanization, Christianity, and capitalism while it was tranformed into a mineral-exporting enclave with a vast underdeveloped hinterland. In the cities and towns, traditional tribes were not present, hence true tribalism did not exist either. Rather, politicians appealed to their ethnolinguistic brethren (fellow tribesmen) to draw on their local power bases in their struggles for power and prestige in the parties and the government. It is in this light that early Zambian politics, seen as incipient class politics, specifically inter- and intraparty politics from 1964–1972, might best be understood.

The struggle for independence had produced powerful politicians with their own regional and class power bases and their own distinct notions of what the new government should do. Harry Nkumbula, the Old Lion of the ANC, still was influential, although the party had begun to decline. When Nkumbula rejected a merger with UNIP, he was neatly sidestepped by Kenneth Kaunda (KK), his former coalition partner. KK and his advisers filled the 1964 government with UNIP party faithfuls. At a senior level of government, Kaunda appointed his trusted friends and colleagues.

Yet political rewards were not doled out without friction. The creation of the first cabinet was especially difficult, as serious personality differences surfaced within UNIP. KK and his advisers carefully divided the top posts in government, the civil service, and party among important individuals. Other considerations were latent irredentism in Barotseland and the continued regional power bases that the major opposition party, the ANC, still had in Southern and Eastern provinces. The ANC's continued appeal among the Ila, Tonga, and Lenje speakers has been interpreted as representing specialized interests of the emergent peasants, who by then were producing for the marketplace.[24] As the nation was still primarily one of peasant farmers, it was imperative for UNIP always to include representatives from those areas in cabinet and at high levels of the party. Also as the result of continued discontent in Barotseland, a disproportionate number of posts within the cabinet were reserved for Silozi-speaking politicians.

Thus, personality, party, and regional politics played their roles in the formation of the early cabinets. In 1964 Kaunda appointed Simon Kapwepwe to the key area of foreign affairs and another northerner Justin Chimba, with long experience in the trade unions, to the sensitive post of labor and mines. KK kept the defense portfolio. The Wina brothers, Arthur and Sikota, well-educated men with power bases in Barotseland and also family ties to the old Lozi ruling class, became ministers of finance and of local government and housing respectively.[25] Another Lozi politician, Nalumino Mundia, became minister of commerce and industry, while the fiery Munu Sipalo took the portfolio of health. Reuben Kamanga and Grey Zulu, longtime nationalist politicians, became the first vice president and minister of transport and works respectively, and the militant Dingiswayo Banda received the

TABLE 4.4
Chronology of John Mwanakatwe

November 1, 1926	Born in Chinsali in Northern Province to Bemba-speaking parents; attended Munali Secondary School in Lusaka.
1948	Took teacher's degree at Adam's College in South Africa.
1950	Received B.A. from Adam's College in South Africa and taught for many years until became African Officer in the Northern Rhodesian Government.
June 1961	Joined Northern Rhodesian Government as Assistant Commissioner for Northern Rhodesia in London.
1962	Returned to Zambia and entered politics; was UNIP's representative on the LegCo. and in the UNIP/ANC coalition government; then Parliamentary Secretary for Labour and Mines.
January 1964-1967	Elected M.P. and appointed and served as Minister of Education; also studied law and was received at the bar.
1967-1968	Minister of Lands and Mines.
1968	Defeated in bid for re-election as M.P.; appointed S.G. to GRZ.
July 1969	Won (uncontested) by-election and became Minister for Luapula Province in the Central Committee.
1970-Oct. 1973	Served as Minister of Finance.
1973-1979	Served as M.P., chairing several commissions including the 1975 Salaries Report (Mwanakatwe Commission).
January 1979	Retired from public office and became full time lawyer with Jaques and Co. in Lusaka, private legal firm.
1980-1986	From a private capacity, often issued mildly critical statements about the regime until charged by President Kaunda with being a "dissident" in April of 1981.

Source: Kelvin Mlenga, Who's Who in Zambia, 1979. Zambia: Roan Consolidated Mines Ltd., August 1979, and personal interviews.

portfolio of housing and social development. Mainza Chona, a lawyer, became the first minister of home affairs; the Irish-born lawyer James Skinner took over both justice and the attorney generalship. Solomon Kalulu became the lands and natural resources minister, and Peter Matoka, from the sparcely populated and very underdeveloped northwestern region, took over posts and information.[26]

To strengthen the professional skills of the cabinet, Kaunda appointed two men with long records of service in the government who had not been party militants. John Mwanakatwe had served in the colonial administration and became the first African minister of education (see Table 4.4), while Elijah Mudenda took the vital job of agriculture. In the early years when UNIP was still quite a democratic party, KK was retained as general secretary; Kapwepwe became the national treasurer and Kamanga, the vice president.

For the first three years, reshuffling and politics based on personality or region managed to "keep the lid on" within UNIP and made positions available to many members of the forming governing class. Yet personal and ethnic antipathies erupted in February 1967 in a by-election campaign and became particularly bitter in the intra-UNIP elections in August 1967.

By February 1968 squabbling within UNIP at the national council meeting had become so serious that Kaunda resigned as president. He later retracted the offer but the "tribalism" persisted. Now, however, this tribalism was becoming a struggle between individuals for powerful positions, appealing to followers on any grounds possible, including ethnicity. For example, in 1968 a new conflict festered within the Bemba camp. Some politicians from Luapula Province felt dominated by fellow Bemba-speakers from Northern Province.[27]

Interethnic struggles were visible in the election of December 1968 when the members of parliament (MPs) and the president ran for election. Then in August 1969, many UNIP members demanded the resignation of the controversial Kapwepwe from the vice presidency, a demand to which he acceded temporarily. KK then dissolved the central committee, assumed the new post of secretary-general of UNIP, and appointed an interim executive committee to run the affairs of the party until a new central committee was elected. Also a commission reviewed the party's constitution and a special disciplinary body was appointed.

KK and his allies were developing a new form of ethnic balancing. Each ethnolinguistic group was to be granted a certain number of high-level positions based in part on the "numerical, political or bargaining strength of a particular group within the ruling party."[28] Because at root this was not an ethnic dispute but one of fractions within the newly forming upper class trying to get access to power and prestige, "ethnic balancing" did not end the struggles. Antagonisms temporarily abated but reemerged with Kapwepwe's group (Northern Province, Bemba speakers) angrily asserting that now it was the Bemba speakers as a whole who were being discriminated against within the party. In 1971 Kapwepwe broke with UNIP and went on to head a new party called the United Progressive party (the UPP). His move threatened to separate key UNIP strongholds in the north and on the Copperbelt. Intraparty strife now spilled over into the interparty domain. These early political battles, although expressed in the idiom of tribalism, reveal an eager grabbing for the spoils of the new system. Politicians turned to tribal appeals for backing but also shifted their claims and rhetoric as the political winds dictated.

These struggles eventually led to the demise of the multiparty system. Although the UNIP leaders were uncomfortable with the continuation of ANC's opposition, they were aware that the ANC had shrunk to a limited regional party without wide appeal in the rest of the country. KK insisted that an end to other parties should come through the ballot box, and that was where UNIP cadres put their energies. In the 1967 by-election, UNIP had won both seats, confirming the feelings that a de facto one-party system would come about through the atrophy of the other parties. Then, in early 1968 the ANC staged a comeback and won four by-election seats. Now the opposition was beginning to threaten UNIP's hegemony and additional sectionally based parties sprang up. When Nalumino Mundia was expelled from UNIP in March 1967, he took over the presidency of a Barotse-based

United party, the UP. The UP was banned in August 1968; then its leaders threw their support behind the ANC, causing an upset victory for the ANC in Western Province in the December 1968 elections, when the ANC took all the seats as well as most of those in Southern Province. They now held twenty-three seats as compared to UNIP's eighty-one, not enough to threaten UNIP's hold over government but an indicator that the ANC was not going to disappear voluntarily.

The appearance of the UPP from within the ranks of UNIP and led by the popular Simon Kapwepwe seemed to have caught KK and his advisers by surprise. It certainly was the last straw for the UNIP militants. Outbursts of violence on the Copperbelt occurred between UNIP and UPP supporters. The last years of the multiparty system have been detailed elsewhere,[29] but the basic story is as follows. Pressed by growing violence between party militants, the GRZ detained one hundred UPP members, excluding Kapwepwe. When the UPP still contested the December 1971 by-elections (for twelve seats) and won only one (Kapwepwe's in Mufulira West), UNIP leaders still were not placated. Within UNIP ranks came cries for an end to multiparty system.[30] According to Tordoff and Scott, "the awful prospect for UNIP was that at the general election due to be held by December 1973 ANC would retain its hold over Southern and Western provinces and that the UPP might wrest control from UNIP in the Northern, Luapula and Copperbelt provinces."[31] UPP was banned and its leaders detained in February 1972. The freedom for the opposition parties to operate openly was drawing to a close.

In 1972 there were rumors that Kapwepwe, Mundia, and Nkumbula were holding discussions. Although all members of a privileged upper stratum, their claims on powerful posts, especially the presidency, threatened KK and his backers. Ethnic balancing and reshuffling, introduced to forestall possible loss of power for both UNIP and the president, temporarily augmented the power of the chief executive, who also headed the party, but a continuation of multiparty opposition threatened his claims to office and patronage. "Too much democracy" within UNIP also undermined KK's pinnacle of power, and he and his supporters were faced with some difficult choices. Should they continue to have a multiparty system, hoping to stay in power? Should they ban all opposing parties and become a de facto one-party state? Or should they follow the lead of other African states (like Tanzania) and begin the process of controlling politics through a de jure one-party state? They chose the last and began the process of making Zambia a one-party state.

Back in 1969 the general electorate had voted a referendum permitting the national assembly to alter the constitution without fulfilling the rigorous requirements of the entrenched clauses.[32] This referendum removed legal barriers to the creation of a one-party state as well as to other momentous changes that were to follow in the economic field. In 1972 after banning UP and UPP, Kaunda appointed a commission headed by the then vice president, Mainza Chona, to explore *how* to bring about a one-party participatory democracy, *not* whether to do it.

Many of the commission's recommendations submitted in October 1972 were accepted, but others were rejected by UNIP.[33] Despite some court challenges, by December 1972 all steps had been completed to end the multiparty system. Legislation was passed and Zambia became a "one-party participatory democracy" on December 13, 1972.[34] Thus the national politicians within UNIP ended some internal rifts in the political system, rifts that had attacked their power positions. The social conflicts persisted and found other outlets, as tactics of ethnic balancing and reshuffling fed the growing power of the executive.

PRESIDENTIALISM

A thread that runs through the prior discussion of the politics of the First Republic and administrative changes is the slow evolution of Kaunda from a compromise candidate, riding a tide of militant nationalism and then heading an untried government, to an individual possessing great status, whose personal actions of reshuffling and ethnic balancing have held the disintegration of UNIP at bay. Accompanying this growth of personal power had been the accumulation, expansion, and centralization of power, the hypertrophy of the executive, with the attendant loss of power by other institutions, especially the cabinet and national assembly.

The cabinet's decline is remarkable, given the collective political power of the individuals who sat there and headed ministries in 1964. Although the executive president under the first constitution inherited the wide-ranging and arbitrary powers of the colonial governor, still the early cabinets had considerable countervailing power to the president's. Kapwepwe, Chimba, Zulu, and Sipalo commanded the confidence of the party and had regional power bases as well. Yet, in part because of crises such as the Unilateral Declaration of Independence (UDI) by Rhodesia and in part because of the tendency toward stagnation within the cabinet and administration, Kaunda began to act independently, using his executive powers to the fullest,[35] noting that he was not obliged to follow the advice tendered by any other person or authority. Kaunda's unilateral actions lessened the power of competing national politicians who under the reshuffling situation did not know how long they would stay in any one post. Because the vice president and all cabinet ministers held office at the discretion of the president, their removal or reappointment could be made without prior notice to the incumbents. Also as head of the party, KK could alter internal regulations of UNIP, which he did in August of 1967, precipitating the sectional battles that led to the departure of Kapwepwe and the eventual demise of the multiparty system. These specific outcomes may not have been foreseen by Kaunda, but their effect was a further enhancement of his personal power and that of UNIP.

The size of the executive also inflated over the years of the First Republic. In August 1969, along with other important announcements, the president reorganized many top posts within the executive and reshuffled high-level politicians. The office of the president, which already included the portfolio of defense, the cabinet secretariat, the establishment division (including manpower planning, training, and deployment), the legal division, the newly formed commission for technical and vocational education, and provincial and local government, now also housed the Ministry of Foreign Affairs and a newly created Ministry of State Participation.[36] This accumulation of power accelerated when KK reorganized UNIP, eliminating the post of vice president, infusing the office of secretary-general (SG) of the party with more power and status, and appointing said official to serve at the discretion of the president.

Using such tactics, Kaunda eclipsed all likely contenders. By 1972 he was executive president, the head of state (independent of a vote of confidence of the national assembly), and head of the party. Under the new constitutions (party and national), the national executive now included the president, the cabinet, the prime minister, and the party hierarchy of the central committee. In practice, it is larger still with the inclusion of advisers to the prime minister and president from Freedom House (party headquarters) and State House (government headquarters).

In summation, the power of the president expanded rapidly during the First Republic as did the wider bureaucratic powers of the executive. When the one-party state blended together party and government (the phrase after 1972 has been "the Party and *its* [emphasis added] Government"), this inflated the powers of the president yet further. The security of the president was also reinforced when the ability to contend for the office from outside the party was eliminated. Under the one-party system, candidates have to be nominated by the national council of UNIP, which is firmly under KK's thumb.

There is a tendency among many writers on Zambian politics to picture His Excellency as standing above politics, arbitrating among contending forces.[37] Instead, Kaunda is very much a national politician and thus a member of the new governing class. He depends on his mastery of power in the state and party to ensure his position. He and others share a power base (state and party) that is to some degree open to pressure from all sectors of Zambian society. For example, it was of vital concern to Kaunda and other top national politicians during the multiparty era that they survive in office. To some degree they also had to protect the unity of the nation that actually allowed them to govern. These two ideas combined to make them receptive to some demands issued from Zambians of all classes. From many different material and political positions, pressures were on KK to find more posts to offer party loyalists (patronage) and also to open the economy to local ownership. Following the pattern of centralizing power in his own hands, KK announced a set of major economic reforms starting in 1968. This he did with little consultation of his party or even the top levels of the civil service. Kaunda and a few advisers launched a new economic era for Zambia that was part of a wider reorganization of the economy. He justified his actions by reference to his own populist ideology, but these moves also grew out of his desire to lessen or deflect growing inter- and intraclass contestation.

HUMANISM AND SOCIALISM

At the time of independence, UNIP's announced ideology was African democratic socialism, which was similar to the policies of *Ujamaa* (or familyhood in Kiswahili) of President Julius Nyerere of Tanzania. The Zambian politicians had interpreted African Socialism to mean policies to lessen overt colonial inequalities and to extend civil rights to citizens regardless of color or race. Also included were freedom for the press and the goals of raising living standards through a more equitable distribution of the national wealth and of extending social services to the majority of the population.

In 1967 President Kaunda introduced a new doctrine called "Humanism," whose main points were put forward in a booklet entitled *Humanism Part I* (1967), since updated in *Humanism Part II* (1974). KK tried to marry basic ideals of Christianity and antiracism to egalitarian precepts of nineteenth century liberalism and Fabian socialism. He included a healthy dose of idealization and admiration of traditional African culture, emphasizing communal values of precapitalist Zambian societies and denying the existence of class in precolonial and postcolonial society. Conflicts between the prior doctrine of African Socialism and Humanism were considered overcome by Kaunda's argument that "socialism is one instrument for building a Humanist society."[38]

In *Humanism Part I*, Kaunda emphasized that Humanism seeks to establish a "Man-centered society" with "people above ideology" and "man above institutions." These vague populist principles were used to justify the nationalizations of foreign companies that KK initiated beginning in 1968, bringing panicky denunciations of militant Zambian socialism from the Western financial press. Professor Tordoff felt that socialism was not the real goal of Humanism. Rather, KK's intentions were to "socialise the economy by the instrument of State control in order to bring this important sector of our life closer to the people who now own it."[39]

In retrospect Humanism did not offer the ideological or programmatic clarity necessary to build the newly independent state during times of transformation. Internal contradictions abound within the doctrine itself. For instance, the denunciation of international capitalism and exploitation of man by man did not translate into a ban on private ownership, either local or foreign. Instead Humanism provided some philosophical support for the introduction of welfare programs while an incipient Zambian capitalist class was substituted for a foreign one in commerce, and state ownership edged out the multinational corporations in mines and manufacturing. Those changes required substantial restructuring of the economy, begun during the First Republic.

RESTRUCTURING THE ECONOMY

The Need for Restructuring

In 1964 the economy was sharply divided, not only between local and foreign owners but also in the productivity and living standards between urban and rural dwellers and between black and white. The copper industry was prospering with a good producer price and London Metal Exchange (LME) price (see Figure 4.1), but many people were desperately poor. The economy was so dominated by the copper industry that any serious problems in that sector (notorious for price instability) threatened around 90 percent of all export earnings and a third of the revenues of the government (see Table 4.5). Outside the mines and the commercial farms on the line of rail, almost no physical or social infrastructure existed. In a nation of three and a half million, "in 1963 there were 225,000 Africans in paid employment, earning an average of £160 per year which should, however, be compared with the £1,600 per year average for the 32,000 non-Africans in employment."[40] In the rural areas, probably 70 percent of the people were living as subsistence farmers with an annual cash income of about £10 per head.[41] The declaration of independence by Southern Rhodesia's white politicians (UDI) in 1965 and Zambia's participation in the international sanctions program meant that overnight Zambians needed to establish or expand their own railroad, coal, oil pipeline, and electricity systems to avoid economic blackmail. Yet this lopsided, inequitable, and highly vulnerable economy also contained wealth for the nation as a whole and for the small, incipient class that had fallen heir to it. Where and how to begin to reorganize and change this economy?

Initially the leadership of UNIP and the civil service took an incremental, conservative approach to adjusting the economy. When they did follow one dictate of socialism, it was to introduce national development planning by asking foreign advisers to draw up a transitional national development plan[42] for the period January 1, 1965, to June 30, 1966. These advisers suggested a moderate strategy based on a slow diversification of the economy without threatening or interfering with the "smooth functioning and development of the mining sector."[43] The primacy of the mines was not to be questioned, as it was the major source of government funds and also of moneys to develop the manufacturing and agricultural sectors—it was a true "copper goose." Taxation and investment policies were designed to make Zambia attractive for business, both local and foreign. One deviation from basic neoclassical prescriptions was that the state should introduce industrial enterprises and help develop technology either by itself or in joint venture with foreign companies. Overall, the development strategy did not threaten the existing power structure. Its costs were easily covered by the plentiful revenue that the government had to draw upon in the first decade of independence.

FIGURE 4.1 Copper Prices, 1963–1972[a] (in Kwacha)

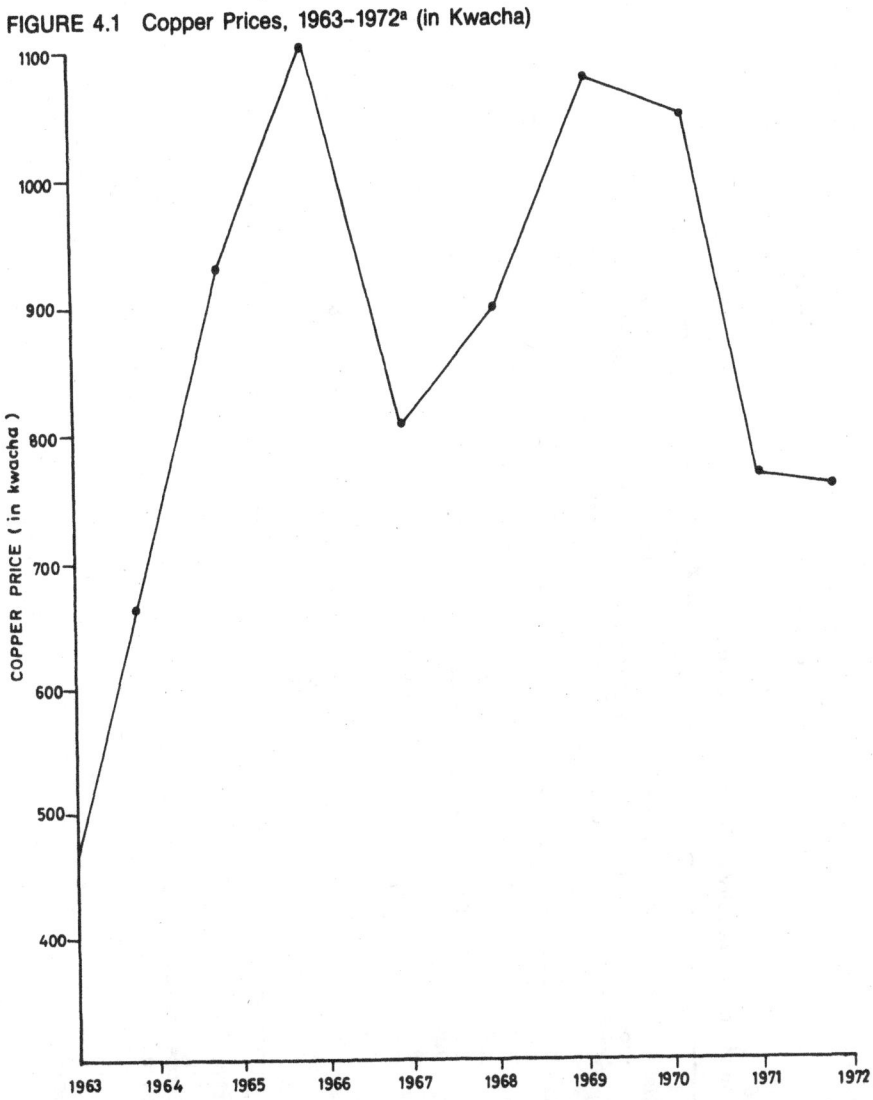

Source: Republic of Zambia, Central Statistical Office, *Monthly Digest of Statistics* 9, 11 (November 1977), Table 53, p. 53.

[a]Calculated on electrolytic wirebars sold at "Settlement and Cash Sellers' Price," which is how Zambian copper is quoted; yearly average/metric ton.

TABLE 4.5
Contribution of Copper Industry to Gross Domestic Product, Revenue, and Exports, 1963-1972

Year	Net Domestic[a] Product (K million)	Contribution to Gross Domestic Product (K m) (%)		Government Revenue (K million)	Contribution to Government Revenue (K m) (%)		Copper and Cobalt Value of Exports (K million)	Contribution to Exports (%)
1963	394	173	44	72	25	34	239	92
1964	474	215	45	108	57	53	302	92
1965	611	246	40	189	134	71	347	93
1966	742	342	46	255	163	64	465	95
1967	842	334	40	276	146	53	440	94
1968	930	365	39	306	183	60	520	96
1969	1,164	631	54	401	237	59	729	97
1970	1,063	453	43	432	218	52	688	97
1971	1,034	254	25	309	116	38	454	95
1972	1,150	278	24	311	69	22	498	93

[a] At market prices.

Source: Copper Industry Service Bureau, Mindeco Mining Year Book 1972 (Ndola, Zambia: Monterey Printing and Packaging Ltd., 1972), Table 2, p. 20.

TABLE 4.6
Growth of the Manufacturing Sector, 1954-1967

Category	1954	1963	1967
Contribution of Manufacturing to GDP	K 9.2 m.	K 24.2 m.	K 78.9 m.
Manufacturing as a Proportion of GDP	3.3%	6.1%	10.8%
Average Annual Rate of Growth of Volume of Manufacturing Output		1954 - 1963 11%	1963 - 1967 22%

Source: Michael Faber, "The Development of the Manufacturing Sector," Constraints on the Economic Development of Zambia, ed. Charles Elliott (Nairobi, Kenya: Oxford University Press, 1971), p. 299.

Income of the government was augmented dramatically by three important changes in the tax structure. The first was the reversion of royalties formerly paid to the BSAC into the Zambian treasury. Michael Faber, an economist, estimated that these mineral royalties accounted for K 34 million in 1965 alone.[44] An end to the payment of federal taxes to Salisbury, the second change, meant an additional £9 million per year redirected to Zambian coffers. Third was the introduction of an export tax on minerals in 1966. The new tax on the export of copper, although a bit regressive for the less productive mines, brought the government additional revenues, which varied with the LME price. Royalties and taxes inflated the level of the mining industry's contribution to government revenue from K 25 million in 1963 to K 163 million in 1966 alone (see Table 4.5). Thus the productivity and profitability of the mines underwrote the welfare programs begun in 1964 as well as the introduction of new industries begun in 1966. But the government's dependence on mining was enhanced rather than lessened. Whereas the mines contributed 34 percent of the government's revenues in 1963, by the end of the transitional plan period (1966), they were contributing 64 percent.

The vulnerability implicit in such a monoeconomy thus continued and even increased. Furthermore, despite plentiful profits, the mine owners had not attempted to integrate the mines into the economy any more than absolutely necessary. The mineral industry remained exclusively oriented toward the production and export of copper, cobalt, lead, and zinc. No fabrication was done locally nor was there much integration of this industry outside the enclave of the Copperbelt itself. One result was the perpetuation of the lopsided economy.

Although manufacturing grew a bit in Northern Rhodesia in federation days, the overall contribution to the gross domestic product (GDP) was tiny in comparison with that of the mines (see Table 4.6). In 1964-1965 some expansion by private firms in manufacturing did occur and according to

Faber, continued until 1968. Yet the amount was small, reflecting manufacturing at an infant stage at best. Ann Seidman, another economist, attributed this early growth to consumer goods industries that were not linked to intermediate and capital goods located within Zambia.[45] She pointed out that the technology chosen was capital intensive, thus limiting expansion in employment. One unusual feature of the manufacturing sector even as early as 1966 was the presence of a basic metal products and fabricated metal products industry. It was located on the Copperbelt and served the needs of the mines, railroads, and government public works. These companies only made parts and did repairs, but they did represent the nucleus of a capital goods industry for the country. By and large, these companies were owned either by resident expatriates who had formerly worked for the mines and left to establish their own small businesses[46] or were subsidiary companies of the Anglo American Corporation of South Africa Ltd., the larger of the two mining groups operating in Zambia. Anglo had established these feeder industries and a foundry on the Copperbelt to provide inputs such as drill bits. Not surprisingly, these Anglo subsidiaries had not diversified into products for other sectors, because their sole purpose was to make the mines more efficient and profitable.

Although the enclave itself demonstrated industrial integration, the economy as a whole did not fit together in a way to encourage spillover effects or economic self-reliance. Thus basic wage goods for the majority of Zambians—clothing, shoes, food items, matches, hoes—were imported, mostly from South Africa and Southern Rhodesia. Domestic production supplied only about a third of the local market.[47] The multinational corporation Lever Brothers, for example, had a subsidiary in Zambia producing soaps and edible oils, but never expanded into other sectors.

With UDI, manufacturing imports increased rapidly: The level in 1969 was more than double that of 1964 despite budgetary restraints imposed in 1969.[48] The tiny state Industrial Development Corporation (INDECO), whose net assets in 1967 were only K 35.6 million,[49] was practically and ideologically unsuited to redirect manufacturing development in an aggressive fashion. There seemed to be no natural forces speeding the process of diversification and lessening the country's vulnerability and dependence.

Zambia's agriculture reflected the same pattern of imbalance and regional underdevelopment. Forty years of industrial mining had left Zambia with an especially peculiar agricultural system. According to Robert Klepper,

> most marketed agricultural output was produced by slightly more than one thousand European farmers half of whom left in the first five years of the post-colonial period. African farmers who produced a surplus for the market, and who were in the cash economy, were concentrated in Central, Southern and Eastern Provinces. Other areas of Zambia without access to agricultural markets and with virtually no agricultural services suffered severe emigration to urban areas. The underdeveloped rural areas of Zambia suffered shortage of labor, they had virtually no fixed or working capital for agriculture, and agricultural technology and skills were limited to traditional subsistence meth-

ods. The outlying provinces of Northern, Luapula, Northwestern and Western [formerly Barotseland] are also areas of poor soils and the traditional crops in these regions are cassava, sorghum, and finger millet which have limited markets in the urban economy.[50]

A serious crisis loomed for the new government with the departure of many commercial farmers and rapid decline in production of stable crops such as maize. Potentially, food shortages could lead to serious instability or even starvation in urban centers. Also there was a political issue in the wind as some peasant farmers had been part of the coalition that brought the majority government to power; they expected some returns on election promises as well. Government and party debated strategies to transform agriculture. One option was to encourage foreign agribusiness firms to establish plantations in Zambia as in Malawi. Another idea was to establish village cooperatives based on socialist models and backed with plentiful credit facilities. A third was more typically Soviet tactic of introducing state farms with technology-intensive cultivation methods. Everyone agreed that something had to be done, but there was little agreement as to what.

Despite some improvements in infrastructure under the transitional plan and some improvement in the manufacturing sector, by 1966 the new nation rested on a fragile and dependent economic base that would require far more aggressive actions than the timid prescriptions of the early plans. The vital influx of funds from foreign sources did not materialize, despite favorable tax arrangements. Rather, foreign owners were externalizing their profits, neither reinvesting in new areas nor plowing a portion of profits back into existing enterprises.[51] If this pattern continued, the wealth of the nation would be quickly drained.

Members of the new governing class inside and outside the formal state apparatus had ideas about gaining personal access to this national wealth. Few had entrepreneurial skills or sufficient capital to take over the larger expatriate-owned businesses, but many were interested in at least small-scale ventures.[52] In order to obtain an entry to profit-making businesses in areas currently dominated by foreigners or resident expatriates, these aspiring entrepreneurs needed the state to intervene. Others in the governing class, civil servants and technocrats (people with specialized skills that they sell for their livelihood), less personally concerned with accumulation, wanted to localize the economy for national benefit. A few farsighted individuals argued for the creation of state-owned companies to fill gaps in the domestic economy, create employment, and satisfy the needs of the masses for cheap consumer goods. Representatives of organized labor also had their say about better wages and working conditions. The long period of low wages under colonialism had begun to change when the Brown Commission Report in 1966 recommended a 22 percent wage increase for all Zambian miners. Similar awards to the civil service followed.[53] Nonetheless, these wage increases did not defuse the desires of the unions to improve conditions. The number of man-hours lost in industrial disputes rose from 124,738 in 1964 to 579,406 in 1966. Organized labor was also putting pressure on the new regime to live up to the preindependence political alliance and promises made therein.

Not surprisingly these different fractions of the governing class as well as distinct classes sometimes had opposing notions of how to restructure the economy and who should benefit. Ultimately, the president attempted a compromise based on the twin stools of strategies laid out in national development plans and active state intervention through nationalization. Chronologically the first was the new, more aggressive development policy introduced in the First National Development Plan (FNDP) announced by the president at a UNIP rally in 1966.

The First National Development Plan (1966-1971)

Although the objectives of this new plan were wide ranging, the major thrust of the plan was to establish the economic and social infrastructure of the country and encourage manufacturing in order to lessen the predominance of mining. The planners carried over several ideas from the transitional plan, especially the idea of encouraging the mines to be productive and profitable. But they set out to use state intervention more aggressively to develop the physical infrastructure of the nation and to invest in factories and agricultural projects. Over the four years of the plan, vital services such as electricity (at the time generated by the station in Kariba on the south bank of the Zambezi River and thus under control of Ian Smith's government) were to be initiated and if possible completed. Heavy expenditures were allocated to build up the railroads (K 19.5 million), K 69.8 million to improve the roads in general, with K 39 million to extend and improve the Great East Road to Malawi and the Great North Road to Tanzania, K 7.6 million for an international airport; a pipeline to the East African coast for K 40 million; hydroelectric power generating stations for K 53.4 million, and other projects. Paralleling the investment in physical infrastructure were the already mentioned costs (K 98 million) of developing the social infrastructure, especially in education and health. Planners had calculated that foreign investment would flow into the country in these four years despite the shortfalls in the first two years. Out of the minimum capital investment for 1966-1970 of K 858 million, K 294 million was estimated to come from the private sector, particularly for investments in the mining industry.[54] Assuming that the mines would be provided for by the private sector, the government would be free to use its capital for developing the manufacturing plants to produce goods that previously had been imported (the basic logic of import substitution) and to invest in agriculture, especially in those regions most underdeveloped.

A plant to produce nitrogenous fertilizers and explosives was to be established, as well as a textile mill, a copper fabricating project, a hessian (burlap) and grain bag plant, a tire and tube factory, and a drugs and nutritional foods plant. These enterprises were to be launched with government capital, though it was hoped that the private sector would later buy into the companies, thereby producing a larger and more diversified industrial base, still primarily private.

Agriculture for its part was to receive K 87 million, which meant a doubling of the rate of annual expenditure of the transitional plan with most of the funds to go to crops and livestock. The target group within the rural population was "emergent farmers," who were beginning to participate actively in the cash market by increasing agricultural output through new methods and attitudes. Also the government was to sponsor some settlement schemes, cooperative farms, and technical assistance projects. Most hopes were pinned on the existing commercial farmers and the new African emergent farmers. It should be noted, however, that only 12 percent of investment was to go to agriculture. The true focus, rhetoric aside, was on infrastructure and manufacturing.

This first four-year plan mixed capitalist incentives and expectations with state direction to diversify the industrial economy, giving priority to construction of physical and social infrastructure. In many ways, the FNDP was the most successful of all the Zambian national development plans to date, at least in terms of the plan's ambitious infrastructural objectives. This was in large part because of the high price that copper fetched from 1966–1970. An assessment of Zambia's economic progress at the end of the First Republic would be incomplete if it were based only on the plan's figures and sectoral achievements. Another strategy was set into motion in the middle of the FNDP period. Direct state participation and the introduction of a large parastatal network began with a presidential announcement in April 1968.

The Nationalizations and Economic Reforms

To assembled UNIP members at Mulungushi Rock, Kaunda proclaimed that the GRZ was requesting twenty-six firms—foreign-owned retail, commercial, building material, construction, road transport, and brewery—to sell a majority (51 percent) of their shares to the government. Suddenly the GRZ was actively nationalizing foreign investment in infrastructure and a few key industries. Twenty-five of the nationalized companies complied; in return they received generous compensation and several former owners stayed on as managers or consultants to the new joint-venture companies.

The GRZ's shares were placed in the newly enhanced INDECO, which had in 1965 gained a capable new managing director, Andrew Sardanis, a Zambian businessman of Cypriot origin. Under his guidance,[55] the new INDECO companies were organized into streams or subdivisions.[56] From 1968 to 1972 their numbers were joined by totally new companies that the government built, such as Nitrogen Chemicals of Zambia Ltd. (NCZ), a product of FNDP investments. Together these subsidiaries formed a sizable parastatal[57] industrial complex with net assets worth K 167.9 million by March 31, 1972.[58] As a political payoff, the number of new posts to be given to "clients" by KK vastly expanded as did the recurrent expenditures of the government.

More controversial than the national development plan, these state takeovers were part of a wider interventionist strategy that included revising

TABLE 4.7
Important Dates in the Economic Reforms of 1968-1972

Date	Venue for Speech	Major Provisions
April 1968	Mulungushi I	GRZ requested 51% of shares of 26 foreign - owned companies; shares placed in INDECO.
August 1969	Matero	GRZ requested 51% of the mining assets of Anglo American and RST (AMAX). Announcement that oil refinery and other industrial concerns to be built.
January 1970	Lusaka	RCM and NCCM (joint venture mining companies) established to run mines under Anglo and RST management; Government's 51% placed in MINDECO.
November 1970	Mulungushi II	GRZ attempted nationalization of Barclays, Grindlays, and Standard Chartered banks; actual takeover of insurance and building societies; Government's shares placed in FINDECO.
January 1971		More GRZ takeover of firms; parastatals reorganized and Zambia Industrial and Mining Corporation (ZIMCO) to become omnibus parastatal.
1971/1972		Copper slump.

the tax and foreign exchange laws. Outlined in the long address by the president, these provisions generally became known as the "Mulungushi Reforms," although the government publications persist in calling them the "Mulungushi Revolution" (see Table 4.7). When reflecting on his actions, Kaunda said that he had been motivated by the continued outflow of capital from the country and the failure of the foreign-owned companies to reinvest in Zambia despite the liberal exchange control policies and tax incentives.[59] One object of the reforms had been to "reorganize the Zambian economy so as to increase capacity of Zambians to control their own economic destiny."[60] Equally, of course, it increased the area for patronage by central government into the productive sectors. As well, there were some limited rewards to rural capitalists in that there was a ban on licenses, retail and trading, to non-Zambians in the rural areas.

In 1968 the president said that the mines would not be touched, as they were "too big" for the GRZ, but he cautioned Anglo and RST to reform their reinvestment and local borrowing policies, adding some power to his words by curtailing local financial facilities and restructuring the proportions of profits all private companies could pay to external shareholders yearly.[61] The mine owners chose to take a wait-and-see approach and allowed their unrepatriated profits to remain in Zambian banks ("the blocked funds") rather than reinvesting them in either the mines or other available enterprises in manufacturing or agriculture.

In August 1969 Kaunda took the offensive at a UNIP national council meeting in Matero, a suburb of Lusaka. This time he demanded a 51 percent share in the mining assets owned by Anglo and RST, excluding companies outside direct mining operations. At the same time, KK announced the government's intention to build an oil refinery (Indeni) for the oil piped in from the Indian Ocean ports; an agricultural implements factory; a glass industry (Kapiri Glass); and an integrated iron and steel industry. These new manufacturing ventures were overshadowed by the scale and importance of the GRZ assumption of a majority share in the mines.

Initially Anglo and RST reacted angrily to what they said was a surprise move by the government. How surprising it could have been is doubtful, given all the steps leading up to the action. Still, the Western financial press denounced this "rampant socialism" and the U.S., South African, and British embassies and representatives were brought into the fray.[62] The president, in his capacity as minister for state participation and advised by his permanent secretary Sardanis, stuck to his guns. Sardinis drew around himself a team of advisers and researchers and began negotiations over the actual financial meaning of the "Matero Reform" and the future relationship between the government and the foreign mining houses.

The institutional outcome of the 1969–1970 takeover was two new joint venture companies—the Roan Consolidated Mines Ltd. (RCM) with the GRZ holding 51 percent; AAC, 12.25 percent; RST (later AMAX directly), 20.0 percent; and with 16.75 percent in the hands of small shareholders represented by AMAX; and the Nchanga Consolidated Copper Mines Ltd. (NCCM) with GRZ holding 51 percent and Anglo, the remaining 49 percent. Although the government held the majority of the shares in both companies and thus did appoint most of the directors to the board, the articles of association of the new companies limited the freedom of the GRZ to press its will on the mines if these desires contradicted profit-making behavior.[63] Financially, Anglo and RST (AMAX) came out of the negotiations very well, especially when compared with the far more contentious and costly nationalizations of Anaconda and Kennecott Copper in Chile at about the same time. For management, sales, and consultancy services to NCCM and RCM, Anglo and AMAX received generous fees (approximately K 5.3 million to AMAX from RCM and K 10.16 million to AAC from NCCM in 1971) as well as dividends from their remaining minority shares when the mines made profits.[64]

Despite the rhetoric that accompanied it (the Matero speech was entitled "Towards Complete Independence") and the surprise of the president's announcement, the GRZ takeover of the mines was done in a controlled manner with an eye to the money markets in Europe and North America from whence the top-level decision makers still hoped to attract

PHOTO 4.1 Anode casting plant, Luanshya Division.

foreign investors. A few sentences often overlooked by analysts also implied a changing relationship between those who controlled the state and their old allies, the unions. In the same Matero address, KK announced an injunction against strikes by the miners, introduced both to calm the Copperbelt and to reassure foreign capital.

In early 1970 the GRZ's shares in NCCM and RCM were vested in a new parastatal body, the Mining Development Corporation (MINDECO), a sister organization to INDECO. MINDECO was meant to be a watchdog over the mines with its foreign managers. In some circles it was hoped that MINDECO would offer some creative ideas for using the wasting assets of the mines. Under the managing directorship of Sardanis and later Dominic Mulaisho, MINDECO struggled to do its job, recruiting a professional staff and presenting technical proposals to the minister of mines. One such proposal was the controversial anode casting plant for Luanshya Mine (see Photo 4.1). In general and for a variety of reasons, MINDECO was never as powerful a parastatal as INDECO, and in 1974 it was demoted to covering the smaller mines of Zambia.

Next KK turned to a third major sector—the foreign-owned banks, insurance companies, and building societies. In November 1970, His Excellency returned to Mulungushi to demand a majority share in the local financial institutions of Barclay's, Standard Chartered, and Grindlay's, all major banking multinationals. The banks resisted, and after a readjustment in January 1971, a compromise was struck. The GRZ established its own bank, the National Commercial Bank, to receive all the government's business. The foreign banks agreed to be registered in Zambia, which gave the government some indirect control over their operations, although not direct share holding. The insurance companies and building societies were nationalized and amalgamated into monopoly parastatal subsidiaries and subsumed under the newest umbrella parastatal, the state's Financial and Development Corporation (FINDECO). This Mulungushi II Declaration also included some smaller-scale reforms so that all trading activities, wholesale and retail, and especially those in the rural areas had to be owned by genuine Zambian organizations and individuals. This was a step directed primarily against Asian merchants and traders and meant to benefit the Zambian petite bourgeoisie in the rural areas who might be able to take up the licenses and buy out the shops. A third aspect to the Mulungushi II Reforms was an extension of INDECO's interest in the manufacturing sector, with the GRZ starting negotiations to take over the Zambia Sugar Company; Duncan, Gilbey & Matheson; the National Milling Company; the Northern Drug Company; Zambia Oxygen; Lever Brothers; Refined Oil Products; and Central Cigarette Manufacturers (formerly Rothman-BAT).[65]

Mulungushi II completed early efforts to "capture the commanding heights of the economy"[66] during the First Republic, although incremental company takeovers continued until 1978. The reforms had led to a substantial reorganization of the economy, placing more and more of the productive assets of the nation in state hands, at least as far as share holding was concerned. In 1971 INDECO, MINDECO, and FINDECO were reshuffled to fall under an omnibus parastatal, the Zambia Industrial and Mining Corporation (ZIMCO), whose chairman was the president. Over time, noncommercial parastatal companies such as the Zambia Electricity Supply Corporation (ZESCO) and the National Marketing Board (NAMBOARD) were also subsumed under ZIMCO. According to Ben Turok, by 1971 ZIMCO's total assets were worth K 713 million, of which the copper mines constituted 75 percent.[67] Total state assets were roughly K 1,009 billion in 1971, as compared with K 234 million at independence.

Although state takeovers did not contradict the major principles of the FNDP, the introduction of a large parastatal sector affected the course of the economy, altering the context for the development plan in a variety of ways. The state's nationalizations, for example, although conducted in a friendly fashion, with the GRZ payment "prompt, adequate and effective compensation,"[68] ended investment from abroad. The hope that private and public sectors would both diversify and expand, always a chimera, was displaced by a more aggressive state investment policy. Fortunately in those days, the GRZ had the money. Second, the takeover of existing firms meant an unconscious adoption of already existing technology and operating system of the plants. For example, the takeover of the Lever Brothers plant in Ndola in 1970 meant that the new parastatal company inherited a system of production and product lines that were capital intensive and depended upon imported raw materials. Again, so long as the foreign exchange receipts were high, this was not a serious problem for day-to-day production. Yet when copper was in trouble, the problems spilled over rapidly to manufacturing.

Although Mulungushi I and II had begun to pry open sectors of the economy for small- and medium-scale African businesses, especially in retail trade and construction, the bigger companies were absorbed into the state. Subcontracting could be (and often was) directed toward indigenous businesses, but the overall thrust was for the party and government to dominate, rather than private Zambian capitalists. One can say that this outcome to some degree was intentional and consistent with Humanism. In 1970 Kaunda said that "I do not want to create 'business barons' here . . . we will introduce limits to the development of private enterprise."[69] The private entrepreneurs within the new governing class were still small businesspersons; meanwhile, the civil servants and national politicians allied to the state grew in power as the state asserted more control over major sectors of the economy. The managers of the newly nationalized businesses, in general, were instructed to continue to be productive and profitable and were not required to change any major features of their operations except to localize their personnel (employ more Zambians). State involvement introduced by the Mulungushi Reforms did not lead toward socialism but rather toward state capitalism.[70]

Achievements and Effects of the Economic Restructuring During the First Republic

Early economic indicators led some analysts to deem the first eight years of independent rule as highly successful. By 1972 much of the infrastructure begun in the transitional and FNDP was established or nearly so, although some projects such as the electricity-generating stations demanded more capital expenditures then envisaged (K 75 million rather than K 55 million).[71] Stage two of Kafue Dam hydroelectric project was near completion; the Victoria Falls generating station was operating and a second station under construction; the principal cities, industrial centers, and majority of towns along the rail line were supplied with cheap electric power. As far as transport was concerned, by the end of 1971, 3000 km of tarmac had been laid and the Great North Road (822 km to the Tanzanian border) and the Great East Road (430 km to Malawi) were completed. A K 10 million railroad workshop at Kabwe had started operation in October 1971. Other infrastructural projects included an oil pipeline (Tazama) completed in August 1968, the Indeni petroleum refinery being built in 1972; the Lusaka International Airport finished (though costing over K 13 million), and the list went on.[72]

Manufacturing, although still the weak sister behind mining, had expanded. Its overall contribution to the GDP had gone from K 28.2 million (6.1 percent) in 1964 to K 162.7 million (11 percent) in 1972. Many large-scale industrial units were completed and in production: Zambia Clay Industries (1969), INDECO Milling Company (1968), Lusaka Brewery extension, Truck Assembly Plant at Luanshya, Chilanga Cement Ltd. expansion, Dunlop Zambia Ltd. (1969), Kafue Textiles Ltd. (1970), Kabwe Industrial Fabrics Ltd. (1970), Nitrogen Chemicals of Zambia Ltd. (1970), Kafironda Explosives (1970), and Mwinilunga Fruit Canning Factory (1970).[73] Not surprisingly, given the boom in building of plants and infrastructure, construction firms also expanded in size and numbers at a growth rate of 13.8 percent per annum, providing employment for 73,870 persons as of December 1970.[74] Overall employment figures were very positive, with formal sector employment increasing from 283,600 in December 1964[75] to 326,550 in December 1972.

The picture of the mines was slightly less positive, because production had not increased at the planned rate and productivity per worker decreased slightly. A mining disaster at Mufulira Mine in September 1970 cost eighty-nine lives and temporarily shut one of the most productive mines on the Copperbelt. Despite these unfavorable trends and happenings, the high price of copper on the world market meant that the value of the minerals exceeded the FNDP's target by 36.1 to 98.2 percent of original high and low estimates respectively.[76] Parts of the mining operations were mechanized in order to increase productivity. The lack of foreign investment did not restrain growth or the creation of new industries—the Zambians financed themselves out of their copper earnings.

The weakest sector, agriculture, lagged far behind the rest of the economy, expanding less rapidly than expected (3.3 percent as opposed to the plan target of 9 percent). The relevant authorities spent only 76 percent of the capital allocated to that sector,[77] which implies that despite the rhetoric of the FNDP, agriculture continued to be overlooked and overshadowed by events in the urban arena.

Because of the boom in the urban-based economy, statistics paint a very encouraging national picture. GDP increased by 83 percent from 1965 to 1970, averaging an annual rate of 10.6 percent, which compared favorably with the plan (and very optimistic) target of 11.7 percent.[78] Average earnings for African workers rose 97 percent from 1964 to 1969, while the consumer price index rose by only 37 percent. For those Zambians in formal wage employment, they were very good years.

Despite these extremely positive indicators, the whole edifice rested on the ready supply of foreign exchange (FOREX) from the mines. In the early 1970s some critics pointed to disturbing features in the expanding economy, especially in manufacturing. Ann Seidman argued as early as 1973 that the new and nationalized parastatal companies were too concentrated in consumer goods production, using capital-intensive technology, often oriented toward luxury production for the few, rather than necessities for the many, and often dominated still by their "minority partners," the multinational corporations (MNCs). She detected a trend that the value of local production was declining in these boom years as parastatal firms relied heavily on imported materials, technology, machinery, spare parts, and skilled expatriates' manpower. In some industries (for example wood and wood products, paper and paper products, chemicals, chemical petroleum, and plastic products, basic metal products, and nonmetallic mineral products), import intensity was growing rather than declining, despite the overall strategy of import substitution.[79] Contrary to the expected outcome of such a strategy, the Zambian manufacturing industry was shifting its vulnerability from the stage of finished imports to dependency on imported inputs and technology.

The human and political consequences were many. For example, the inherited capital-intensive technology meant that after an initial increase in employment, the growth rate would level off. Suspicious of the MNCs, Seidman argued that the government's majority shares did not guarantee it the necessary control over these "state" firms. Weaknesses in the bureaucracy and the lack of transformation of many institutions meant that the Zambian economy was caught in a trap that the civil servants were unlikely to understand or to fashion a way out of. Seidman predicted that soon the economy would face some serious economic difficulties. Subsequent events have done much to bear out her predictions.

A chill went through the economy in the last years of the First Republic (1971 to 1972) when the price for copper temporarily plummeted, cutting the government's revenue by almost a third. The comfortable cushion in the balance-of-trade accounts dwindled; Zambia experienced its first balance-of-payments' deficit since independence. The downturn delayed the completion of many projects begun during the FNDP, requiring an extension of the plan for an additional year. Nevertheless, in 1972 stringent foreign exchange controls and import licensing readjusted the balance of trade, and in 1973 the copper price picked up again. Breathing a deep sigh of relief, the GRZ did not alter policies to meet the criticisms of academics about the long-term frailties of the overall development strategy. Why were so few efforts made to redirect the economy at this time? Answers seem to lie in the nature of the local governing class and its relations with other classes.

THE CHANGING SOCIAL BASES OF SOCIETY

The years of the First Republic saw the Zambian governing class forming itself, altering its relations with the other classes, and to some degree changing its relationship to foreign capital as well. The economic strategies undertaken to encourage the economy to grow rapidly (import-substitution industrialization, infrastructure building) and increase the number of jobs for Zambians did not transform the nature of the inherited economy. Still dominated by mining and thus affected by the whims of the international copper buyers via the LME pricing for copper, with an agricultural sector regionally underdeveloped and dependent on pockets of commercial expatriate farmers, and with weak although expanding manufacturing, the Zambian economy remained lopsided and vulnerable. The reforms and development plans did allow elements of the petite bourgeoisie to gain access to the smaller and less capital-demanding areas such as retail shops, construction businesses, and small farms. State employees joined a growing salariat and became part of the politician's clientele. More technically trained Zambians returned from education abroad and joined the government or parastatals. When the national politicians spearheaded a localization of control of mining and manufacturing, the bureaucracy cooperated. Although the embryonic local upper class had its internal divisions, attention was deflected by the fratricidal antics in the multiparty system.

If one analyzes the major speeches reforming the economy for their social content, an interesting pattern emerges about the direction Zambian society was taking. The 1968 Mulungushi Reforms allowed small businesspersons to gain an economic leg up and defused some intraclass combat over political office. The consummate national politician KK, hearing discontent, could now give rewards in the system outside state and party jobs. Under the spirit of Humanism, small capitalists could be accommodated and local Zambian businesses were encouraged so long as they did not become too large. A leadership code was introduced in 1973 to limit the amount of personal accumulation allowed by civil employees. By and large, this code has been ignored. The Matero speech was delivered in August 1969, just a fortnight before Kapwepwe resigned from the vice presidency, provoking serious splits within UNIP. This address also included the first direct action by the governing class against their allies in the nationalist struggle, the trade unions, through a wage freeze and ban on strikes. That same year the GRZ commissioned a report from H. A. Turner on prices, incomes, and wages, which provided the governing class with academic backing for their denial of demands by labor. The Turner report detected a decreasing productivity in industry as a whole[80] despite increasing investment in equipment. Turner recommended that the GRZ link future wage increases to productivity, an opinion that met with hostility in union circles. Although incremental wage increases continued to the end of the First Republic, state participation changed the nature of industrial relations between the local governing class and organized labor. As far as labor was concerned, the owners were now the state and to be treated accordingly. Thus state participation undercut the nationalist alliance, but the significance of this did not manifest itself until well into the Second Republic when the economic situation had rapidly worsened.

The peasantry, many of whose members had been supporters of the nationalist struggle and also had been allied with the local petite bourgeoisie, was the weakest and least rewarded portion of the population. The underdeveloped circumstances and grinding poverty of the rural areas were mentioned frequently in official statements. The review of the FNDP in the introduction of the Second National Development Plan (SNDP), however, showed that not much was done for the peasantry. Commercial agriculture still dominated, although production had declined with the exodus of white farmers after independence. Into the vacuum came new semicommercial Zambian farmers. According to Baylies and Szeftel, in the 1970s "356 individual Africans held state land under freehold or leasehold title covering 430,000 acres. Some 263 of these had holding over 50 acres, the average for this group being 1,630 acres but reaching 3,100 acres in Kalomo District and 3,500 acres in the Choma area."[81]

Overall, these black capitalist farmers were few, but a trend had begun. In remote rural areas the people who benefited from access to credit or extension services tended to be party or government people or those with friends in high places. In general, however, most rural areas remained underdeveloped and underproductive.

CONCLUSION

The political struggle concluded with a one-party state and a dominant central government under a strong and personalized executive leadership. The governing class was consolidating its position relative to other classes both domestic and foreign. The basic compromise between the urban population and the government continued at the expense of the rural masses. Still, fissures had begun to appear within this upper class; embryonic capitalists pulled in one direction, civil servants and technocrats in another over some issues. These cracks were papered over during the general boom period, but the history of the Second Republic has been different in political, economic, and social terms, underscored by a marked and sustained decline in the worth of Zambian copper.

5
The Political Economy in Decline, 1973–1985

The ebullience of the first decade of independence gave way to serious concern over the decline of the economy, a decline not matched by creative policies to deal with a hostile international trading environment. Income gaps widened rather than narrowed[1] and frictions between the evolving classes sharpened. Material conditions worsened rapidly, though changes in social relations, buffered by ethnoregional rivalries and the extended family system, adjusted more slowly. Many observers, both local and foreign, were misled in the 1970s by the verbal commitments of the Zambian leaders to narrow the gaps, to introduce true socialism, and eventually to a policy of "return to the land." Although political life ultimately turns on the viability of the economy, the one-party system muted political discourse after 1972. Early successes of the First Republic left many leaders self-satisfied and insensitive to the signs of economic decline. As the 1970s unfolded, however, the true parameters of the crisis and the paralysis of the government were manifest. After 1975 the drive for money and power by the local governing class became more naked, accompanied by growing corruption and inefficiency at all levels of government. The "rot started at the top." Yet the regime remained stable, remarkable in the violent waters of southern Africa at the time. Why did the economy collapse so rapidly, and what are the chances for a recovery? How did the regime, initially committed to Humanist principles now clearly devalued, cling to power?

The basic reasons for the economic downturn were the ailing mining industry and the negative international terms of trade for Zambian base metals. In essence, the economy was always a house of cards balanced narrowly on the prosperity of the copper mines. The reforms undertaken in the First Republic had failed to make the economy more self-sustaining, and when foreign exchange receipts declined, all sectors contracted. Public finances dried up (government revenues shrank by 30 percent from 1974 to 1983).[2] The political ability or will to alter the economy evaporated as the country reeled under successive waves of imported inflation and low prices for Zambia's minerals. Cumulative balance-of-payments deficits forced a country that was proud never to have begged from the West into substantial external debt (K 6.418 billion or approximately U.S. $4.1 billion by 1984).[3] Pressing demands from the population for more social services and from the mines, farms, and factories for imported inputs meant that the government borrowed more and more to cover its spending.

This downward slide of the economy did not happen overnight: The effects accrued over time. Different conditions prevailed from 1973 to 1985, leading to different policies and official attitudes. The political economy of the Second Republic is divided into three periods for clarity. From 1973 to early 1975 the economy was affected by international inflation, yet copper revenues were still high, so society was protected from some immediate effects and social spending continued apace. Politicians' attentions were directed at the consolidation of power within the one-party state. From mid-1975 through 1980, the copper price fluctuated, the terms of trade became negative, and foreign reserves dried up. The GRZ then began to devalue the currency, which drove up the scale of debt and increased domestic inflation. Production and transport problems throttled the mines, also cutting into manufacturing and commercial agriculture. Yet foreign loans and grants were still available to cover the deficits, and the regime negotiated with the IMF for large and short-term balance-of-payments' loans. In these bad years, serious corruption and growing apathy began to infect the national scene (see Table 5.1).

From 1981 through 1985 the economic and social circumstances have been dire. Soft loan options have evaporated and the country is living on foreign aid. As a quid pro quo, politicians and planners must now incorporate policies demanded by major lenders and donors for restructuring the economy. By late 1985 the signs of political rot pervaded national politics and rumblings of discontent made the regime uneasy and sometimes vindictive. UNIP had withered at its roots despite its uncontested position, and the monopoly of the president and his advisers continued and expanded. To begin the analysis of how all this happened, we start with the features of the economy and weave in the story of the collapse of development planning, the fiscal crisis of the state, the political decline, and what the economic crisis means for the majority of Zambians.

1973 TO EARLY 1975: THE DOWNTURN BEGINS

The extreme degree of Zambia's external economic orientation (so dependent on foreign buyers as well as external suppliers of raw materials, technology, and consumer goods) meant that the international recession that started in 1973 and the negative changes in the prices for raw materials redounded severely on the national treasury. As with other oil-importing nations, Zambia was negatively affected by the hikes in the price of oil from 1973 onward. The petroleum bill, which had stood at K 14.9 million in 1970, reached K 57.6 million in 1975. Furthermore, this fuel bill had to be paid in foreign exchange, primarily U.S. dollars. Unlike many other Third

TABLE 5.1
Major Events in the Second Republic, 1973-1986

January 1973	Border with Rhodesia closed.
May 1973	New constitution announced.
June 1973	Nkumbula joined UNIP; Kapwepwe went into retirement.
August 1973	New constitution adopted by National Assembly and General Conference of UNIP.
December 1973	First election under Second Republic, low poll (39% of voters); KK won overwhelmingly.
June 1975	KK rebuked MPs for "anti-party and anti-government mouthings"; Watershed Speech and Land Act; Rural Reconstruction program introduced.
Late 1975	Tanzania-Zambia Railway opened.
1976	Central Committee decentralized.
February 1976	University of Zambia closed; some staff and students arrested.
March 1976	Mozambiquan route for cargo also closed.
April 1976	At 8th meeting of UNIP's National Council, condemnations of "tribalism" voiced.
July - August 1977	Several senior ministers dismissed for corruption and abuse of power.
October 1977	Emergency session of National Assembly, KK's address on the economic crisis.
November 1977	Mwanakatwe Report advised equity between civil service salaries and parastatals'; Industrial Development Act.
December 1977	11th meeting of UNIP's National Council with statements against corruption.
January 1978	Austerity budget introduced.
March 1978	Kwacha devalued 10 %; Zambia Railways Corruption Report issued.
September 1978	General Conference of UNIP amended constitution to exclude Nkumbula, Kapwepwe and others from contesting presidency.
October 1978	Border with Rhodesia reopened.
December 1978	Elections, 67% turnout; 80% "yes" vote for KK.
Late 1978	Kanyama flood and subsequent scandal.
September 1980	Kapwepwe died of natural causes.
April 1980	Elias Chipimo's speech against a one - party state
August 1980	Corrupt Practices Act.
October 1980	Railway strike.
October 16, 1980	Coup attempt failed, Treason Trial began.
January 1981	17 labor leaders temporarily expelled from UNIP.
June 1981	Diplomat suspended for taking bribes.
July 27, 1981	Labor leaders detained and rolling strikes began.
September 1981	Abortive attempt to release Treason Trial defendents.
October 1981	Labor leaders released under High Court order.
November 1982	Wife of senior UNIP official arrested in England for drug smuggling.
April 1982	University of Zambia students protested; University closed.

(Continued)

TABLE 5.1
Major Events in the Second Republic, 1973-1986 (Continued)

January 3, 1983	KK rebuked "self-proclaimed elite"; IMF loan of SDR 34 million extended to help pay shortfall for imports.
January 7, 1983	Kwacha devalued 20%.
January 20, 1983	Six men sentenced to death for treason; petition court about "inhuman treatment."
April 1983	Standby loan from IMF.
May 1983	IDA/World Bank extended loans; Paris Club rescheduled K 113 million in debt; various senior politicians and parastatal managers arrested in connection with drug smuggling.
July 1983	Kwacha floated; UNIP National Council proposed KK as sole official candidate for president.
August 1983	9th UNIP General Conference, elected new central committee.
October 27, 1983	Parliamentary general elections.
October 1983	Nkumbula died.
December 1983	KK reelected.
January 1984	IMF standby facility sought.
July 1984	Paris Club rescheduled.
August 1984	Third National Convention of UNIP held on restructuring the economy, Economic Crusade announced.
June 1985	Miners' strike, 4,364 dismissed.
July 1985	Fuel shortage brought transport to a halt.
September 1985	More prominent Zambians arrested for drug smuggling.
October 1985	Auctioning introduced; 100% inflation begins; some demonstrations in cities.
January 1986	Zambia Consolidated Copper Mines Ltd. launched five-year production and investment plan with closure of seven units, 3,000 jobs lost.
May 1986	South African troops attacked ANC buildings in Lusaka.

World countries, however, Zambia's basic export of copper was fetching a high price for most of 1973 to early 1975, earning the precious FOREX for the nation. The price of a wirebar (1 metric ton) of copper on the LME went from £727 ($1,786 and K 1,156) in 1973, to peak at £878 ($2,059 and K 1,327) and then to dip to £557 ($1,237 and K 794) in 1975 (see Table 5.2). So the oil shock was delayed.

But what could Zambia buy in these years with the mineral revenues—that is, what were the terms of trade for Zambian copper? What could the kwacha buy?[4] In 1970 to 1974, copper's value was high relative to Zambia's major imports, consisting mostly of manufactured goods, fuels, foods, and fertilizers. In 1974 the trend began to turn against Zambia's exports such that the buying power of Zambia's copper was almost halved by 1975 (see Figure 5.1). Zambia was caught in a classic bind: A weakening market for the main exports cut into the FOREX earnings, which were in turn necessary to purchase the more and more expensive industrial and consumer goods from abroad. Unable to supply manufacturing and agricultural needs locally,

TABLE 5.2
Copper and Cobalt Prices, Production, Exports, and Value of Exports, 1973-1984[a]

Item	1973	1974	1975	1976	1977	1978	1979	1980*	1981*	1982*	1983*	1984**
Copper Price												
£ per metric ton[b]	727	878	557	781	751	710	936	941	865	847	1047	1037
$ per metric ton[c]	1786	2059	1237	1401	1309	1309	1985	2183	1742	1742	1591	---
K per metric ton[d]	1156	1327	794	1007	1016	1090	1572	1719	1514	1374	1985	2099
Copper Production[e] (in metric tons of blister and electrolytic)	681.2	702.1	640.3	712.9	659.8	655.8	584.8	609.5	560.7	584.5	576.0	551.0
Copper Exports[e] (in thousand metric tons)	680.0	673.4	641.2	745.7	666.6	589.8	651.8	681.1	551.8	606.6	588.3	589.0
Value of Copper Exports[e] (in million Kwacha)	698.3	838.5	472.0	688.6	644.9	597.7	897.2	872.4	835.4	855.4	867.8	1279.0
Cobalt Price (in Kwacha[f] per metric ton)	4455	4158	5462	6913	9529	20,389	43,300	41,667	17,727	10,792	14,655	15,652
Cobalt Production[e] (in thousand metric tons)	1.9	2.0	1.8	1.6	1.7	1.6	3.3	3.3	2.6	2.4	2.4	2.7
Cobalt Exports[e] (in thousand metric tons)	1.1	1.9	1.3	2.3	1.7	1.8	3.0	2.1	2.2	2.4	3.4	3.1
Value of Cobalt Exports[e] (in million Kwacha)	4.9	7.9	7.1	15.9	16.2	36.7	129.9	87.5	39.0	25.8	49.9	58.9
Total Value of Copper and Cobalt Exports (in million Kwacha)	703.1	846.4	479.1	704.5	661.1	634.4	1027.0	959.9	874.5	881.2	917.7	1338.0

* Provisional and likely to undergo revision. ** 1984 figures are for the corporate year ending March 31, 1984.

Notes to Table 5.2

a Zambian copper has been quoted on the basis of electrolytic wire bars' "cash and settlement sellers' price" with effect from June 1968 as listed on the London Metal Exchange. Cobalt figures are based on Zambian official statistics.
b £ price for copper taken from the LME figures averaged for the year.
c US$ price for copper taken from World Bank, Commodity Trade and Price Trends, 1983–84 edition.
d Kwacha price for copper taken from GRZ, Central Statistical Office, Monthly Digest of Statistics, Zambia Mining Yearbooks and ZCCM Annual Reports.
e Production and export figures vary due to different stockpiling methods used by the mining companies.
f Kwacha price for cobalt calculated through dividing export value by tonnage exported.

Source: Copper figures from 1973-79 are taken from the Zambia Mining Yearbooks, 1970-1979; copper figures from 1980 to 1983 and all cobalt figures from Monthly Digest of Statistics, 20, 12 (December 1984) Table 15, p. 14, Table 21 p. 20, Table 48, p. 45; 1984 statistics from ZCCM Ltd., 1984 Annual Report.

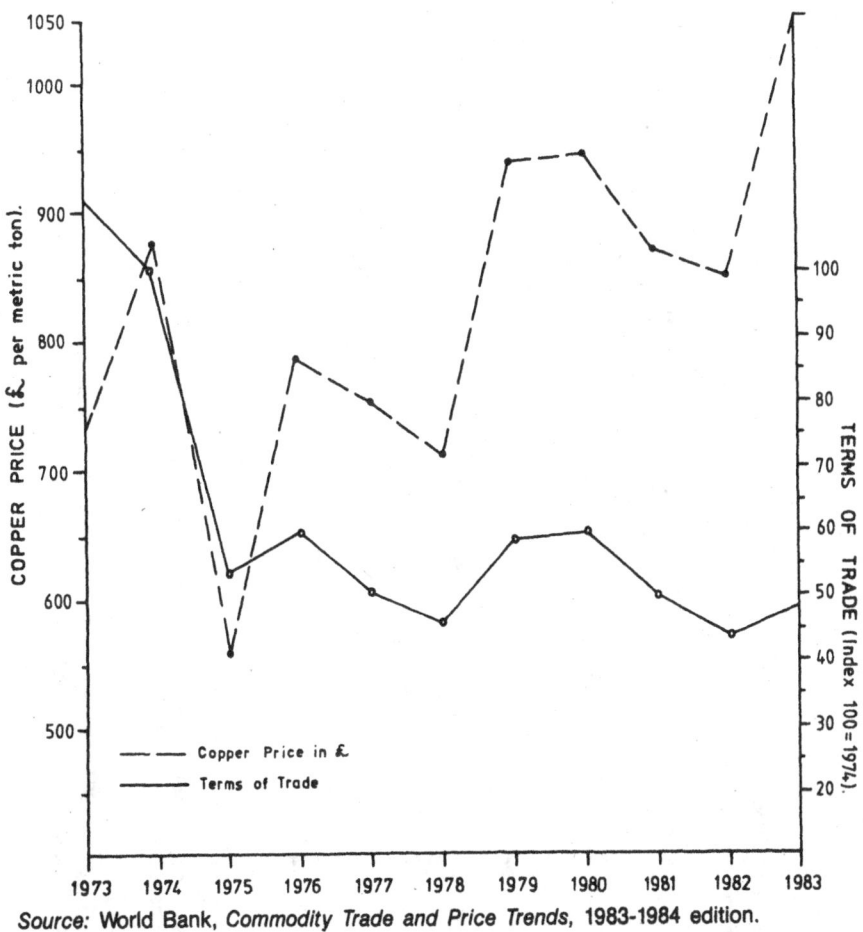

FIGURE 5.1 Copper Prices in Pound Sterling (£) and the Terms of Trade for Zambian Copper, 1973-1983 (1970-1974=100)

Source: World Bank, *Commodity Trade and Price Trends*, 1983-1984 edition.

Zambian officials could only hope that the copper price would skyrocket again, which it did not. Instead, the economy stagnated and then declined; employment, a sensitive indicator, shrank also. Although industrial production continued to expand slightly, the import bill inflated far more rapidly, from K 346.9 million in 1973 to K 597.6 million in 1975.[5]

Government revenues were particularly hard hit by the slump in the copper price and the negative terms of trade. The vulnerability of the government during cyclical downturns in the copper price is illustrated in Table 5.3. In 1973 (a good year) the copper industry accounted for 32 percent of the gross domestic product (GDP). Company and export taxes plus mineral revenues meant that total revenues from the mines to government rose to K 108 million, 29 percent of the government's total revenues. Copper and cobalt alone represented 95 percent of the nation's export earnings. The boom year of 1974 saw the mines supplying over half (53 percent) of the government's revenues.

TABLE 5.3
Contribution of Copper Industry to Gross Domestic Product, Revenue, Exports, and Value of Exports, 1970–1983 (at current prices)

Year	Gross Domestic Product (K million)	Contribution to Gross Domestic Product (K million)	(%)	Government Revenue (K million)	Contribution to Government Revenue (K million)	(%)	Value of Exports (K million)	Copper and Cobalt Contribution to Exports (%)
1970	1,278	455	36	435	251	58	688	97
1971	1,189	268	23	316	114	36	454	95
1972	1,348	317	24	302	56	19	500	93
1973	1,591	506	32	385	108	29	703	95
1974	1,893	607	32	647	341	53	846	94
1975	1,583	204	13	448	59	13	479	93
1976	1,941	330	17	443	12	3	705	94
1977*	2,024	223	11	449	-1.2	nil	661	94
1978*	2,259	271	12	550	0.1	nil	633	94
1979*	2,566	450	18	685	-9.8	nil	1,034	96
1980*	3,038	520	17	719	42	6	960	80
1981*	3,449	473	14	820	11	1	875	88
1982*	3,564	382	11	940	nil	nil	882	89
1983*	4,206	639	15**	957	42	4	n.a.	n.a.

* Figures are listed as provisional in the official statistics. ** Adrian Wood estimates that the 1983 mining contribution to GDP was as low as 5.9% in "An Economy Under Pressure: Some Consequences of the Recession in Zambia," Paper read at Annual Conference of British Geographers, Durham, U.K., January 1984, p. 6.

Source: for 1970-1980, Zambia Mining Yearbook 1980; for 1981, interviews with NCCM and RCM personnel; and 1982 and 1983 figures calculated using data from the Central Statistical Office, Monthly Digest of Statistics, 20, 12 (December 1984), Table 21, p. 20, Table 27, p. 25, Table 50, p. 47, and Table 52, p. 49.

Buoyed up by good production and temporary high prices, in 1973 the GRZ extended its participation in the mines. At a press conference held on August 31, 1973, President Kaunda announced the cancellation of the management contracts between the GRZ and the two foreign companies (AAC and RST/AMAX) that had run NCCM and RCM respectively. Almost immediately the government redeemed the outstanding bonds (which were the form of the GRZ debt to the multinationals) at a cost of $226.3 million, all in hard currency. Zambian managers were appointed to head NCCM and RCM and the restrictive clauses of the old articles of association were dissolved. Unfortunately for the GRZ, these unilateral actions violated the terms of the 1969/1970 contract with AAC and AMAX. The government became embroiled in eighteen months of negotiations with AMAX and AAC representatives, which in the end cost the government an additional K 55 million (ca. $85 million) in penalty fees. These penalties also were to be paid in hard currencies, and the nasty wrangle embittered relations between the majority and minority partners.

Nevertheless, expectations were that the mines, now under direct government control, would provide even more revenues to the state. These hopes proved to be misplaced. By the time the negotiations with the companies had ended (in February 1975), the cash-flow situation of the mines had rapidly deteriorated. The plummet of the copper price in late 1974 meant that by 1975 the mines' contribution shrank to 13 percent, and their overall contribution to the GDP diminished to the same figure.[6] This sudden constriction of funds had consequences for the Second National Development Plan and also led the government to indebtedness. Nationalizing the mines further had not alleviated the fiscal problem at all; rather, the money spent absorbed much of the nation's reserves just as it entered a period of serious fiscal crisis.

One consequence of the rapid drop in government revenues was that the Second National Development Plan (SNDP), launched in an era of prosperity and optimism, now ran into serious financial difficulties. The first three years of the plan had gone quite well. After 1974, the drop in the copper price and inflation of imported goods meant that the growth in all three productive sectors—mining, agriculture, and manufacturing—slowed down. As the authors of the Mid-Term Review of the Plan predicted in 1975 (somewhat understatedly), a shortfall in finance would undermine many of the general objectives of the plan. The official reasons given for the failure to complete some objectives were shortages of FOREX and transport problems. Less generally accepted was criticism of the industrialization strategy itself. The choice of an import-dependent, capital-intensive, and consumer-goods-oriented strategy for the parastatal companies meant a long-term dependence on foreign manufactures and therefore a reliance on the foreign exchange that only the mines could generate. The physical and social infrastructure that the regime embarked upon in the First Republic was very popular, and money continued to be put into those areas. Not until late 1975 was it apparent to the leaders that the optimistic goals of the SNDP would have to conform to the realities of an economy in recession. Yet in the political arena, there was little acknowledgment of any need for change in the overall development strategy. Politicians' attentions were focused elsewhere.

POLITICS IN A ONE-PARTY STATE

Despite the economic undertow, Zambia's leaders were preoccupied with solidifying UNIP's control over the one-party state as well as reworking the relationship between the party and the bureaucracy. By implication, this meant adjusting power relations between national politicians, civil servants, and technocrats. Maneuvering took place from 1973 to 1975; the strongest current was the steady accumulation of power in the hands of the president and his executive establishment. By 1975 the trends were well established.

The new constitutions introduced in 1973—one for the party and another for the nation—contained the skeleton of the structures and processes of the Second Republic. Yet details and actual power relations of the one-party system were ambiguous. One clear point was that all opposition parties were outlawed. Under the "one-party participatory democracy," as it was known, criticisms were to be aired within UNIP's party organs such as the central committee, the national council, and the general conference.[7]

In the first year, many famous voices of opposition from UPP, ANC, and UP joined or rejoined UNIP's ranks, if with varying degrees of grace. Harry Nkumbula and Nalumino Mundia joined, while the militant Simon Kapwepwe opted for temporary retirement (see Table 5.4). Grumbling over the end to legal opposition did not tip over to violence; the December 1973 general elections (for MPs and president) went off smoothly. KK won easily, but surely a disconcerting note for UNIP organizers was the low voter turnout. Only 39 percent of those registered to vote did so, and there were regional pockets of discontent. Nonetheless UNIP now was uncontested in the political arena and KK preeminent within UNIP.

Adjusting the relationship between the different sections of government (the executive, the judiciary, and the legislature) as well as levels of government (central, provincial, district, ward) and most importantly between the government and the party was more difficult. The new constitutions made it clear that the party was to be supreme over government as the phrase "the Party and *Its* Government" implies (emphasis added). Thus the relationship between national politicians, civil servants, and technocrats was supposed to shift so that politicians in UNIP's central committee gained greater authority over various minister(s) in cabinet singly and collectively and thus over the bureaucracy. Now a member of the central committee (MCC) outranked the minister(s) whose portfolio(s) fell within his/her competence. The cabinet was relegated to "policy implementation rather than policy formation."[8]

Things did not work out as the designers of new regulations expected. With the well-known tendency for any bureaucracy to defend itself tena-

TABLE 5.4
Chronology of an Opposition National Politician, Simon Kapwepwe

April 12, 1922	Born in Chinsali District, Northern Province to Bemba-speaking parents; childhood friend of Kaunda's and also educated at Lubwa Mission.
1945	Teacher qualified and taught elementary school in Kitwe on Copperbelt.
1948	Returned to Lubwa Mission with Kaunda to farm and teach; became active in Chinsali African Welfare Association.
1950	Retired from teaching and went to Bombay University in India to study journalism.
1955	Returned to Northern Rhodesia, became Provincial President of Northern Province branch of the NRANC.
1956	Became NRANC's party treasurer.
1958	Broke with NRANC and became a founding member of ZANC.
1959-1960	Restricted to Mongu (Barotseland, now Western Province).
1960-1967	Treasurer - General of UNIP; in 1962 elected overwhelmingly and made Minister of African Agriculture in the 1962 government.
January 1964	Appointed Minister for Home Affairs.
September 1964-1967	Served as Minister of Foreign Affairs.
August 1967	Involved in interethnic disputes within UNIP; won his seat and was elected the first National Vice President and Deputy Leader of UNIP.
January 1969	Became leader of House of Assembly.
August 25, 1969	Resigned both Vice Presidency of Republic and Deputy Party leadership of UNIP; called back by President Kaunda to serve in UNIP and as Minister of Culture.
January 1970	Took additional portfolio of Provincial and Local Government.
October 1970	Lost job as Deputy Leader of UNIP to Mainza Chona but kept two ministerial portfolios.
August 1971	Resigned from government; founded UPP with Justin Chimba.
December 24, 1971	In by-elections, won Mufulira West seat.
February 1972	UPP banned and Kapwepwe arrested along with followers.
December 31, 1972	Released.
January 1973	Brought libel suit against The Times of Zambia and won; was awarded K 20,000 by court.
February 3, 1973	Charged with possession of two guns but received two-year suspended sentence.
1973-1977	Returned to farming in Northern Province.
September 9, 1977	Rejoined UNIP.
September 1978	Contested UNIP election for president and was outmaneuvered at the General Conference of UNIP.
1979	Supreme Court dismissed petition against UNIP General Conference ruling; Kapwepwe again drops out of politics; again charged with possession of firearms and prohibited literature.
September 1980	Died of natural causes.

Source: Kelvin Mlenga, Who's Who in Zambia, 1979 (Ndola, Zambia: Roan Consolidated Mines Ltd., August 1979); W. Tordoff, "Introduction," Administration in Zambia (Manchester, U.K.: Manchester University Press, 1980), pp. 1-42; Times of Zambia and Zambia Daily Mail.

ciously, the civil servants and technocrats clung to power through their control over day-to-day administration. In some highly publicized incidents, a MCC's decision took precedence over an already announced decision of a minister, permanent secretary, or senior civil servant. But such occurrences were rare. According to Ian Scott's study of the Zambian bureaucracy, in the long run the conflict between party officials and civil servants was "entirely resolved in favour of the latter" under the one-party state.[9] In class terms, the fractions of civil servants and technocrats held their own against the politicians.

Whatever the power allocations below, at the apex of the new combined party and government hierarchies sits the president. His first lieutenant is the secretary-general of the party (the SG) who outranks the prime minister (the PM). The SG heads the party apparatuses, oversees the work of the subcommittees of the central committee, and acts as the public spokesperson for the party to the nation. With these expanded duties, the SG is more instrumental to the executive's power: He can reach into any ministry and force an explanation or change of policy. Potentially, he can pose a threat to the president, so occupants of this office tend to serve relatively short tenures.

In the Second Republic the PM's power has been curtailed, although he sits on the central committee of UNIP. The post of secretary of state for defence and security emerged from within the president's office to become the fourth-ranking position in the central committee. The president keeps a close eye on this post with its sensitive connections to the military and its wealth of information on the citizenry. KK appoints only close associates to this job. All districts now have an office of security forces located there; the employees have a palpable presence in the town with "ears" in most bars and shebeens.

In institutional terms, the game of musical chairs in the Second Republic ended with the cabinet losing ground, primarily to the president and senior civil servants. The central committee, which was supposed to gain power, does not wield it as a unified political force but rather acts as the closed shop for national politicians. Although some key positions have grown in power and influence—most pointedly the SG—all important positions in the party and its government are clearly subordinated to the president and State House (government headquarters), whose powers have grown commensurately.

Executive power has also expanded in parliament.[10] Bills originate (by and large) in the departments, ministries, and the president's office. They move on to the cabinet office and Freedom House (party headquarters) for clearance and then to the national assembly. If the president withholds his assent to a piece of legislation, the assembly cannot override him. After 1972 MPs became unwilling publicly to oppose the president directly, perhaps because individuals running for office now had to be vetted by the central committee, firmly under KK's control. Despite these structural diminishments of its autonomy, the national assembly elected in December 1973 did not immediately become a rubber stamp for the executive. Those members who represented an aspiring bourgeoisie[11] were vocal in their sentiments, which were often probusiness and critical of the regime's policies. In June 1975 KK publicly rebuked MPs for the "anti-party and anti-government mouthings."[12] In the Watershed Speech delivered on June 30 of the same year, the president reaffirmed the country's committment to socialism. He reinforced this with the last of the major reforms, the abolition of freehold tenure of land. He attacked the inefficiency of the parastatals and denounced the capitalistic tendencies appearing in Humanist Zambia, pointing a finger again at the MPs. By the end of 1975 even sympathetic observer William Tordoff noted that the national assembly was functioning primarily to legitimize government policy through debate and passage of bills rather than as an independent and countervailing force to the executive.[13]

In contrast, the judiciary managed to hold on to many powers handed down in the independence constitution. The Supreme Court remains the final court of appeals and the superior court of record, although in practice it is the High Court that usually gives the final word. The president appoints judges to both of these courts (on the advice of the Judicial Service Commission) but can revoke the appointment of a justice only after investigation by a tribunal. This accords a judge a considerable degree of security of tenure. Members of the legal profession point to the autonomy of the judiciary with pride, as they do to the government's good record on civil liberties.[14] Most lawyers qualify their assessment of the freedom of the judiciary and peoples' rights, however, in light of the extensive presidential detention powers.

In summary then, the accumulation of power in the hands of the executive under the one-party system occurred at the expense of the legislature, cabinet, and to a lesser degree the central committee and the courts. National politicians, loyal to the president, and civil servants have tended to develop competing loci of power—one based in the party and the other in the bureaucracy. Ultimately, the president controls both party and government and governs more and more unilaterally with his advisers.

Unleashed from any constraints built into the multi-party system, Kaunda has fashioned the presidency into an institution dominated by one man. Despite this overt accumulation of power, Dr. Kaunda remained (at least until late 1986) quite popular with the average citizen. Charges were often raised against politicians and grumbling was heard over the avaricious behavior of the *apamwamba*, but little negative commentary was aimed at KK. Some silence may be attributed to legislation that prohibits strong public criticism of the chief executive. But Zambians are notoriously outspoken. The lack of criticism stems from a widespread recognition of the president's own austere life-style (he is both a teetotaler and a vegetarian) and his warm and friendly personality (Photo 5.1). Kaunda's charm and political deftness have allowed him to refine a particular brand of personal politics (see Table 5.5) that disarms his opponents and tends to protect other national politicians when the public comes for an accounting.[15]

PHOTO 5.1 President Kaunda's official portrait.

The biblical parable of the Prodigal Son is an apt analogy for a public drama played again and again on the national stage. A rising young politician, technocrat, civil servant, or diplomat appears in national politics and is shown public favor by the president in a "fatherly role." At some point and for widely differing reasons, this "son" is seen to reject the "father" and is cast out of the political house to poverty, abuse, and obscurity. After some time in the political "wilderness," if the prodigal makes a public apology, castigating himself for his behavior and throwing himself on the beneficence, charity, and mercy of the president, KK publicly reaches down, forgives the prodigal, raises him up, and reinstates him in some appropriate position.

One result of this political drama is that unlike the case in so many other societies, political battles and rapid changes in the fortunes of prominent individuals do not end in bloodshed. President Kaunda is outstanding as a restrained national leader; Zambia has a well-deserved reputation as a country with a good human rights record. Yet there is a negative side to the parable as well. Capable young politicians, civil servants, and technocrats whose ideas vary from those of the president or the accepted orthodoxy of the day are unable to express these opinions in public without risking the loss of office and sometimes even of their livelihood. An example of this is the former Zambian high commissioner to London and former chairman

TABLE 5.5
Chronology of the President, Kenneth D. Kaunda

April 28, 1924	Kenneth David Kaunda born at Lubwa Mission near Chinsali, Northern Province, eighth child of missionary teachers, Helen and David Kaunda, originally from Malawi.
1924 - 1942	Kaunda educated at Lubwa Mission, then at Munali Secondary School in Lusaka where he took teachers' training course.
1943	Returned to Lubwa Mission as teacher.
1944	Headmaster at Lubwa, scoutmaster and athletic coach.
1946	Married Betty Banda with whom he raised nine children.
1947 -1948	Taught in Tanganyika and on Copperbelt at Mufulira; worked as welfare assistant at Nchanga Mine.
1949	Returned to Lubwa to farm with old friends, Simon Kapwepwe and John Sokoni; became active in the Chinsali Welfare Association then a local branch of the Northern Rhodesian African National Congress (NRANC).
1950	Elected secretary for Chinsali Association.
1951	District organizer for NRANC.
1952	Organizing Secretary for Northern Province.
August 1953	NRANC Secretary - General, second to Nkumbula and editor of the Congress News.
November 1953	Arrested but not imprisoned.
January 6, 1955	Arrested and sentenced to two months in prison where he began his austere life style.
May 1957	Visited England as guest of Labour Party.
May 1958	Traveled to Tanganyika and India.
October 24, 1958	Broke with ANC to form ZANC; became president of ZANC.
March 1959	Northern Rhodesian government baned ZANC; sentenced to nine months imprisonment in Kabompo in the northwest.
January 9, 1960	Released.
January 31, 1960	Elected president of UNIP.
April 1960	Wrote Black Government with Colin Morris; campaigned vigorously against the Federation.
October 1962	UNIP contested elections and formed coalition with NRANC; KK became Minister of Local Government and Social Welfare in the first black majority government.
1963	KK served as president of the Pan African Freedom Movement of East, Central and Southern Africa; he was awarded an honorary doctorate (Doctor of Laws) from Fordham University, New York.
January 1964	In new elections UNIP won and KK appointed Prime Minister.
October 24, 1964	KK became first President of the Republic of Zambia.
1966	Took post as Chancellor of University of Zambia.
1964 -1970	Held the portfolio of defense in president's office.
1967	Resigned temporarily over ethnoregional dispute within UNIP.
1970 -1971	Served as chairman of the OAU.
1970 -1973	Chairman of the Nonaligned Movement.
December 1972	Introduced one-party state in the Second Republic.
December 1973	Reelected.
December 1978	Reelected.
December 1983	Reelected.
August 9, 1985	Elected chairman of the Frontline States.

Source: Fergus Macpherson, Kenneth Kaunda of Zambia: The Times and the Man (Oxford: Oxford University Press, 1974); Kenneth Kaunda, Zambia Shall Be Free: An Autobiography (London: Heinemann, 1962); Kelvin Mlenga, Who's Who in Zambia, 1979 (Lusaka, Zambia: RCM Ltd., August 1979); the Times of Zambia and Zambia Daily Mail.

of the Standard Bank of Zambia Ltd., Elias Chipimo. In April 1980 he had the temerity to criticize the one-party system (and by implication KK) saying, "the multiparty system was the surest way of avoiding coups and eliminating the disgraceful tendency of presidents ending up with bullets in their heads."[16] Kaunda took umbrage at this comment, charged Chipimo and others with attempting to incite the army to overthrow the government and assassinate him. In October 1980 Chipimo was arrested with others and charged with treason. Although later released, he lost his post with the Standard Bank, and after a long period of domestic troubles, his wife left him as well.

Opponents and critics of one-party system and Kaunda's leadership are effectively silenced by the combination of paternalism and the iron fist of the state. Presidentialism in Zambia is not just the accumulation of power in the hands of one person. It has evolved into the centralization of political power and the use of that power to monopolize major policy decisions, to sideline or threaten contenders, and to offer patronage to others, leading to a general inflation of the government. In 1975 when Zambia desperately needed critical, challenging voices, the waters of political debate outside the party were becalmed. Also Zambia's involvement in the struggles in Angola, Mozambique, and Zimbabwe (to be discussed in Chapter 6) were used to stifle dissent at home. The only prescription for economic ills coming from the president's office was to continue as before and hope for a major recovery in the fortunes of copper.

MID-1975 TO 1980: THE MINES FALTER

Luck did not visit the Zambian people in the next half decade. The mines began to run into serious internal production problems as well as obstacles to sales. The consequences for the dependent manufacturing and agriculture were disastrous, as was the effect on the economy as a whole. Now the GRZ became entangled in the merciless debt trap in which, by 1985, it was deeply ensnared. In these years the decline of the party and the growth of corruption became more evident.

First let us look at some general economic indicators. The terms of trade for Zambian copper stayed at a low level from 1976 through 1980. Zambian exports were able to purchase no more than 60 percent of what they had bought in 1974. In 1978 the proportion dropped as low as 46 percent. Private and government firms were unable to purchase the imports that they needed without resorting to more loans, suppliers' credits, and the like. The volume of imports declined from 2.1 million metric tons in 1974 to 1.6 million metric tons in 1980,[17] yet public and private debt grew. Mirroring the low copper price, the contribution of the mines to the GDP fluctuated between 11 and 18 percent. In 1977, 1978, and 1979, when the mines supplied the GRZ with little or no revenue, shortages of funds for the running of government became critical. The leaders began to borrow money abroad.

To understand the seriousness of the Zambian economic dilemma (and also to see why some prescriptions offered by outside funders are unlikely to work), we need to explore the mining industry in some depth, as that is the linchpin of the whole economy. A useful way to understand the domestic and foreign aspects of the crisis in the copper business is to look at two sets of measurements. Free on rail (f.o.r.) figures tell one how much it actually costs in kwacha terms to produce a ton of copper or cobalt. Cost-insurance-freight (c.i.f.) charges include the domestic costs plus nonfactor services such as insurance, freight, port charges, and so on. C.i.f. charges, then, reveal what it costs to get a ton of copper or cobalt from landlocked Zambia to its far-distant markets.

Although in the 1960s Zambia was known as a low- or medium-cost producer of copper, by 1976 the Commodity Research Unit, based in New York, estimated that Zambia was one of the highest-cost producers of copper in the world.[18] Testing such a judgment is difficult, as the companies were reluctant to divulge information as well as the complication that NCCM and RCM had different accounting methods and years until 1979/1980. Still some comparisons and assessments can be made.[19] Indeed a general pattern of escalating domestic *and* c.i.f. costs appears.

The domestic costs of production increased for both NCCM and RCM. As 70 percent of the operating costs of the Zambian mines are said to be "fixed," the ability to managers to reverse this trend of increasing f.o.r. costs was limited. The basic choices for them were to expand output, rationalize domestic operations, or press for greater labor efficiency by introducing more machinery. In general from 1975 to 1980 they chose to expand production and to rationalize operations.

Expanding production proved very difficult. Lack of sufficient skilled manpower combined with growing technical problems with the orebody itself (the latter problems go along with deepening of the mines) meant declining production rather than increasing output. Rather than "economies of scale" operating for them, the copper managers found that shrinking tonnages meant a steady increase in the costs of production per ton of copper hoisted. One glimmer of hope was cobalt. Cobalt occurs in several Zambian mines, and high quality cobalt was produced almost as a by-product of copper production (see Photo 5.2). Prior to 1978 the price had been so low (ca. $5.00 per lb.) that it was marginally profitable, gaining the mines only K 16 million in 1977. In 1978 and 1979 the producer price moved upward when Zambia and Zaire, as the world's major cobalt exporters, formed an informal cartel. Also Zaire's production was disturbed by the invasion of Shaba Province,[20] driving the price higher still. The Zambian industry gained K 37 million from cobalt sales in 1978 and K 130 million in 1979. The market was so strong that the companies airfreighted cobalt overseas in some of these years because of the railroad blockages. Unfortunately, the arrangement with Zaire fell apart in 1980. The price dropped although profits remained higher than in the pre-1978 period. The Zambian mines were trapped in a vise between static or declining production and rising costs to extract and refine the metals.

PHOTO 5.2 Worker pulling cobalt starting sheets at Chambishi Mine, ZCCM.

Undermining profitability still further were the escalating and uncontrollable additional costs of selling their minerals abroad. Of all the c.i.f. charges, transportation contributed the most to making Zambian copper expensive and also losing the companies some buyers because of unreliable deliveries. In the most troubled years (1975–1980), two out of the three major railroad routes for the country were either blocked or inefficient. The third route, the Tanzania-Zambia Railway Authority (TAZARA), to Dar es Salaam completed by the Chinese in late 1975, was not able to carry the total weight of the imports and exports. The port of Dar rapidly became overwhelmed by the volume of Zambia's international trade. When regional wars cut Zambia's transport lifelines, the overall effects on the mines were twofold. Domestic costs of production (f.o.r.) were pushed up because of lack of spare parts and equipment, while the costs of sales (c.i.f.) skyrocketed from more insurance, freight, port charges, and the like. Mine managers found themselves, after 1976, producing and selling minerals at or below the break-even point. The pressures to export did not abate, however, given the mines' desperate need for revenues (especially FOREX) to buy spare parts, fuels, and technical services.

The state was in much the same straits. Now other sectors began to feel the pinch. Manufacturing had always been heavily dependent on the mines' FOREX receipts to purchase foreign inputs such as technology, raw materials, machinery, and specialized manpower. As the mines were not providing enough FOREX for the national economy, factory production stagnated at the 1973 level. Predictions made earlier by Seidman (rising unemployment, declining domestic value-addedness, increasing import-intensity) were borne out. Wage employment in existing industries, for example, contracted except in a few service areas, although the addition of some new firms meant a little increase in jobs in manufacturing overall. The contribution of manufacturing to the GDP (when measured in 1970 constant prices) shrank from K 170 million in 1976 to K 152.4 million the following year, only recovering to K 162.9 million in 1980.[21] Agricultural production, also affected by a drought, dropped dramatically. Maize, the staple food crop, dropped from 750,000 metric tons marketed in 1976 to 696,000 in 1977, 582,000 in 1978, 336,000 in 1979 and 382,000 in 1980.[22] Slowly starved of vital imported items, agriculture and manufacturing were less productive and less profitable.

The cycle of FOREX shortage and declining production was completed with lower contributions from all sectors to overall government revenues. Four general trends in the central government's finances deserve mention here. First, despite some temporary reductions, total expenditures continued to expand, moving from K 855 million in 1975 to K 1.302 billion in 1980. Capital expenditures, however, had a declining share, while recurrent costs (such as salaries, general operating expenditures) took the lion's share.

Second, revenues grew slightly but not as swiftly as expenditures, so a chronic deficit appeared on the national accounts. Third, the government increased direct and indirect taxes to obtain finances, making the burden more regressive. Finally, the GRZ repeatedly resorted to deficit financing to bridge the gap, borrowing locally from the Bank of Zambia and from external sources. Debts accumulated both in kwacha and in FOREX. International debts expanded rapidly. Before 1975 a generally positive balance of trade meant that Zambia had not incurred heavy debts, although the government did resort to occasional deficit financing to pay for social programs. After 1975 the external debt shot up from U.S.$1.377 billion to $2.657 billion (1980), according to the World Bank's Debt Reporting Service.[23] National politicians and civil servants were faced with a dilemma: how to continue to respond to the public demand for more welfare programs while experiencing declining revenues. They chose to squeeze capital projects and borrow externally on an increasing scale. Although in 1980 the debt was not enormous by Third World standards, servicing it required a growing proportion of the declining FOREX receipts from the mines. In a delayed reaction to the economic bind, the GRZ in 1978 announced austerity measures, cutting food subsidies and placing tighter controls over import licensing and remittances. The drain continued. An early casualty was the national development strategy.

Inevitably, the overall development strategy was derailed in the economic crisis. An official evaluation of the SNDP when it concluded in 1977 acknowledged that it had started with "excessively optimistic targets" and had then been swamped by factors such as the collapse of the copper price.

Yet the original strategy never could have worked except in rare instances of very positive terms of trade for copper as in 1969–1972. Few intermediate goods and no new capital goods industries had been introduced in the first and second plans. Factories heavily dependent on foreign technology, imported machinery, and sometimes imported manpower were doomed in an era of FOREX shortage.

Perhaps little could have been done to introduce appropriate technology to the mines, but few efforts were made even to locate and promote local materials and techniques for state-owned companies. In 1979 the general manager of ROP 1975 (Refined Oil Products—a parastatal that produces cooking oil, bath soap, detergents, and toiletries) estimated that 70 percent of the raw materials in ROP's processing was imported.[24] Certainly the drop in returns for copper and the rapid increase in the costs of imports hurt the economy. Yet inappropriate planning and expenditures during the years preceding the squeeze meant that the monetary birthright of the nation had been squandered.

When the Third National Development Plan (TNDP) was introduced in 1980 (a year late), its goals reflected some new thinking but were so far from economic and political reality as to be in the realm of fiction. The announced intentions were to coordinate economic activities, to move toward true socialism, to shift investment to agriculture, and to emphasize labor-intensive industrialization and the informal sector. These aspirations sound like wishful thinking when contrasted to the funds available and in light of the steps taken in the prior two planning periods, when more funds had been available. For instance, despite assertions that the TNDP would emphasize agriculture, the budgetary projections for 1983 indicated a reduction by 34 percent of the revenue available to the two key ministries that deal with agriculture: the Ministry of Cooperatives and the Ministry of Agriculture and Water Development.[25]

Lacking political muscle, the Planning Commission was subverted by a coterie of private individuals and public officials. "Long range planning ha[d] become anachronistic and crisis management ha[d] taken its place."[26] Attempts to control public spending and to direct investment into the most vital areas were often futile. Rather than designing a well-integrated industrial and agricultural plan, the party and its government permitted various parts of the economy greater autonomy. This was partly the outcome of struggles within the government class itself, partly because of the weakening of UNIP, and partly a reaction to pressures from outside.

INTRACLASS STRUGGLES, CORRUPTION, AND THE ATROPHY OF UNIP

In 1978, dramatically, Kapwepwe and Nkumbula contested KK's ascendancy within the party. For the Zambian presidency, there are two elections: a party election followed by a popular election. Any political aspirant has to start at the general conference of the party, where cadres select the candidate who then runs in the national poll (and who must receive at least a 50 percent "yes" vote to be elected president). Kapwepwe and Nkumbula appealed to the UNIP cadres and to the nation as a whole, criticizing KK and the general economic and foreign policies of the regime. They gained some support before they were outmaneuvered by UNIP officials in September 1978.[27] Despite some fears within UNIP circles, Kaunda received an 80 percent "yes" vote in the December 1979 elections, with 67 percent of the electorate turning out.[28] Since 1978, KK's powers have continued to expand, while the era of the flamboyant early politicians dimmed with the deaths of Kapwepwe in 1980 and Nkumbula in 1983.

An end to opposition did not translate into coordinated and unified national policies however. Sections of the petite bourgeoisie and aspirant bourgeoisie connected to the state and the party directed their energies to the grab for personal wealth and power, leaving politics to national and local politicians. Sizable amounts of the nation's precious FOREX went for personal consumption,[29] while private entrepreneurs skillfully eluded state supervision. Some state enterprises resisted government direction too. Some civil servants as well as managers of the state firms (often technocrats) and national politicians milked state firms and engaged in all sorts of illicit behavior.[30] The yearly reports of the auditor general turned up improper activities ranging from misuse of funds by ministries to actual corruption by public officials.[31] From January through March 1979, eleven leaders were suspended for corruption or involvement in illegal activities such as poaching.

To give one a flavor of these happenings, in 1976 the governor of the Bank of Zambia was dismissed for allegedly receiving government property illegally. (He later appealed to the Supreme Court, was successful and reinstated in January 1981.) In 1977 a senior army official in charge of the Mechanical Services Division was caught in corrupt practices and three senior ministers were dismissed from the cabinet for alleged corruption and abuse of power. A Railway Commission reported in 1978 the existence of widespread corruption, ineffiency, and tribalism in the railway system. About the same time, public officials (including another former cabinet minister, a provincial secretary, a district governor, and a district secretary) were accused of selling relief supplies donated to victims of a flood (the Kanyama Scandal).[32] In 1979 the minister of labour and social services was suspended, pending investigations into his involvement in poaching. Ultimately he was dismissed in August 1980. These are not just isolated incidents. The number of corruption cases handled by the police had increased 500 percent from 1979 to 1980.[33]

In 1980 the government introduced the Corrupt Practices Bill, which was supposed to give the authorities more power to stem this trend. But the avaricious and increasingly blatant behavior of those with money or power had not been tempered. When ready cash dwindled and when adequate financial backing for public and private ventures became more scarce, many civil servants, national politicians, technocrats, and entrepreneurs scrambled for whatever available means for accumulation there were, legal or not. Sometimes friends and relatives turned against each other to entrench a position or defend the potential to accumulate land, businesses, or money, poisoning social relations. Battles within the governing class affected the ability to plan and enact policies in every conceivable area.

In the midst of such struggles, the core institution of the new regime, UNIP, began to wither at its roots. Indirectly UNIP's decline was linked to the national economic disaster. Many UNIP officials had looked eagerly to the introduction of the one-party state to protect the fragile unity of the party and to augment their power in struggles with bureaucrats. The political slogan that "it pays to belong to UNIP" took on a double meaning as party officials expected salaries and perquisites for their activities. The party invested heavily: for example UNIP made a joint venture in Zecco with the Yugoslavs; it bought outright Duly Motors and invested in the South African–owned firm E. W. Tarry.[34] The downturn in the economy after 1975 and the tenacity of the civil servants meant that jobs for middle- and lower-level party faithfuls were not forthcoming. Scott argued that this lack of opportunity led to a distinct loss of morale among party officials, worsening when the national leaders rejected the suggestion that UNIP party and constituency workers be paid allowances.[35]

Soon thereafter, many UNIP local organizers left the party. Not surprisingly the party then lost membership as well.

> On the Copperbelt alone, membership declined from about twenty-five per cent of the population in 1968 to around eight per cent in 1974 and had apparently declined even further by 1976. In parts of the country (*The Sunday Times of Zambia* reported) the only card-carrying members of UNIP are those holding posts in the section, branch, constituency and regions ... men and women entrusted with the big task of being the vanguards of the party and thus the revolution, are there purely for cupboard love.[36]

In 1982 the SG announced that only 89,000 out of 3 million Zambian youths were members of UNIP.[37] Unofficial reports indicate that women do not enroll in the Women's League in large numbers either. Below the ward chairman level, the party effectively had atrophied in Zambia especially in the rural areas. The economic downturn plus declining party subscriptions meant that not enough money was available for UNIP, and as a result some loans were unsecured.[38]

Disillusionment with the party became public. On the front page of the *Times of Zambia* on September 25, 1984, an editorial started with: "Could the United National Independency Party UNIP have spearheaded the freedom struggle at its present administration and organisation? The Answer to this question is an emphatic NO. UNIP is thriving on its past glory. This is how political observers look at the Party now. Except for a few leaders at the top echelons, the majority are no longer committed to the cause of the nation." The average Zambian was alienated further and further from decisions that affected his or her life. Certainly there was growing perplexity at the inability of the leaders to protect the people from the economic tidal waves that threatened to engulf the nation. The next five years were even worse

worse for the economy and for the middle-income people and urban and rural poor in particular.

FROM 1981 THROUGH 1985: THE CRISIS DEEPENS

The leaders failed to make substantive economic reforms for most of this period, and a stubborn negative terms of trade continued. By 1981 the economy and society had entered a true crisis, the proportions of which deepened over the next four years. Serious production problems on the mines became more intractable, and the dependent manufacturing sector began to fall apart. Only agriculture held its own in production terms, albeit tenuously because of a drought and the dependence of commercial agriculture on imported inputs such as fertilizers, pesticides, and machinery. To indicate what this has meant for the "common man or woman," when adjusted for terms of trade (i.e., when calculated for what a person can buy with his or her income), the GDP per capita had sunk from K 184 in 1980 to K 168 in 1983.[39] Behind this collapse lay the ailing mining industry, with consequent effects on FOREX receipts and import constraints.

Effects on Key Sectors

The Mines. In 1980 President Kaunda directed NCCM and RCM to merge into one giant company, the Zambia Consolidated Copper Mines Ltd. (ZCCM), to avoid duplication of spare parts, plants, and double administrations. By 1982 this merger was accomplished and new managers ordered a major review of the industry. They found that from 1980 to 1983 (when the report was concluded), Zambian copper averaged only 51 percent of its 1970–1974 indexed value (purchasing power). Despite some upward movement in the price after 1982, FOREX receipts neither covered escalating costs nor provided the government with enough hard currency to keep afloat the import-dependent manufacturing and agricultural sectors. Inflated c.i.f. charges on mineral exports pared away the profitability of the mines, while marketing managers could not raise the price and remain competitive. Despite efforts at increasing production, the tonnage of copper mined and sold stayed stubbornly below the 600,000 metric ton mark, automatically constraining increase in export earnings through increasing scale.

The inability of the mines to generate enough FOREX meant that by 1982 Zambia was importing only about one-third (34.4 percent) of what it had imported in 1970, although its population and its local demand were higher. Charges for nonfactor services cost the nation in 1982 what it had paid back in 1970 for a much larger bulk of imported goods. Faced with such problems, ZCCM's managers looked at a limited number of options. Growing awareness of the short resource life of the mines (most experts predict that Zambia's mines will become uneconomic by the turn of the century, based on current resource calculations), managers began to take vigorous, often unpopular, actions.

They closed some of the less profitable mines and plants. Bwana Mkubwa Mine was shut in April 1984.[40] Some expensive projects begun in the buoyant early 1970s, such as the Torco Plant at Nkana Division, were shut. In coordination with the government, ZCCM began to seek international aid to rehabilitate the existing mines, specifically to pay for spare parts, equipment, and consumable stores.[41] And the company began to emphasize cobalt, entering into several purchasing agreements with companies or foreign governments willing to underwrite new projects.

The chronic problem remained of how to cut domestic costs of production and stabilize transportation to markets. ZCCM's financial people estimated that an investment of K 160 million would increase production by at least 50,000 metric tons per year. This tonnage could reduce the unit costs and thus lessen ZCCM's losses in a bad year and in a good year, provide more FOREX. The problem was whether to increase production in a period of world oversupply. In 1985 the World Bank sponsored several private consulting firms to explore what rehabilitation and reorganization would entail and whether to expand production. In January 1986 the government announced a five-year production and investment plan for ZCCM. Seven mining operations were to be closed (Kansanshi Mine, Konkola III shaft, Chambishi Mine, Luanshya smelter, Ndola Copper Refinery tank house, Nkana oxide concentrator, and Chambishi concentrator), and approximately 5,000 workers were to be affected.[42]

The thrust behind the consultants' recommendations and the ZCCM plan is to lessen domestic costs of production by cutting out the less efficient units, lowering labor costs, and using less precious FOREX. This would mean lower production, but it was hoped that cheaper copper and cobalt could then find more markets. Still haunting ZCCM is the reality of new and cheaper materials substituting for copper, limiting its market, and keeping the price down. Conventional copper wire cables are being replaced with optical fibers in some countries, for example. Such considerations temper optimistic assessments that cheaper copper necessarily will give a comparative advantage to copper producers such as Zambia. The mines, despite their key position in the economy, are unable to reverse the negative trends themselves.

Manufacturing. How has manufacturing fared with the eclipse of mining? In 1985 parastatal companies still dominated manufacturing, and from 1980 to 1985 most INDECO companies had done poorly. Many INDECO firms utilize well below 50 percent of their capacity. The capacity utilization rates are low in many companies whose products are crucial to other enterprises. For instance, Consolidated Tyre Services (CTS) retreads tires, Zambia Steel and Building Supplies (ZSBS) and Monarch make construction inputs, and Livingstone Motor Assemblers (LMA) and Luangwa Industries make motor vehicles and bicycles respectively. All were operating at about a third of capacity. This trend was expected to continue, for these abysmal capacity-utilization rates are connected to the shortage of allocations of foreign exchange to purchase raw materials, machinery, and spare parts. In the 1982/83 financial year, INDECO's share of FOREX allocations measured only 45 percent of its requirements. As one INDECO spokesperson put it,

TABLE 5.6
Marketed Production of Some Selected Crops, 1979/80-1983/84*

For year ended[a] 30th April	Maize[b] ('000 bags)	Sugar[c] Cane ('000 tonnes)	Seed Cotton ('000 tonnes)	Sunflower[d] ('000 bags)	Shelled[e] Groundnut ('000 bags)
1979/80	3,733	888	14,916	238	34.2
1980/81	4,247	920	22,913	345	25.4
1981/82	7,704	893	16,752	384	16.5
1982/83	5,672	1,010	12,786	426	9.6
1983/84	5,902	1,086	31,230	609	13.0

* Figures are provisional.

[a] The marketing year begins in May and ends April 30th of the following year.
[b] A standard bag of maize weights 90 kgs.
[c] The year ends on March 30th.
[d] A standard bag of sunflower seed weighs 50 kgs.
[e] A standard bag of shelled groundnuts weighs 80 kgs.

Source: Republic of Zambia, Central Statistical Office, *Monthly Digest of Statistics*, 20, 12 (December 1984), Table 8, p. 6 (Lusaka: Central Statistical Office).

"when inflation is considered, it means that the little forex given cannot even purchase one quarter of goods imported five years ago."[43] The underutilized capacity means shortages of essential goods and low or no profitability to many firms, thus fewer revenues to the state's coffers.

Agriculture. The picture of agriculture by late 1985 is complex and slightly less depressing than manufacturing. This is fortunate because agriculture may be Zambia's economic mainstay for the future. Despite serious droughts in 1979, 1980, and 1982, marketing of many crops continued to be adequate. Maize began to recover from a slump in 1979/80 in an apparent response by peasant and commercial farmers to the 100 percent increase in the producer price from 1980 to 1984. In 1980 the president launched "Operation Food Production," a ten-year program costing $500 million, with most of the funds to come from outside. The idea was to feed the nation through developing agriculture and secondarily to encourage more urban Zambians to return to farming.

Despite the fanfare, in most years since 1975 the country has not produced enough maize to meet annual consumption. In 1981, K 50.7 million was spent on importing food;[44] in 1983 Zambia signed a commodity agreement with the United States for 18,600 tons of wheat, a crop fast becoming a vital urban staple.[45] Yet the picture is not all bad. Seed cotton, sunflowers, and sugar have better growth rates and are feeding raw materials to INDECO companies such as Kafue Textiles, ROP, and ZAMSUGAR (see Table 5.6).

Zambian farmers, both commercial and smaller scale, are producing more for the market. The bottleneck for agriculture is on the state's side—poor distribution of inputs such as fertilizers and seed and late collection of crops by the national marketing board and provincial cooperative unions. Local councils have also often failed to grade roads and repair bridges, making private haulers unwilling to risk their trucks to collect crops. Endless tales of maize left uncollected until soaked by the rains; fertilizers, pesticides, and seed delivered long after planting season; and farmers facing delays of several months in payment for their crops pepper the national press. The blame for such inefficiency often falls on incompetent or corrupt managers. Shortages of vital imported inputs such as tires and diesel fuel for the trucks undercut efforts of both the farmers and some employees of the provincial marketing boards.

New Policies. Against all odds, agriculture is holding its own and even making substantial contributions to feeding the nation and supplying raw materials to the factories. Manufacturing remains the weakest link, while mining, in a bad year, drains rather than generates income for the nation. In order to squeeze more revenue from the economy, the government ended most subsidies in January 1983 by announcing the introduction of "economic pricing." Essentially, "economic pricing" has meant rapid increases in the price of basic consumer goods, allowing merchants and state shops to raise prices to levels that are officially controlled but in practice have no limit except the consumers' wallets. For the same goods and services purchased in 1975, low-income consumers in 1983 were paying over 150 percent more. Official calculations were that inflation was around 20 percent annually, but most evaluators placed it between 30 and 50 percent annually in 1983/84.[46] After 1983 it became "open season" on Zambian consumers, yet the astronomic prices had not reduced shortages of locally produced essential commodities in mid-1985. Long lines outside the state-owned shops were a permanent fixture in Zambian cities, as consumers and traders hoped for detergent, cooking oil, and milk. Many commodities, such as salt and flour, seemed only available on the black market at prices from two to four times the official stated price (used in calculating the rises in the consumer price index!). Despite such unpopular policies and some negative outcomes, the government was still desperate.

Public Finances: Fiscal Crisis

From 1981 through 1982 revenues to the state stagnated while expenditures expanded. Deficits of five hundred million kwacha or more became the rule rather than the exception. Each year budgetary projections for deficits prove smaller than the reality. When in 1983 and 1984 there was an improvement in government revenues, expenditures still outstripped the moneys coming in. What accounts for the chronic overspending? Allocations to directly productive ministries (agriculture, mines, commerce and industry, tourism) remained around 10 percent from 1980 through 1984 (see Table 5.7) while support for infrastructure varied only to a small degree.

TABLE 5.7
Central Government Expenditures by Functional Classification in Percentage Terms, 1980-1984

Expenditure by Percentage Distribution	1980	1981	1982	1983* Budget	1984* Budget
Directly productive**	9	6	11	9	10
Infrastructure support	11	8	11	12	10
Social services	16	18	22	24	26
Administration	16	20***	20	21	17
Nonministerial expenditure	48	48	36	34	37
TOTAL	100	100	100	100	100

* Figures are those budgeted, not the final actuals.
** Agriculture, commerce and industry, mines, and tourism.
*** Administrative expenditures included K 82.0 million for general salary and wage increases and K 32.2 million for Zambia National Service and Rural Reconstruction Centers, which, prior to 1981, had been under Constitutional and Statutory Expenditures.

Source: Adapted from World Bank working document, Zambia: Country Economic Memorandum: Issues and Options for Economic Diversification (Washington, D.C., April 1984), Table 5.03, p. 92.

The major changes appeared in social services and administration. Money allocated to education, health, information and broadcasting, labor, and social services increased while funds for all remaining ministries and some nonministerial areas such as the rural beer surtax, pensions, subsidies, and constitutional and statutory expenditures (including debt financing and defense) were cut. GRZ's commitment to populist programs continued despite a quandary over where to find the funds. Within ministries, wages took a steadily increasing bite (from 20 percent in 1980 to 29 percent in the 1984 budget) as did general operating expenses. Debt servicing grew to absorb 19 percent of the domestic budget by 1984 while capital expenditures shrank to 13 percent.[47] With the prevailing patronage system, it was not easy for national politicians to reduce the number of civil servants. Furthermore, the governing class' commitment to its own aggrandizement meant that slashing top-level salaries and the number of supernumerary posts was not likely either. So wage expenditures continued to grow, while marginal increases in revenues (partially from indirect taxes and grants) did not make up the difference. When the Third National Development Plan terminated in 1983, it was widely acknowledged as a fiasco, primarily due to the scarcity of investment resources both domestic and foreign.

When medium- and long-term external debt increased 47 percent in December 1984 over December 1983,[48] experts estimated that by 1985 servicing the total debt would require 86 percent of all export earnings.

This would leave a paltry 14 percent to be fought over by the mines, factories, farmers, and bureaucrats. Because the country's balance of payments remained in the red, suppliers became reluctant to extend Zambians more credit. Clearly something had to be done. This is where the IMF, World Bank, and Paris Club entered the story.

ZAMBIA'S WALTZ WITH INTERNATIONAL LENDERS

Facing frequent and impossibly steep balance-of-payments deficits, officials from the Bank of Zambia and Ministry of Finance negotiated a series of facilities with the International Monetary Fund, the World Bank, as well as loans from private banks and foreign donor governments. Loans from the IMF have loomed large, and the conditions imposed have been socially and politically controversial, so they are the focus of the following discussion.

Drawings from the IMF started in 1971 in a small way but escalated from 1976 onward with the worsening of the economy. As of April 1984 Zambia had drawn an oil facility, a compensatory financing facility, and regular credit tranches totaling 635.3 million of the IMF's unit called the Special Drawing Rights (SDR) (see Table 5.8). The end is not yet in sight. In November 1984, President Kaunda announced that the GRZ had just concluded negotiations for another IMF loan (amounting to K 410 million),[49] with promises of intensifying the stabilization program. What had such stabilization programs meant for Zambians by late 1985?

The IMF espouses a certain economic doctrine that demands that the chronic borrower try to set its "house in order" through controlling consumption and freeing funds for investment while reducing other government intervention in the economy. Commonly, Third World nations are encouraged to export more primary commodities; devaluation of their currencies is supposed to make these exports more competitive internationally. Often the IMF strongly suggests that the debtor try to create a "favorable investment climate" for foreign investors to offset the outflow of capital for loans, dividends, and so on under liberalized tariff regulations. If the recipient country does not follow the IMF's suggestions, the fund is empowered to cut off remaining amounts of money (tranches) of existing loans. Frequently the borrower does not live up to all conditions, so the IMF suspends funds. Negotiations begin again when the country is desperate for the money and willing to bow to IMF pressures.

The pattern in IMF/Zambia relations has been a steady increase in borrowings matched by accelerating stringency of conditions, which essentially demand a major restructuring of the economy. The IMF acts on behalf of other major foreign lenders; IMF and World Bank conditions have been much the same. Although the path has not been smooth for the IMF in Zambia, the most acrimonious era began with the announcement of a K 800 million (ca. U.S. $1 billion) drawing to be disbursed from 1981 to 1984.[50] In line with fund guidelines, the GRZ promised to devalue the

TABLE 5.8
Zambia's Transactions with the IMF (millions of SDRs), 1971-1983

Year	Drawing	Repurchases*	Net Credit from IMF	Use of Fund Credit	Charges Paid on Use of Fund Credit
1971	19.0	-	19.0	19.0	-
1972	38.0	-	38.0	38.0**	0.1
1973	19.0	-	19.0	57.0	0.6
1974	-	-	-	57.0	1.6
1975	56.9	38.0	18.9	75.9	1.3
1976	38.5	19.0	19.3	95.2	4.1
1977	19.0	19.0	-	95.2	5.3
1978	148.8	-	148.8	245.1	7.9
1979	100.0	26.3	73.7	320.0	13.3
1980	50.0	44.0	6.0	308.3	20.0
1981	359.3	47.3	312.0	627.8	25.3
1982	41.5	86.2	44.7	575.6	48.6
1983	173.7	114.0	59.7	635.3	49.6

* Repurchases mean repayment to IMF in foreign exchange equal to the SDR.
** Reserve position in Fund (SDR 19.0 million) was used to reduce net use of Fund credited to SDR 38.0 million.

Source: Adapted from World Bank working paper, Zambia: Country Economic Memorandum: Issues and Options for Economic Diversification (Washington, D.C., April 1984), Table 3.08, p. 35.

kwacha, lower imports, reduce price controls on many staples, and invoke rigorous foreign exchange restrictions on Zambians' personal bank accounts while liberalizing them on foreign company accounts.[51] A very unpopular part of the package was the low ceiling (10 percent) placed on wage increases, which in the end, provoked a series of strikes. In August 1981 a tranche was temporarily suspended for noncompliance by government, but the funds flowed again when the GRZ promised to follow IMF dictates.

The GRZ really has had little choice in these confrontations. Of the massive 1981-1984 IMF loan, SDR 500 million went immediately to foreign creditors who were threatening to cut off new deliveries to Zambia until arrears had been paid.[52] By late 1981, imported items, especially spare parts and raw materials, arrived in the country; parastatal managers and private entrepreneurs alike breathed sighs of relief. Throughout 1982 and 1983, however, trade unions and consumers criticized the IMF because of the serious effects conditions were having on the average household budget. When resistance by the GRZ (noncompliance with some conditions) grew too overt, the IMF simply withheld the quarterly release of funds. Facing the cutoff from vital funds, again and again the GRZ knuckled under and implemented more "stabilization" policies.

In 1982 the IMF suspended funds for the announced reason that Zambia had failed to settle arrears with its major creditors. A quick way to pay these external debts was to squeeze the major FOREX consumer, the mines. The mines were forced to cut operating costs by 17 percent, costing approximately 2,600 jobs.[53] The unions grumbled and grumbled louder still when in December of that year prices were decontrolled. Local businesspeople were angered too, as the new interest rates substantially increased the cost of domestic loans.

Using these methods, the GRZ pared down its deficit but could not end it. Money for administration and infrastructure support was reduced, yet the debt still worsened. In May 1983 the GRZ met its major creditors in Paris (the so-called Paris Club) to announce terms for reducing the backlog of commercial payments and renegotiate Zambia's external debt. In response to conditions suggested in Paris, in July 1983 the GRZ floated the kwacha by putting it on a flexible exchange rate. The "floated kwacha" sank. From January 1983 to March 1984 the kwacha was devalued 42 percent against the SDR.[54] Imports decreased and the slow starvation of manufacturing and commercial agriculture began again.

Much of the burden of these IMF/Paris Club-inspired policies was borne by those Zambians least able to bear it—the working class, the unemployed, and the middle-income group. In 1983 alone, K 72.6 million was earmarked to be withdrawn from consumer price subsidies despite its being an election year and the rising inflation. Still the debt crept upward. When Zambia returned to Paris to meet its eleven major creditors in April 1984, the total national debt had risen to around U.S. $7 billion.[55] The Paris Club agreed to reschedule K 297 million on the condition that the arrears of interest (K 66 million) were to be repaid in twelve equal and successive monthly installments beginning August 1984.[56] Again the GRZ did not live up to these promises. Slowly creditors, led by the IMF and World Bank, intruded further into Zambian economic policy. More offers that Zambia "could not afford to refuse" followed.

So far, Zambia's leaders have not rejected major foreign loans even though the prescriptions suggested are unlikely to help the country out of its economic chaos. Forced to undertake IMF prescriptions, the designers of the national budget and development strategies have an impossible task. Because the conditions attached to external funds undercut consistent plan implementation, the bureaucrats never know whether the funds will be forthcoming or not. More and more the domestic economy is directed from outside Zambia. In July 1985, for example, a serious fuel shortage caused ground transport almost to grind to a halt. The GRZ had not paid for the oil shipments necessary to sustain local demand. A FOREX shortage had followed another temporary cutoff (late 1984) of IMF funds and was the likely reason for the failure to pay the fuel bill. The IMF had cut off funds because of the GRZ's reluctance to devalue the kwacha to the full degree (rumored to be an additional 40 percent) demanded by the Paris Club.

In October 1985, following strong IMF advice, the GRZ undertook a new FOREX allocation system called auctioning. The Bank of Zambia allows all citizens and resident expatriates with kwacha to bid for FOREX, using their local and foreign bankers as intermediaries. In this exercise in Alice in Wonderland economics, the World Bank and other foreign donors lend or grant Zambia around U.S. $5 million weekly for a national auction. Bidders send in blind bids, guessing at the exchange rate average. The marginal bid sets the rate, which had averaged at about sixteen cents ($.16) to the kwacha through the end of 1985. As a result of auctioning, the price of imported commodities (and locally produced commodities with a foreign exchange component) jumped overnight. The price of fuel increased by over 100 percent at the end of the first week following the start of auctioning. The Zambia Sugar Company and soap manufacturers raised prices between 50 and 100 percent on October 22, barely two weeks after they had last been raised.[57]

October was a tense month in urban Zambia. In one well-publicized case, police used riot control measures to disperse demonstrators at the Lusaka central bus terminal after drivers demanded major fare increases and customers rioted. Overnight, conditions had worsened for the average Zambian, and a common question was why had the GRZ turned to auctioning? The logic of the system is that free bidding should establish the real value of the kwacha and drive out the black market in currency that had been thriving in Zambia. Auctioning is supposed to encourage the most productive and profitable of managers and entrepreneurs, because it is those with the largest amounts of kwacha who can obtain the FOREX. There are few restrictions on the purchases to be made with this FOREX (import licenses are automatic), so supposedly the free market should reign. How had auctioning worked by late 1985?

One eminent economist, Dr. Jacob Mwanza (also the vice chancellor of the University of Zambia), commented that auctioning had proven a more efficient and less corrupt way to distribute the limited FOREX available. However, the "free market" logic threatened to be distorted by the import of luxury goods and the lure of fast money, already so prevalent in the governing class. Vital raw materials for industry (especially the parastatal companies) are not given priority. Many firms are "going to the wall." How long will auctioning go on, and how are the major creditors (especially the World Bank) going to be repaid? No one knows the answers to these questions, so Zambia goes on day by day on hope and foreign money.

Certainly such mechanisms allow foreign governments and multilateral agencies to increase their influence in Zambian economic planning and policies. Bilateral donors now fund the chronic deficits with grants and loans; they direct sectoral policies to an increasing degree.[58] Some foreign policy implications of these debts are explored in the next chapter, but one effect has been to pull national development planning in so many directions as to leave no discernible direction at all! How does the regime stay afloat under such conditions? Why do not Zambians fashion an alternative strategy to adjust the imbalanced economy and lessen domestic pain?

Briefly, the regime stays afloat on loans extended by the industrial nations of the West as well as on some socialist aid.[59] A tacit agreement, with roots in foreign policy alliances and compromises, seems to exist between Kaunda's government and Western countries. Despite Zambia's clear inability to repay and frequent noncompliance with conditions, the IMF, Paris Club members, and private international banks still lend money to Zambia on moderate terms.[60] Such infusions of funds keep the government operating and sustains the fractions of the governing class most dependent upon the state—the politicians, civil servants, and technocrats within the GRZ. GRZ spokespersons use the IMF and others as whipping boys on which to blame domestic ills and unpopular policies. For instance, the GRZ had been trying to reduce subsidies since 1976, but in the 1980s an end to subsidies and introduction of "economic prices" were blamed on the IMF. Presumably such claims do not disturb IMF and World Bank officials safely ensconced in Washington, D.C. And they are convenient for the governing class to deflect anger and criticisms as well. Some of the tacit agreement between Western countries and the governing class in Zambia is based on shared perspectives. Zambian technocrats and civil servants have cooperated with foreign consultants in drawing up many of the suggested policies for stabilization and restructuring. What direction Zambian development policy is likely to take in the future is a very difficult question to answer, however, because of the prevailing economic crisis and because of considerable disagreement over a national development trajectory.

No clear policy position on the economy had been declared by the GRZ or UNIP by late 1985. Rather, the rhetoric of socialism and Humanism continued. Nevertheless, indicators suggest that the regime is conforming to the IMF/World Bank/Paris Club's wishes and has been slowly moving in that direction for some time. Many direct links between the parastatal company managers and the actual central ministries were severed after 1981.[61] Since 1981 the budget deficits have been controlled primarily through trimming infrastructural costs, cutting back on administration, and constraining social welfare programs. The mines contracted with the African Development Bank, the European Economic Community (EEC), and the International Finance Corporation (IFC) of the World Bank (IBRD) for a U.S. $900 million, five-year (1984–1988) investment program to reduce the unit costs of production without expanding production.[62] This is an euphemism for introducing more capital-intensive technology on the Copperbelt. In response to external pressures, the government altered its FOREX policies for the mines, so that after 1983 the government began to credit ZCCM's account directly with a specified percentage of its own FOREX earnings, thus circumventing the slow and cumbersome import-licensing provisions.[63]

Such changes have met with positive responses from those Zambians disillusioned with socialism or at least with Humanism. Yet opposing voices exist as well, based primarily in the unions and secondarily at the university. Some analysts[64] argue for genuine import substitution, as well as policies to stimulate and diversify exports, export routes, and trading partners, without slashing benefits to the average Zambian or losing the commitment to socialism still current in party statements. They call for increasing efficiency in parastatals not by more autonomy but rather by closer state supervision and with clearer direction from central government. A key aspect is to protect carefully and foster interindustry and intersectoral linkages within the Zambian-owned enterprises, both private and public, rather than to open the economy further to foreign competition.

Such policy disarray is one sign of the growing fragmentation of the governing class and the shattering of the consensus that brought UNIP to power in 1964. As one wit put it back in the 1970s, it is not clear whether Zambia suffers from "planning for chaos or chaos in planning!"[65] What happened to the nationalist coalition and Humanist ideals? What is happening to the social fabric of the nation?

SOURCES AND SIGNS OF OPPOSITION

Resistance from Within the Governing Class

In October 1980 eight men were arrested and charged with treason. The charges were that they hired a mercenary army, provisioning this army at the farm of one of them, and then attempted to purchase arms and to corrupt members of the armed forces. As the story unfolded in the press, these men had plotted to kidnap President Kaunda and fly him to another country while the conspirators, backed by "Katangese mercenaries" and some South African troops, executed a bloodless coup d'état. The individuals arrested included highly placed members of the governing class, both civilian and military, some of whom were later released without charge. Those who went on to trial included Valentine Musakanya, a former governor of the Bank of Zambia and local manager for IBM; Edward Shamwana, then a High Court commissioner and potential nominee to the Supreme Court; Goodwin Voram Mumba, former manager of the Industrial Finance Company; Godfrey Miyanda, an army brigadier general; Air Force Major Anderson Mporokoso; and an assortment of businessmen and Zairean nationals.[66] By May 1981 the number of those accused had swollen to thirteen. All were committed to summary trial on treason charges, which hold a mandatory death sentence under Zambian law.

From 1981 to 1984 the nation was treated to a public spectacle of the treason trial, enlivened by an apparent attempt by a lawyer (G. Haamaundu) and an air force warrant officer (Christopher Chawinga) to release the detainees in September 1981.[67] Lusaka High Court Judge Dennis Chirwa found seven men guilty, handing down a five-hour judgment in January 1983. Those condemned to hang included Musakanya, Shamwana, Mumba, and the Zaireans, but not the military men. Mporokoso initially was given a ten-year sentence for misprison (concealment) of treason; General Christopher Kabwe, who had been brought into the trial as a defendant later, was indemnified against prosecution by turning state's witness; and the only European, lawyer A. Pierce Annfield, who had fled the country, was tried in absentia.[68]

Several of the principals petitioned the court against inhuman treatment and appealed for clemency to the president. The appeals process was laboriously complied with; eventually Musakanya was acquitted on appeal, and Haamaundu was pardoned by KK. The fate of the others was still in doubt when 1985 came to an end. Most observers expect the president, in his paternal role, to commute the death sentences of the Zambians to life imprisonment.

One interpretation of the treason trial events is that fractions of the governing class (specifically new entrepreneurs, more independent technocrats, and some comprador elements) threatened the supremacy of the national politicians. Since the mid-1970s many prominent civil servants and party men had left state employ and established themselves as independent entrepreneurs, technocrats, or as local representatives of international capital. Between September and December 1981 alone, 145 entrepreneurs registered new firms in Zambia. Their ranks included prominent ex-leaders such as former parliamentary secretary-general Mainza Chona and former Lusaka Province central committee member Fwanyanga Mulikita.[69] These individuals joined the ranks of others who had already left government employ for greener pastures, such as Emmanuel Kasonde, the chairman for the Standard Chartered Bank of Zambia Ltd., who had been permanent secretary in the Ministry of Finance in the early 1970s. Kasonde now owns a 2,500-hectare farm, fifty kilometers from Lusaka. Although many government and party officials accumulated farms and businesses before leaving office, their behavior was tolerated by the political leadership, despite violations of the Leadership Code.[70] When individuals began openly to criticize the regime, however, a reaction was not long in coming. The harshness of the treatment of the treason trial defendants (loss of personal and familial belongings, the horrible jail conditions) may have been meant to serve as a warning to others on the "right wing" of the governing class. The temporary detention of a few technocrats and former civil servants[71] may have been a threat from the president. Despite a common class interest to remain on top and accumulate the surpluses of the society, there are deep fissures within the governing class.

Worker Militancy

Another potential threat to the UNIP government comes from organized labor. The unions had been key to the early nationalist coalition. Under the one-party state, UNIP had carefully manipulated the structures by placing party faithfuls into leadership of the Zambia Congress of Trade Unions (ZCTU) and making ZCTU a branch of UNIP.[72] As the ZCTU has substantial power bases in sixteen affiliated unions, including the Mineworkers' Union of Zambia (MUZ), this had meant considerable UNIP influence over organized labor. The rapid decline of living standards after 1975, the introduction of such policies as the 10 percent ceiling on wage increases (in a period of 20 to 30 percent inflation), and cuts in subsidies broke down the symbiosis between the unions and the "Party and Its Government." Now ZCTU (with a membership of 380,000) has adopted the role of an informal opposition outside parliament.

Issues that provoked much hostility and worker resistance in the 1980s (e.g., the introduction of decentralization in 1980 and the new pensions program in 1984/85) seem small and certainly could have been resolved more peacefully. Yet relations between the unions and the regime had hardened. Head-on and sometimes violent conflicts have flavored the 1980s. In January 1981 seventeen union leaders (the executive committee members of the ZCTU and MUZ) were expelled from the party. They were charged with "working with outside forces to try and divide the nation."[73] Although these labor leaders were later readmitted into UNIP in April 1981, by July unrest had erupted on the Copperbelt. Miners burned the official car of the minister of mines when he came to negotiate with them. Some time thereafter, four important leaders were detained—Frederick Chiluba, chairman of ZCTU, Newstead Zimba, general-secretary of ZCTU, Assistant Secretary Chitalu Sampa, and the chairman of the MUZ, Timothy Walamba. They were charged with inciting workers to disrupt industrial peace and eventually to overthrow the government.[74] Although the High Court later released all the men (and several union leaders were then offered seats on the boards of directors of parastatal companies), relations between the party and the unions remain cool.

The leadership's commitment to narrow economic benefits for their members (economism) and the absence of any ideological basis for organized resistance tend to constrain militant behavior by the unions. Yet industrial actions continued, sometimes union sanctioned and sometimes wildcat. From January 1981 through March 1983, 233 strikes took place, costing the nation 4,570,792 man-hours.[75] In 1985, 4,000 miners were fired and K 16 million in revenues were lost to ZCCM over industrial actions.[76] Given the relatively small size of the work force (ca. 380,000 in the formal sector), this represents a considerable loss of national productivity. Such data reflect the deepening polarization between the governing class and the most powerful section of the working class.

Student Opposition

Another source of resistance comes from within a privileged stratum of society, the university and college students. Between 1971 and 1984 there were four major episodes of militant student opposition at the University of Zambia (1971, 1976, 1982, and 1983) and many at other colleges such as Evelyn Hone and the Zambia Institute of Technology (ZIT). Issues have stretched from opposition to UNIP's foreign policy in 1976 to boycotting classes over poor food in the cafeterias, as at Evelyn Hone in 1984. Although college administrators might have been able to negotiate settlements with the student leaders, the regime has been unwilling to tolerate any criticism from that quarter and has taken harsh and sometimes savage actions against the students.

These battles inevitably terminate in a closure of the institution, the blanket dismissal of the students, and sometimes the expulsion of foreign lecturers for "fomenting rebellion." Privileged though the students are (they represent only 1.2 percent of those who start primary school, and many are children of the governing class), they enthusiastically voice their criticisms of foreign, domestic, and university policies. The refusal of the student union at the University of Zambia (UNZA) to affiliate with the party creates a permanent canker in those relations.

Although student militancy is a perennial in Zambian politics (in 1985 UNZA students were protesting the reintroduction of boarding school fees at primary and secondary schools), resistance to the regime tends to be short-lived after departure from college. Once the graduate finds himself or herself struggling to find a job and survive in the inflationary climate, overt criticism gives way to general grumbling about the system. Of great concern to many young college-educated Zambians is the rising tide of corruption that makes government inefficient and eats away at the nation's resources. Worse still, some of the perpetrators block the upward mobility of the younger, more educated in the public service.

Flagrant Corruption

The incidence of publicly acknowledged (and reported) corruption in high places multiplied in the early 1980s. Illicit activities expanded from domestic graft, poaching, and theft by public servants in the late 1970s to an involvement of diplomats, businesspersons, and politicians in smuggling heroin, marijuana, and the regional specialty, Mandrax. Mandrax tablets are "uppers," which have strong effect when taken with alcohol or *mbanje* (local marijuana). The tablets are legally produced in India. Various middlemen go there, buy the tablets, and then illegally export them to other parts of the world, often using Zambians as intermediaries. The trade is enormously lucrative. The rumor that the tablets end up with the South African defense forces based in Angola and Namibia is reminiscent of heroin and the American GIs in Vietnam. Since 1981 several high-level officials and their wives[77] have been caught in the drug trade, often at European airports. Outraged by behavior that sullies the name of Zambia, President Kaunda demanded that embassies and high commissions remove the passports of Zambians caught in the drug trade and withdraw diplomatic immunity from any Zambians caught in such dealings.

In 1983 the long-time nationalist leader Sikota Wina (former cabinet minister and central committee member) was detained in India, implicated in Mandrax smuggling. When a New Delhi court released him after five months in jail, Wina returned to Zambia on a Sudanese passport using the name "Hussein." Upon returning home, he publicly disavowed any wrongdoing, suggesting that some politicians were out to get him. Then he went on to regale reporters with his plans to return to politics to help KK out! Whatever was the final straw in the Wina affair, he was eventually detained in Zambia in 1985 for some of his Mandrax-related activities.[78]

Although only one case, the Wina story points to the end of the nationalist era and the disappearance of the high moral tone of independence.

Many prominent individuals have slid into corruption despite the great advantages they already had. In September 1985 Zambian residents were shocked to hear that the former minister of foreign affairs and member of the central committee Vernon Mwaanga had been detained, implicated in the drug trade.[79] Mwaanga was one of the Zambians who had served in prominent positions in the early years and then had left government to set up their own businesses. In the 1980s he became the head of ZINCOM (Zambia Industrial and Commercial Association), an organization that acted as the mouthpiece for entrepreneurs. His statements on the economy were widely publicized, especially when they were at variance with government policy. He was later released without trial so it is difficult to know whether the charges were legitimate or part of the intimidation of opponents.

Corruption and venality of the governing class bring to mind Frantz Fanon's indictment of the group that he saw taking power in Africa in the 1960s.

> [T]he dynamic, pioneer aspects, the characteristics of the inventor and of the discoverer of new worlds which are found in all national bourgeoisie are lamentably absent. In the colonial countries, the spirit of indulgence is dominant at the core of the bourgeoisie; and this is because the national bourgeoisie identifies itself with the Western bourgeoisie, from whom it has learnt its lessons. It follows the Western bourgeoisie along its path of negation and decadence without ever having emulated it in its first stages of exploration and invention. . . . In its beginning, the national bourgeoisie of the colonial countries identifies itself with the decadence of the bourgeoisie of the West. We need not think that it is jumping ahead; it is in fact beginning at the end. It is already senile before it has come to know the petulance, the fearlessness or the will to succeed of youth.[80]

With such examples at the summit of society, it is not surprising that petty corruption and thievery permeate through the layers of society. Cases of banditry and personal violence have increased dramatically. The average citizens' concern with national politics is displaced by an immediate fear for their personal safety and that of their extended family.

Corruption, growing militant resistance, and the inability of the governing class to construct and carry out consistent policies are harbingers of a sad future for Zambia. The social glue that held together Zambian society for the first twenty years is coming undone. Such trends usually mean an alienation of the majority of the people from the regime. Yet the lack of an organized political alternative of a truly reformist or revolutionary character gives the one-party state longevity.

CONCLUSION

Tinged with moral decay and too paralyzed to develop a strategy out of their economic nightmare, Zambia's leaders seem to take refuge in the world of international politics where Kaunda's name is highly respected.

Intermittantly the UNIP government has blamed its ills on external forces—the heavy costs of UDI or the IMF conditions, for example. Although it is easy to dismiss such explanations as mere excuses, regional politics have been a true quagmire for Zambia's leaders. The story of the collapse of the political economy in the 1970s and 1980s is not complete without a review of how international and regional politics impinged dramatically on the new nation, twisting the fragile economy and limiting options of the leaders.

6
Zambian Foreign Policy

Like all nations, Zambia conducts its foreign policy on a variety of levels from global to regional and with bilateral or multilateral organizations. This chapter focuses on the southern African context because that has been, since independence, the most immediate and potentially threatening arena. Then the discussion shifts to Zambian policies toward African and other Third World institutions, including an abortive copper cartel. Official nonalignment is reviewed briefly in order to make an overall argument that Zambia's inherited exclusive dependence on Britain and South Africa is now more complex, although the nation is still primarily linked to the West. At all levels, the personality and beliefs of President Kaunda have been fundamental to the style and content of foreign policy in the first twenty years of self-rule.

REGIONAL GEOPOLITICS

At the time of Zambia's independence in 1964, four of its eight direct neighbors were ruled by colonial or minority settler regimes. By 1985 only one bordering country remained unfree, Namibia (South-West Africa), although the apartheid regime in Pretoria still ruled giant South Africa. In the intervening years, wars of liberation swirled around Zambia's borders, bringing military conflict onto Zambian soil. Such provocations necessitated the new leaders to take a stand. Economic factors constrained the actions open to the nationalist politicians, however. Two imperatives have lain behind Zambian foreign policies—a genuine moral commitment to peace, racial equality, human brotherhood, and national self-determination, on the one hand, and a pragmatic need to hold the economy together and perhaps even to prosper, on the other. The focal point of regional policies has changed as struggles have altered the colonial order. A constant threat until 1980 came from the southern neighbor Rhodesia, but wars in both Mozambique and Angola also drew in Zambia. With South Africa, relations in which moral commitments often have contended with perceptions of economic necessity have been behind the scenes. Zambia's current active participation in regional economic and political alliances, such as the Southern African Development Coordination Conference (SADCC), stems from a long-standing desire to develop alternatives to the dependence on South Africa for transport routes and trading ties. At independence, two questions were current: How far could the Zambians oppose the two strongest regional economies—South Africa and Rhodesia—upon which Zambia depended so heavily?[1] And which of the liberation movements should the Zambians support?

ZAMBIA'S PREDICAMENT AND POLICIES, 1964 TO MID-1975

Less than one year after independence, Zambia's economic and political survival was challenged when its former federation partner, Southern Rhodesia, rebelled against British rule. Avowedly racist white settlers of the Rhodesian Front under Ian Smith took over the government in November 1965, unilaterally declaring Rhodesia independent (UDI) from Britain. This militant regime now sat astride Zambia's main transport route, aggressively threatening the security of Zambia's population. Later in the 1960s, wars of liberation erupted to the east and west as Angolan and Mozambican nationalists began the long struggle to overthrow extremely repressive Portuguese colonial regimes. By the mid-1970s the South African military was invading western Zambia with impunity, pursuing Namibian freedom fighters, and partisans in the civil war in Angola moved in and out of Zambia. Hovering behind immediate physical threats was the full economic and military might of South Africa. Although the GRZ continued to oppose publicly racial and colonial oppression, leaders emphasized the country's commitment to policies of noninterference and nonviolence. By 1974 such nuanced positions proved impossible to uphold as the region was caught up in wars of liberation.

Relations with Rhodesia were particularly difficult and immediate. In 1963 when the federation was finally dismantled, Zambia and Southern Rhodesia were linked together through a series of common services including the railroads, energy sources, and airlines. The three existing interterritorial services became international agencies, namely, the Central African Airways Corporation, the Central African Power Corporation (CAPCO), and the Rhodesia Railway. Although the assets of the railroad and the power corporation were divided equally between Rhodesia and Zambia, Rhodesia effectively controlled most of Zambia's exports and imports[2] because of its intervening position between the Copperbelt and the ports of Beira and Lourenço Marques (now Maputo) in Mozambique (see Map 6.1). Coking coal from Wankie Colliery in the south continued to feed the copper mines.

Hydroelectric power for the Copperbelt was generated by the Kariba Dam power station placed on the south bank of the Zambezi River. The colonial Southern Rhodesian government controlled over 60 percent of the electricity used in Zambia and 90 percent of the Copperbelt's needs.[3] In 1964 the Zambians began to disentangle these two countries' infrastructure, but it was projected that this would take some time and perhaps some of the agencies would continue to be jointly run.

MAP 6.1 Road and Rail Routes in Southern Africa, Specifically Zambia, Between 1975 and 1978

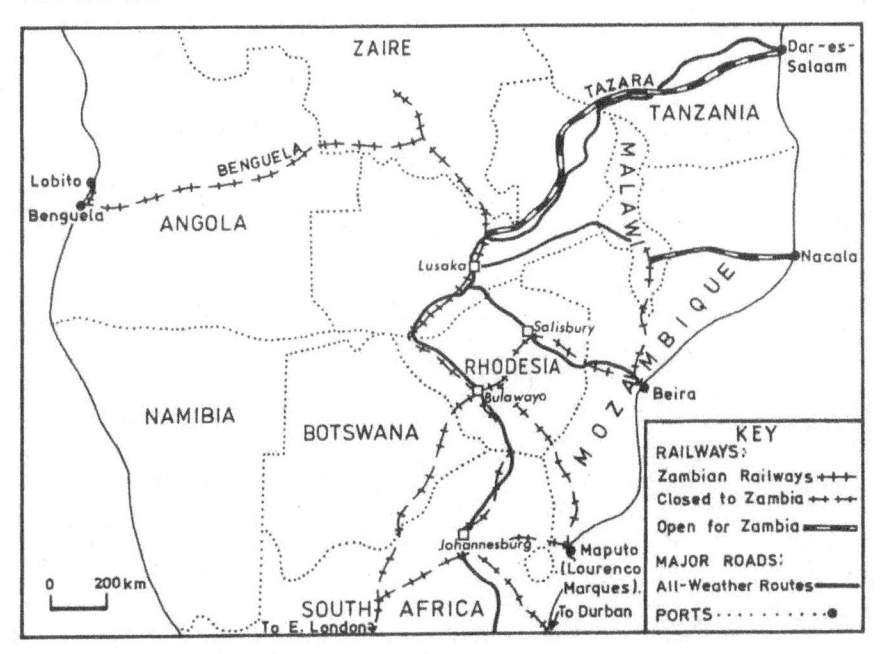

After UDI in November 1965 the whole exercise took on a new urgency, because Zambians were seriously concerned that the Smith regime could dislocate the Zambian economy simply by interrupting the jointly run services. Ninety percent of the fuels and lubricants on which Zambian industry depended came via Rhodesia Railway. At the time of UDI, Zambia's oil supply had been reduced to fourteen days, although the oil corporations had built up Rhodesia's supply to ninety days.[4] Switching some of Zambia's international trade to the only real alternative route, the Benguela Railway (which goes westward from the Copperbelt through the Katanga region of Zaire and on through Angola to the port of Lobito on the Atlantic Ocean), was legally constrained by agreements signed in 1964.[5] When the United Kingdom, the Commonwealth, and finally the United Nations pushed for economic sanctions against rebel Rhodesia for its violation of the rights of the majority of its citizens, Zambia initially tried to implement sanctions, expecting that the rebellion would be short-lived. Then Harold Wilson's government backed away from the military actions that might have brought a swift end to Rhodesia. Nonetheless the nationalist leaders of Zambia were not deterred and even tried to use their minimal economic leverage on Rhodesia by blocking the transfer of railway funds to Rhodesia from Zambia. In general Zambia's efforts were ineffective and very costly. Slowly the Zambian resolve faded; by January 1973 Zambia was relying on Rhodesia Railway for at least three-fourths of all imports, exclusive of oil, and upon

CAPCO for electricity (until the new Kafue Dam in Zambia was fully operational).[6]

But this picture of compromise is not the full story. National politicians and civil servants were not willing to allow this economic blackmail to continue indefinitely. Their general strategy of disengagement had two aspects: to gain some autonomy in strategic supplies and to find or create alternative trade and transport routes, notably through economic links to the Eastern Bloc and transport through the friendly country of Tanzania. Thus the first national development plan contained funds to build a new dam on the Kafue River and construct an international airport at Lusaka. A new colliery was set up in Zambia at great expense to supply the Copperbelt, and the mines shifted to more hydroelectric fueling. In 1968 an oil pipeline was completed from Zambia to Dar es Salaam (Tanzania), and an oil refinery was designed for Ndola on the Copperbelt.

After 1965 Zambians explored other transport options, including an emergency airlift (for petroleum products and essential mining equipment) and began plans to revise the transport system altogether, involving the construction and improvement of two key roads, the Great North Road, which runs from central Zambia to Tanzania's seaport capital Dar es Salaam, and the Great East Road, which runs east from Lusaka to Chipata and then to Salima in Malawi. From there goods can be railed to the Mozambican port of Beira.[7]

Rail transport posed other problems. Expanding shipments via the Benguela Railway was tried but proved ineffective. At best the Benguela route was a short-term solution for it simply switched the GRZ's reliance to the colonial regime of Angola rather than the settler regime of Rhodesia, truly not much improvement! The long-term solution seemed to lie in building a new railroad from Zambia to Dar es Salaam (DSM) on the Indian Ocean. This route would parallel the Great North Road but be capable of carrying heavy goods though all sorts of weather, features not true of the notorious Hell Run of the northern road. Accordingly, plans were laid for a new rail link to the coast.

Building the Tanzania-Zambia Railway (TAZARA) drew in many important foreign policy issues. Most essential were the development of close relations with Tanzania and the location of financing to build the route. Kaunda dedicated much time to solidifying relations with Dr. Julius Nyerere, the president of Tanzania; they also became allies on wider questions. Financing the railroad was more troublesome: Several Western governments and aid agencies were approached, to no avail. In 1967 the People's Republic of China (PRC) offered to build the TAZARA and to extend a K 200 million interest-free loan for the purpose, as well to supply manpower, equipment, and initially the supervisory personnel.[8] Zambia and Tanzania signed an agreement with the PRC in 1968 that included various promises to buy Chinese commodities equal in value to the local construction costs incurred by the Chinese. Although the railway gave clear expression to Zambia's policy of disengaging from the south, it also heralded the cultivation of closer relations with the socialist bloc. The solution to the transport dilemma was still distant; only in 1970 did the Chinese begin to build the 1,000-mile railroad. Almost daily the country was drawn more deeply into conflicts with Rhodesia, South Africa, and the Portuguese colonies.

Acting upon a deeply felt commitment to end colonial rule, Kaunda had since 1965 permitted liberation fighters, their families, and other refugees to use Zambia as a sanctuary on the condition that no military actions would be permitted within or launched from Zambia. Zambian diplomats attempted to convince the Rhodesian, Portuguese, British, and South African authorities that Zambia would neither attack nor be the base for attacks on neighbors. In the Lusaka Manifesto of 1969, the GRZ emphasized its essentially nonviolent stance in the light of continued moral backing for the freedom fighters. As the wars heated up, however, Zambian noninvolvement became impossible to maintain. In 1970 KK signed the Mogadishu Accord, accepting the need for some violence to overthrow the racist regimes in the region. This new policy brought Zambia more in line with Tanzania but lessened the credibility of its claims of noninterference in the eyes of Pretoria, Salisbury, and Lisbon.

Zambia remained vulnerable to economic blackmail. In January 1973, in reprisal for the actions in Rhodesia of nationalist guerrillas alleged to operate from Zambia, the Salisbury government closed its border with Zambia. Overnight, Zambia lost its principal southern supply and export route. Once again the country was totally reliant on the Angolan route and on Hell Run to Dar. Much to everyone's surprise, Kaunda picked up the Rhodesian gauntlet and maintained the closure from the Zambian side even after Smith's government had relented. Copper revenues permitted such an expensive move, as the closure meant extensive rerouting of Zambia's imports and exports. Now diplomacy with Angola and Mozambique took on more importance for the country's economic survival. Relations were complicated by Zambia's support of the liberation movements dedicated to the overthrow of the colonial governments in these Portuguese-controlled territories in Africa.

In 1969 and 1970 the Portuguese bombed the border area between Mozambique and Zambia. Near Chadiza in Eastern Province, the bombing was so severe that two thousand people were evacuated and many Mozambican refugees arrived in eastern Zambia, to be placed in camps near Petauke. Land and air incursions took place on Zambia's eastern and western borders, but the Zambians refused to respond in kind. Officially, the Zambians were partisan to the freedom fighters but unwilling to engage directly in combat on their behalf. In 1969 the Zambian courts even undertook to return to Portugal some soldiers who had been captured within Zambia, a move that was very unpopular in Zambia and raised some eyebrows in other African countries.[9]

In the years following, the Front for the Liberation of Mozambique (FRELIMO) gained ground over the Portuguese colonial troops in the border area with Zambia, and these small skirmishes lessened. The revolution in

Portugal in April of 1974 signaled the impending demise of these colonial holdovers. On June 25, 1975, Mozambique became an independent state under a FRELIMO government. This major political victory for FRELIMO provided President Kaunda with a new ally in regional, continental, and world affairs, President Samora Machel, as well as some respite from the tensions of the border raids to the east.

In 1974 the western border with Angola suddenly became troublesome. In the struggle to liberate themselves from Portuguese rule the Angolan nationalists had split into three movements: the National Union for the Total Independence of Angola (UNITA), the National Front for the Liberation of Angola (FNLA), and the Popular Movement for the Liberation of Angola (MPLA). Their differences stemmed from ideological and leadership incompatibilities. The MPLA proved to be the best organized of the movements, and its then leader Aghostino Neto had canvassed Western governments, seeking support for ending Portuguese colonialism in Angola. Rebuffed by the West, Neto turned toward the Soviet Union. In 1974 (and earlier) the USSR extended some support to the MPLA. When the South Africans (backed by the United States) invaded Angola in 1975, Soviet aid increased and Cuban combat troops came to bolster the MPLA's military wing.

The smaller FNLA was based in the northeastern part of Angola, led by Holden Roberto and backed by the CIA and President Sese Seko Mobutu of Zaire. In late 1974 this movement controlled a portion of the Benguela railroad and thus affected Zambia's exports westward. UNITA, the last group, was led by the experienced politician Jonas Savimbi and drew its local support from the southern and southeastern parts of Angola. Its military presence was strong along and inside Zambia's western border. By mid-1975 Savimbi had put together an unlikely coalition of backers from the United States, South Africa, and the People's Republic of China! Furthermore, he had established cordial relations with KK over the years; the Zambians were said to be partial to UNITA.[10] By June or July of 1975 the FNLA and UNITA were effectively vanquished, and in the wake of MPLA ascendency came South African and U.S. intervention. Now UNITA revived and claimed to control the Benguela route. The South African military incursions jeopardized all rail transport. By August 1975 the western route was effectively closed.

Yet in early 1975 this outcome was far from clear. The Zambian leadership was puzzling over which of these diverse movements they should back. Initially the GRZ attempted to neutralize the issue by announcing Zambian backing for the Organization of African Unity (OAU) Declaration of Support for a Government of National Unity in Angola. In practice, however, by 1975 it was an open secret that Zambia was directly and indirectly supporting UNITA and FNLA.[11] This support was partially based on pragmatic calculations that one or both of these movements had the best potential for keeping the Benguela route open for Zambian goods and partially on an ideological compatibility between Zambian national politicians and Roberto and Savimbi.

Whatever the initial calculations, the Zambians backed the wrong horse. The MPLA gained control over the major cities, routed invading South African troops, and established effective control by early 1976. The gap between Zambian official neutrality and actual support for the two movements embarrassed the government in many continental circles and at home when students at the University of Zambia demonstrated against Zambian support for UNITA. Because the Benguela Railway effectively had closed in mid-1975, Zambia gained little economic advantage from its contentious policies over Angola. Zambia's duplicity left a residue of cool relations with the new MPLA government in Luanda even after official Zambian recognition in April 1976. Thereafter, an internal civil war dragged on in Angola, with South African and U.S. backing for UNITA. This occasionally spills over into Zambia's Western and North-Western provinces and may be said to be a bitter legacy of Zambian policies of 1974–1976.

For Zambia, the first decade of foreign relations with her neighbors were dominated by the transportation problem and economic dependence on Rhodesia and South Africa. With Angola and Mozambique under black majority rule, pressures lessened on Zambia, but the fundamental bottleneck of the Rhodesia Railway was not solved either by the existing roads or the Benguela route. The next decade proved even more difficult and dangerous for the new governing class in Zambia, drawing the country under military attack by Rhodesia and miring its leaders in the diplomatic quicksand of relations with South Africa.

REGIONAL FOREIGN POLICY, LATE 1975 THROUGH 1985

Foreign policy in this second decade was dominated by the war to liberate Zimbabwe and by diplomacy to construct first a political alliance and later an economic coalition to resist the power of South Africa in the region. Again the two imperatives of moral support for freedom fighters and pragmatic concerns for their own economic survival were uppermost in the minds of the Zambian policymakers. As the Zambian economy began to undergo sustained crises, not surprisingly, the second pragmatic strain gained dominance in regional policies. Yet the moral and political support for self-reliance and for other peoples' self-determination have not faded entirely from Zambian policies. Kaunda has been central to new regional alliances—the Frontline States and SADCC—which are meant to hold the line in support of South Africa's eventual liberation and lessen the regional economies' vulnerability to economic blackmail.

The war to liberate Rhodesia affected Zambia in two ways. First, it tightened the transportation bottleneck and began to strangle the local economy. Second, it posed dilemmas again concerning which liberation movement to back, as the winner would form the first independent government of an important neighbor.

The Transportation Bottleneck

Zambia's imports and exports were directly affected by the war to liberate Rhodesia and the protracted civil war in Angola. The border with Rhodesia remained sealed after January 1973. Interrupted service along the Benguela Railway intensified the need to create new routes or reopen routes running through Rhodesia, Mozambique, and South Africa. In mid-1975 TAZARA was not yet in operation and alternative routes had not been developed. Then in March 1976, attempting to put more pressure on the Salisbury government, FRELIMO in Mozambique closed down the access route for the Rhodesia Railway to the ports of Beira and Maputo, indirectly closing off future use of this outlet for Zambian goods as well. Zambia was now left with two potential routes—the railroad to Dar and the southern route via Rhodesia to South African ports.

In late 1975, TAZARA was opened and began to carry Zambia's copper and cobalt. By 1976 this route was carrying the bulk of Zambia's import and export trade. Within a year, however, it was obvious that this line was not constructed to bear the tonnage of the freight. For one thing, the original Chinese engines found the steep inclines over the Great Rift Valley too taxing. Many broke down en route, leaving TAZARA short of engine power. The port of Dar became too congested to process the bulk of Zambia's exports and imports efficiently; stocks built up on the docks, subject to weather and pilferage. Emergency airlifts of precious minerals such as cobalt were attempted but proved very expensive. A dirt track across the Botswana-Zambia border was expanded in 1977, but its ability to carry freight was even more limited than that of TAZARA, and its eventual outlets were still South African ports, as Botswana is also landlocked.

By late 1977 the full impact of the transportation bottleneck was being felt throughout Zambia. The transport squeeze accentuated the collapse of mining and accelerated the rising costs of goods and pervasive shortages. Kaunda now came under great pressure for his decision to keep the border closed to Rhodesia, upheld since 1973. Some senior civil servants, politicians, mine managers, and commercial farmers called for a reopening of the southern route, because the country desperately needed food and fertilizer as well as outlets for its growing stockpile of minerals. Reopening of the border would also have been popular with the wider population, which was suffering the effects of the war, rising prices, scarcity, and lack of jobs. The countervailing force was the top leadership's desire to put as much pressure as possible on the Smith regime, hoping that this would bring an early end to the liberation struggles daily spilling over into Zambia.

Zambia and the Struggle to Liberate Zimbabwe

Bilateral relations with Rhodesia, strained since UDI, entered a new and more violent stage in the mid-1970s. Zambian backing for the freedom fighters attempting to overthrow the Smith regime brought counterattacks by the Rhodesian military. The struggle was attenuated, moreover, by divisions within the ranks of the freedom fighters. By 1974 the Zimbabwean nationalists were divided into four major parties: the Zimbabwe African National Union (ZANU) at that time under the leadership of Ndabaningi Sithole; the Front for the Liberation of Zimbabwe (FROLIZI) led by James Chikerema; the African National Congress (ANC), a coalition behind Bishop Abel Muzorewa; and the Zimbabwe African Peoples' Union (ZAPU) under the leadership of Joshua Nkomo. Nkomo was an old acquaintance of Kaunda's from the days of Zambia's own liberation struggle, and ZAPU's military wing, the Zimbabwe People's Revolutionary Army (ZIPRA), was based in Zambia. ZANU's army, the Zimbabwe African National Liberation Army (ZANLA), had been operating primarily from the liberated zones of northwest Mozambique with FRELIMO's help since 1972 but maintained political representation in Lusaka. When the FRELIMO government took over in Mozambique in 1975, ZANU remained allied to Mozambique, antagonistic to ZAPU and to any suggestions of a merger behind the leadership of Muzorewa's African National Congress.

Relations between ZANU and ZAPU were not good, and occasionally militants had spilled blood within Zambia. There were also serious divisions within ZANU and ZAPU, in which the Zambians became involved.[12] In March 1975 Herbert Chitepo (the national chairman of ZANU and leader of its war council) was killed by a car bomb outside his home in the Lusaka suburb of Chilenje South. Who had done it—the Rhodesians, ZAPU, ZANU dissidents, or even the Zambians? Zambia's subsequent actions towards ZANU are contentious, and few writers have tackled the tangled web of Kaunda's regional policies in this era.[13] Basically Kaunda feared two things: that the continued disunity of the Zimbabweans would extend the war and that with independence in Zimbabwe, a recurrence of the splits of the movements as had happened in Angola could lead to a protracted civil war within Zimbabwe. One major Zambian policy objective was to force unity on the liberation movements, using whatever means at the GRZ's disposal.

In pursuit of this goal, the GRZ blamed ZANU dissidents for the assassination of Chitepo. The Zambian police detained members of the ZANU high command as well as most of the general staff and 1,300 guerrillas. ZANU was temporarily crippled, and rumors spread that Zambian authorities were the actual perpetrators of the bombing of Chitepo in the desire to force the nationalists to negotiate with Smith and to augment the position of Nkomo's ZAPU. Ironically, recent evidence indicates that it may have been Rhodesian agents operating within Zambia who killed Chitepo.[14] Nevertheless, the assassination disrupted the actions of ZANU, and subsequent Zambian actions set back this wing of the liberation movement.[15] Eventually ZANU withdrew most of its personnel from Zambia. After a hiatus in August 1975 (around a peace conference at Victoria Falls), the war continued and inevitably Zambia was drawn into the violence.

In October 1976, ZANU and ZAPU formed a coalition known as the Patriotic Front to negotiate with the Rhodesian government in Geneva over a settlement of the war. When the Geneva talks aborted, Salisbury threatened to attack targets within Zambia. Henry Kissinger even became involved in shuttle diplomacy but to no lasting effect. In 1977 Smith threatened preemptive strikes on the Zambian military as well as on the ZIPRA troops; in return KK declared a state of war with Rhodesia but never activated Zambia's own military. Rhodesians bombed far into Zambia, including an attack on Nkomo's house in Lusaka and various ZAPU camps. The Rhodesian air force bombed Zambian bridges, roads, and even the railways, putting considerable pressure upon the UNIP government.

Zambia's will to resist these pressures was bolstered by the backing Kaunda received from the leaders of Botswana, Tanzania, and Mozambique, who were the original members of the coalition that became the Frontline States. As the Rhodesian provocations escalated, however, Zambia's national politicians leaned more heavily on ZAPU. Meetings were held between Kaunda and Smith in Lusaka and Livingstone. The South Africans were drawn into talks to influence Smith, while the Zambians and to some degree Nyerere and Machel pushed the liberation leaders.

But in 1978 Smith remained intransigent. By 1978 the economic situation was so severe for Zambia that Kaunda began to consider a unilateral compromise. Zambian entrepreneurs and parastatal managers were arguing for new policies to allow Zambia to buy the cheapest possible goods and reopen the southern transport route for Zambia's minerals.[16] The IMF reportedly also was making reopening of that route a condition for further loans.[17] In October 1978, after an austerity budget and the breakdown of another Kaunda-inspired meeting between Nkomo and Smith in Lusaka, the Zambians reopened the border with Rhodesia. This reopening did not stop Rhodesian raids into Zambia but did permit the import of vital fertilizer and maize. In effect, the Rhodesians gave Zambia an economic breathing space while at the same time escalating their military pressures upon both the Zambians and ZAPU. Kaunda identified the purpose of the carrot *and* the stick as one of "crippling the economy and getting Zambia to force more concessions on the Patriotic Front."[18] Despite KK's boast that Zambia would stand firm, according to Lionel Cliffe, the pressures were too great and the Zambians pressed hard on the Patriotic Front for an early settlement.[19] The border reopening breached the economic encirclement of the Smith regime. Some have said that it weakened the hands of the African nationalists by limiting their attacks on the Rhodesian Railway for fear of harming Zambia.[20]

After considerable guerrilla successes, the Patriotic Front entered negotiations with the Smith regime at Lancaster House in London in September 1979. Elections were held in Zimbabwe in March 1980. The results came as another blow to the Zambian backing for ZAPU—ZANU gained fifty-seven seats while ZAPU took only twenty. The new nation of Zimbabwe was born in April 1980, with the government led by Robert Mugabe (ZANU) taking over in Salisbury, soon to become Harare. Zimbabwean independence loosened the transport stranglehold over Zambia, but by 1980 the Zambian economy had entered a sustained decline. In 1982 Kaunda announced that the liberation war had cost Zambia K 2,000,000,000, to say nothing of the immeasurable national and personal opportunities foregone in the same

TABLE 6.1
Zambia's Trade with South Africa, by percent of total imports and exports, 1970-1979

	1970	1974	1975	1976	1977	1978	1979
Imports	17.3	7.6	6.8	7.5	7.2	6.6	10.8
Exports	1.2	.4	.3	.2	.3	.1	.4

Source: Carol B. Thompson, Challenge to Imperialism: The Frontline States in the Liberation of Zimbabwe (Harare, Zimbabwe: Zimbabwe Publishing House, 1985), Table VI-b, p. 114.

period.[21] Whenever Zambians went to the racetrack to bid on the likely leadership of a neighboring country, they lost their bets! Yet Zambia's backing for the liberation of Zimbabwe, costly though it was, proved vital to the decolonization of the region. Now, with Zimbabwe under majority rule, an economic reorientation for the whole region became a possibility.

ZAMBIA AND SOUTH AFRICA

The problems that bedeviled Zambian relations with Rhodesia found resonance in relations with South Africa. In 1964 the unevenness of Zambia's reliance on Rhodesian trade and transport was replicated in relations with South Africa. The GRZ's eagerness to disengage from the republic, strong in the early years, was dampened after 1975 by the expense and unreliability of the alternative trade and freighting routes. Furthermore, the South Africans were eager to keep Zambia within their net. Additionally, the Zambians had to fear the military might of the republic, which by the 1980s was exercising its muscles in the region, bombing Gaberone (Botswana) and invading Swaziland in search of the ANC. So whatever strategy the GRZ undertook had to be measured against the South African willingness to punish Zambia or entice the country. In general the South African approach has been the carrot rather than the stick.

The success of the South African strategy of ensnaring Zambia with economic benefits is visible in the overall trade statistics (see Table 6.1). Sanctions against Rhodesia caused the percentage of trade with South Africa temporarily to increase between 20 and 22 percent from 1965 to 1969.[22] After considerable sacrifice, these links were lessened to represent only 6.8 percent of imports and 0.3 percent of exports by 1975. Thereafter this trend was slowly reversed as Zambia's policies toward South Africa circled around two poles—the desire to continue economic relations with South Africa and the hope of bringing peace to the region. South African consumer goods, maize, and mining equipment began again to enter the Zambian market. After 1978 the South African ports of Durban and East London were used as well. By 1979, 10.8 percent of Zambia's imports came from the republic.

The Anglo American Corporation remained the largest foreign shareholder in the Zambian mines and a minority partner in several parastatal firms as well.

In addition to these trade bonds, Zambia had cause to fear the military might of Pretoria. Zambia supported various freedom fighters, especially the ANC and other agencies such as the South African Congress of Trade Unions (SACTU), which intended to overthrow the South African government. These liberation movements have their offices in Lusaka; some of their refugees live in Zambia. Namibian independence fighters also found sanctuary in Zambia. As South Africa was the power against which the South West African People's Organization (SWAPO) of Namibia was fighting, again Zambia was potentially a target for South African military and political forces.

Fear and pragmatic economic concerns thus led to a set of policies toward South Africa that have been interpreted as hypocritical by some[23] and realistic by others.[24] As far back as 1968 Kaunda had engaged in dialogue with the Afrikaner leaders over détente for the region. In 1971 John Vorster published a correspondence with Kaunda in an attempt to lessen Kaunda's credibility with the other African leaders. Kaunda managed to survive that embarrassment by publishing the full correspondence.[25] Certainly now the other Frontline leaders were aware that Zambia's diplomacy with South Africa extended beyond their alliance. Because so many of the liberation movements were based in Lusaka, Kaunda has been at the heart of many open and secret negotiations. Secret talks were held between Vorster and Kaunda's aides over the Zimbabwean liberation war throughout 1974, for example, culminating in a meeting at Victoria Falls in 1975. When the talks between Nkomo and Smith collapsed later that year and the hostilities began again in earnest, Kaunda continued to extend diplomatic offers to the South Africans, often without consulting either the Zimbabwean nationalists or the Frontline allies.[26]

Kaunda continued his brand of personalized diplomacy toward the political and economic leaders of South Africa into the 1980s. Behind his actions to try to find a compromise that would be economically beneficial to Zambia were increasing pressures from fractions of the governing class. For example in 1978, MPs in the national assembly called for a reopening of the border to the south and more trade with South Africa. It is notable that Kapwepwe and Nkumbula added these issues to their platforms when they ran against KK for the presidency in 1978. Although at the time KK and MCCs publicly denounced these calls, Kaunda's subsequent actions indicate that he responded to those pressures. With the sharp decline of the whole economy in the 1980s, Kaunda has been even keener to find a settlement to the wars over Namibia, Angola, and South Africa, which potentially could destabilize the Zambian economy again. In 1982 Kaunda and the South African Prime Minister P. W. Botha met in a caravan on the Botswana–South Africa border to talk over détente. In February 1984, KK hosted talks in Lusaka between the South Africans and the Angolans; in

May, between the South Africans and SWAPO. Also South African business persons, led by the Anglo chairman Gavin Relly, have met ANC representatives in Lusaka at Kaunda's behest.

In turn, Zambia has received certain benefits—some military and some economic. Until May 1986 South African troops had not violated Zambia's borders beyond some hot pursuit of SWAPO troops into Western Province. Exact items and amounts of South African trade are not public, but several researchers suggest that overall links have expanded considerably since 1980 when Zambian state-owned companies were ordered to seek the cheapest and closest suppliers, that is, Zimbabwe and indirectly South Africa.[27] Particularly enticing is the fact that South African suppliers offer an eighteen-month line of credit and easier terms to Zambia than do companies in neighboring states or the Western governments. In May 1985, when Zambia began to run out of fuel, South Africa provided 5,600 metric tons of diesel on credit.[28] The South African ports remain attractive because the alternative routes are either congested or still caught up in wars. Since the opening of the Zimbabwean border in October 1978, as much as a third of Zambia's copper has continued southward to the South African port of East London.[29] At UNIP's third general convention (Lusaka, July 23-25, 1984), the suggestion was made that as much as 40 percent of Zambia's trade should be rerouted through the "more reliable ports" of South Africa.

Despite Zambia's rhetorical opposition to South Africa then, the reality is a set of long-term economic relations and rather more sporadic diplomatic connections. These economic ties offer benefits but also constrain Zambian politicians because they make the economy vulnerable to blackmail and generate mistrust among the other African leaders. Nonetheless, Kaunda has been crucial in the construction of regional alliances to shore up the black-ruled states in central, eastern, and southern Africa.

ZAMBIA, THE FRONTLINE STATES, SADCC, AND THE PTA

Out of the cooperation among Kaunda, Nyerere, Sir Seretse Khama of Botswana, Machel of Mozambique, Eduardo dos Santos of Angola (replacing the deceased Neto), and their senior ministers around the struggle to free Zimbabwe emerged a permanent political alliance. "At the Ninth Extraordinary Session of the OAU Council of Ministers in April of 1975 the Frontline States won formal recognition as an ad-hoc committee of the Assembly of the Heads of States of the OAU."[30] Frontline allies had some successes in pressuring Rhodesia and South Africa as well as the divided Zimbabwean liberation fighters. Joined by Zimbabwe in 1980, the Frontline States (FLS) have continued to operate as a loose political alliance on the thorny issues of Namibian independence and the war building up to liberate South Africa itself. Kaunda has continued to be a major spokesman for the Frontline; with the retirement of Nyerere in 1985, KK became the head of the FLS.

Among Frontline leaders, there grew the idea of trying to transfer the experience of political cooperation to the economic battlefield by encouraging (and permitting other nations to join) an economic alliance that would embrace other nations of southern Africa. Participating members would try to redirect their trade away from South Africa or develop sectors of their economies that could be viable if based on regional resource availability as well as a much enlarged market. Diversification was seen as "an important element of national self-reliant development strategy [which] will strengthen collective self-reliance."[31] The principal idea was to foster economic coordination, beginning with the functional areas of information sharing, research, transport, and communications and later moving to areas of production.[32]

In April 1980 four countries (Zimbabwe, Malawi, Lesotho, and Swaziland) joined the Frontline States (Zambia, Angola, Mozambique, Botswana, and Tanzania) to form SADCC. As the Tanzanian Industry Minister Basil Mramba said, "SADCC is the child of the liberation movement in southern Africa. It is the economic side of the liberation coin."[33] All nations in the region, with the exception of South Africa and Namibia, became members, including those usually considered economic hostages of the republic (Swaziland, Lesotho, and Botswana).

So far SADCC's goals and achievements have been modest. Its immediate priorities have been focused on rebuilding and expanding transportation systems and improving communications. Each nation was assigned a particular project for its planners and civil servants to work on. Zambians studied the feasibility of a Southern African Development Bank in order to make precious capital available for SADCC projects. The GRZ also coordinated work on mining in the region. Because industrialization is seen as fundamental to self-reliance, an important aspect of SADCC studies has been to assess areas for potential complementarity of manufacturing for the regional economies. As Carol Thompson pointed out, this has meant the evolution of plans for industrial cooperation so that industries can take advantage of economies of scale without promoting inequities in the development of the productive forces and in income.

Much of the SADCC officials' energies to date have been directed to locating foreign donors for the most expensive projects such as the building of airports and the refurbishing of ports. Over 40 percent of the U.S. $600 million pledged at the SADCC II conference (November 1980) was allocated to Mozambique for the improvement of rail and port facilities. This improvement stands to benefit Zambia if the South African–sponsored terrorists operating in Mozambique cease blowing up the rail line and the port of Beira. The pledges also contributed to extending the Kazangula road and bridge between Botswana and Zambia to overcome reliance on ferryboats for the exchange of goods between the two countries. To some degree, SADCC funds could help fill the gap in infrastructural support that has led to a precipitous decline in road and rail maintenance in Zambia since 1980.

Although regional economic cooperation has been tried before and failed (the East African Common Market is the major example), the structure and strategy of SADCC may permit it to succeed. SADCC begins with the advantage of a history of political cooperation, which could form the political will behind economic coordination. To date, the SADCC leaders plan to make the political decisions first and analyze the economic variables for more technical decisions later.[34] The inequalities of the economies of the region are uppermost in the minds of the staff, so all proposed policies are designed with the ideas of complementarity and to some degree equity. Optimists argue that SADCC may reduce member countries' dependence on South Africa in the near future and even possibly aid countries' own internal economic development.[35] More pessimistic observers see SADCC as simply another bureaucracy that will be unable to create true regional initiatives because of the diverse social formations in the member states and also the overwhelming power of South Africa to subvert and disrupt the plans.[36]

In a separate diplomatic initiative in the late 1970s, a Preferential Trade Agreement (PTA) was launched to reduce trade barriers between the eastern and southern African states. The membership is wider than SADCC's— twenty nations belonged to the PTA as of October 1987. Unlike the SADCC plans to coordinate the regional economies, the PTA's aims are to reduce tariff and nontariff barriers, thus promoting trade between the nations based on their existing economies. Under the PTA, internal trade between the members is not completely free; rather, member states accord each other's goods preferential treatment vis-à-vis goods from outside countries. According to the former Zimbabwean Minister of Trade and Commerce Richard Hove, the guiding principles of the PTA were to enable member countries to diversify their exports, to increase trade among African countries, and to increase agricultural production, enabling members to be self-sufficient in food. A central clearing house was set up to lessen the FOREX bottleneck by permitting the members to trade using their national currencies, only settling their accounts at the end of a two-month period, plus fifteen days for settlement.[37] Zambia has also been an active member of the PTA, with KK serving as chairman in 1983 and offering to headquarter the PTA in Lusaka.

The economic barriers to regional trade and self-reliant cooperation are daunting indeed. In 1984 only 4 percent of the total trade of the PTA members was within the region.[38] A specific example of the difficulties of creating regional trade is offered by Zambia's key export, copper. Zambian copper is sold primarily to purchasers in the industrial West, Japan, and China, despite a regional market that could use copper wiring and equipment in the various hydroelectric projects. Mining equipment and much technical expertise for Zambia still comes from "down South," Europe, and North America. How to wean the mines away from this habit? To whom in the region could Zambia sell raw copper? The largest potential market would be Zimbabwe, which produces its own copper. A market for processed or fabricated copper is more likely, but the parastatal company Metal Fabricators of Zambia Ltd. (ZAMEFA) does not always produce enough copper wiring, sheeting, or transformer components for domestic needs, not to mention for export.[39]

In addition to these economic barriers, there are political problems that interfere with the logic of economic cooperation. Most of the regional economies, Zambia's included, have development strategies predicated on the dual notions of economic nationalism (explicit) and fear of neighboring countries' possible intentions (implicit). Lip service is paid to "collective self-reliance," but major domestic projects reveal as much narrow nationalism as any ideas of cooperation. The situation between Zambia and Zimbabwe over hydroelectric power is illustrative. Since full operation of the Kafue Dam in 1972, Zambia has been exporting electricity to other countries in the region, especially Rhodesia (now Zimbabwe). With the slow expansion projected for Zambia's industries, domestic consumption is not likely to cut into the surplus power available for the next fifteen to twenty years. In 1980 Zambia produced 9.221 million kilowatt hours (m kwh) while domestic consumption was only 5.828 m kwh.[40] In 1981 Zambia earned K 25.0 million from electricity exports to Zimbabwe (in hard currency), an 11 percent increase over the previous year. Surely this was an example of the kind of economic coordination that SADCC was meant to promote and also of mutually beneficial regional trade under PTA!

In 1983, however, Zimbabwean officials announced a program of massive dam building and thermal processing of coal, billed as making Zimbabwe self-sufficient in energy. In the short run, the costs to the Zimbabwean consumers, private and corporate, have been heavy. The longer-range effects are less certain, but the future now holds heavy foreign debts for Zimbabwe, incurred to finance and build the dams and the thermal stations. Why do it at all with Zambia so close, willing, and able to sell Zimbabwe the energy? (Mozambique also has the giant Cabora Bassa Dam and underutilized capacity that they are eager to sell Zimbabwe.) The only reasonable answer seems to be a flowering of Zimbabwean economic nationalism. Perhaps the Zimbabwean leaders, mostly ZANU, still distrust the Zambians for the GRZ's historical support for ZAPU?

Another case of political-ideological conflict that could affect lowering of regional trade barriers is the dispute about Rule 21 (a) of the PTA. Rule 21 (a) commits country members to allow firms to participate in the PTA only if the firms have a 51 percent local ownership and if most of the management is in the hands of citizens. Socialist Tanzania and Ethiopia insisted on this rule before they joined the PTA. Both Zambia and Zimbabwe resist these conditions, Zambia arguing that it is trying to encourage foreign investors and not discourage them and that it needs all the skilled foreign manpower it can attract.

Despite the economic logic and unquestioned need for regional economic cooperation, the progress of SADCC and the PTA is uncertain. Zambia has continued to give strong support for both schemes, but whether the diplomatic rhetoric can be transferred into realistic and useful programs is another question. Further issues of ideological complementarity and the class nature of the participating states that may undermine these projects are beyond the scope of this brief survey but may prove to be important aspects in the final analysis.

In summary, the statements of high principles on regional questions have to be measured against the ability and desires of the Zambian governing class to support liberation and decolonization efforts while warding off external threats. In the early years, Zambia was a strong backer of the liberation forces when it had the economic wherewithal to pay for major infrastructural improvements, which gave the country more flexibility in its transport routes. Yet Zambia paid a heavy price in human and financial terms for its support of the liberation movements. The decline of the Zambian political economy after 1975 forced its politicians, most prominently KK, into compromises and occasional duplicity, and nudged the country closer to South Africa. Whether the FLS, SADCC, and the PTA can help Zambia out of its economic quicksand is unclear, especially because the economies of the other participating states often make them as much competitors as allies.

ZAMBIA IN THIRD WORLD AFFAIRS

In the flush of independence, Zambia joined most of the existing major international, Third World, and African organizations. Over the next twenty years, Zambia's voice at the continental and global level had a consistency often lacking in regional matters. As Zambia's central decision maker, "Kaunda's dominating personal and humanistic world view powerfully conditioned the substance and style of Zambian external behaviour."[41] In many ways, the country's policies can be seen as an extension of Kaunda's philosophy of Humanism, with morality (as opposed to realpolitik) the foundation, nonracism as a prerequisite for peace within and between states, and justice as the key to international cooperation.[42] Zambian diplomats voiced lofty ideals in such forums as the UNCTAD (United Nations Conference on Trade and Development) Group of 77, the North-South Dialogue in Paris (1975-1977), the Commonwealth Group of Experts (1975-1976), as well as at the hearings over the future of the ocean's seabed. Kaunda and others like Vernon Mwaanga, an early Zambian ambassador to the United Nations, demanded greater equality in international political affairs and greater equity in the distribution of the world's wealth. KK also championed the rights of colonized peoples to self-determination. Such rhetoric gained Zambia some prestige in international and Third World circles, with the advantage of costing the country little at home, in stark contrast to regional realities. In the mid-1980s, however, such humanitarian concerns seem to fall on deaf ears. Kaunda's frequent trips to various international bodies may be an alternative to his growing paralysis and impotence in dealing with the collapsing domestic economy. Also the frustrating world of regional affairs, revolving around South African intransigence, may appeal less to KK than the international spotlight.

In continental affairs, Zambia had a formative influence on the Organization of African Unity (OAU). Kaunda, chairing the organization from 1970 to 1971, tried to fashion it into an effective instrument of African solidarity. It is his firm belief that such unity is a prerequisite for dealing with the immediate issues of southern African liberation and then the broader questions of imperialism. As a charter member of the Frontline States and an important voice on the OAU liberation committee, Zambia's influence has been marked in the crusades against racism (racialism) and apartheid. Zambia's interests have been wider however.

The GRZ has spoken out against any external (extracontinental especially) intervention in the affairs of OAU members and generally has supported the fragile sovereignty of African states. The policy has been to support the principles of the OAU charter, which include "respect for sovereignty and territorial integrity; non-interference in internal affairs; non-aggression and non-expansionism; refusal to serve as the base for subversion of another member state; mutual defence."[43] These principles, which sound good on paper, have not been easy for Zambia to support, especially when principles contradict or when contending nationalist groups within one territory claim the right to govern, as with Angola from 1975 onward. To deal with such circumstances, Zambian diplomats and politicians fashioned their own, slightly altered, interpretation of the OAU principles. For instance, Zambia avoided violating the prohibition against subversion in the cases of Angola, Mozambique, Rhodesia (Zimbabwe), South-West Africa (Namibia), and South Africa (Azania) by arguing that these political entities did not belong to the OAU and were illegitimate regimes to boot.

The Biafran secession was a more serious test of Zambia's basic support of other nations' sovereignty. In May 1968 Zambia recognized Biafra as independent from the rest of Nigeria. Douglas Anglin, a sympathetic analyst, assigned the GRZ's position to Kaunda's general humanitarian concerns.[44] When the war ended and Biafra had lost, relations between Nigerian authorities and the Zambians were cool. Yet there does not seem to have been a long-lasting effect, for in 1978 Nigerians deeply involved Zambians in attempts to bring Nkomo and Smith together for talks. Later KK established a good working relationship with General O. Obasanjo.[45]

The troubled history of modern Uganda has also forced Zambia into a corner. In 1965 Milton Obote, then president of Uganda, Nyerere of Tanzania, and Kaunda joined an informal alliance called the Mulungushi Club. When Obote was ousted in 1971, Kaunda remained an Obote supporter and bitter opponent of Idi Amin (who took over in Uganda). Kaunda refused to attend OAU meetings when Amin was chairman. However, opposition to Amin did not extend to a willingness to use massive military means to overthrow him, as Nyerere eventually did in 1979. After Obote's second ouster, Kaunda offered refuge to the former Ugandan president and many followers. Housed in the presidential lodge in Lusaka and treated well by their Zambian hosts, the Ugandan political refugees nonetheless were sharply cautioned against using Zambian soil for any attempts to overthrow subsequent Ugandan regimes.

The Zambian line on continental issues, then, has many parallels with the stance towards the Zimbabwean and Angolan liberation struggles—

partisanship but noninterference. Sustaining such a nuanced position in continental diplomacy has been easier perhaps because of the distance between Zambia and Biafra or Uganda and the consequent unlikelihood that faraway battles might spill over onto Zambian soil, requiring a more direct response.

The contradictions between the OAU principles of self-determination and territorial integrity of existing nations have posed dilemmas for Zambian diplomats in the 1980s as well. What faction should the Zambians back in the interminable squabbles over Chad? Should the GRZ support the independence of the Spanish Sahara under a Polisario government or the incorporation of that territory into the Kingdom of Morocco? A genuine humanitarian concern for the suffering and loss of life occasioned by such territorial disputes seems to be the prime motivation in the efforts by KK and his aides (behind the scenes) to effect a compromise. Kaunda also may have ambitions to be seen as a "prince amongst peacemakers," according to longtime observer Colin Legum.[46] In his peacemaking missions, Kaunda has often been joined by Nyerere and more recently by other FLS leaders. Thus the FLS alliance, born in the cauldron of the Zimbabwean liberation struggle, has carried over into continental and sometimes global politics.

As a senior spokesman for the Third World in the Commonwealth of Nations, Kaunda's importance is linked both to longevity in office and his public and consistent stance against racism and apartheid. Back in 1966 it was a different story. Then an angry KK threatened to withdraw from the Commonwealth over the British unwillingness to push the white Rhodesian politicians into a compromise with the representatives of the majority of Zimbabwe's black population. By 1979 however, relations had changed and KK successfully hosted the Commonwealth Heads of Government Meeting in Lusaka. This proved to be a very important piece of diplomacy, as this meeting set the groundwork for the Lancaster House Constitutional Conference on Zimbabwe later that year. In March 1983 KK made a state visit to Britain, the first since independence. Kaunda built bridges to the U.S. government as well. In the 1980s the Zambian president has been seen as a moderate voice of reason by both Britain and the United States, which means he has been included in most regional negotiations.

Zambia's international *economic* relations have a lower profile than international diplomacy but are vital nonetheless. The story of CIPEC demonstrates the complexity of the international commodity markets as well as the weakness of raw material exporters when faced with the demands of the major industrial powers of the world. The difficulties the Zambian leaders encountered in trying to forge a Third World alliance to affect the price of copper were intensified by internal divisions within Zambia concerning strategy and options.

In 1964 Zambia's total economy was tied to the fate of the copper mines, which in turn were owned outright by South African, British, and U.S. interests. Although the new government had initiated diplomatic contacts with many of the world's industrial powers (including most of Zambia's copper buyers), international mining companies conducted much of Zambia's foreign economic policy. For example, Anglo, AMAX, and RST controlled the sale and marketing of Zambia's refined metals as well as the pricing arrangements. From 1964 to 1969 the LME spot market price could have offered the GRZ higher prices for minerals. Then the government's share, based on taxes, would have been higher. Yet European buyers still purchased Zambian copper directly from the foreign companies, based on a three-month forward purchase system. Purchasing arrangements were made by the multinational companies' headquarters in New York, London, and Johannesburg and their local managers, rarely even with consultation of the Ministry of Mines. Furthermore, new financing of the mines came from heavy foreign borrowing, arranged by the international parent companies and based on their evaluation of the needs and payoffs of their Copperbelt facilities.[47] In extending such loans, the banks assessed the stability of the regime and the quality of the "investment climate," based on information primarily from the mining companies and secondarily from the political officers of various embassies. Although far less visible than the arena of international diplomacy, such economic relations and pacts were and are vital to any nation. And from 1964 to 1970 this aspect of Zambia's economic diplomacy was conducted on the nation's behalf by foreign companies, by proxy, one might say.

When the GRZ took over a majority of the shares of the mines in 1969, it soon thereafter established in London its own marketing agency, Metal Marketing Corporation of Zambia (MEMACO) Services Ltd., to draw control over copper exports into local hands. Yet the positive effects of Zambian ownership were limited by the shortages of technical personnel and reliance on private companies as agents for MEMACO. Divisions within the governing class over economic strategies also undercut the effectiveness of national control. A brief review of the events when Zambia joined CIPEC, a Third World effort to control copper price and production, demonstrates how internal class divisions split or undermined consistent economic foreign policy.

Briefly put, at independence national politicians were eager to confront the major metropole (United Kingdom), and the white South, as well as some of the major industrial powers, hoping for domestic political advantage from being seen to have lessened the country's overt dependence on foreigners. Zambia's position on disengagement and opposition to apartheid, colonialism, and imperialism were expressed in many speeches to international forums. Yet politicians were sensitive to threats to their political base from the unemployment of miners; they also were eager for enhanced state revenues to further social welfare programs. As a representative of this fraction, the president initiated contact with other heads of state of copper producers with an eye to improving their mutual situation as raw material exporters from the Third World. Kaunda, along with President Eduardo Frei of Chile, was key to the founding of CIPEC in 1967. The charter members—Zambia, Zaire, Peru, and Chile—consciously excluded from their ranks other major copper producers, notably the USSR and the United States, who are both producers and consumers, in order to help the fledgling organization start with clear Third World priorities. Although the goal of price control was always implicit, early written agreements were limited to CIPEC's interest in world copper supply and in using copper receipts to foster the member states' development programs.[48] On the political agenda, the CIPEC members discussed asserting control over their own copper mines, that is, nationalization.

In the boom years of the late 1960s, the Zambian politicians were eager to increase the GRZ share of the profits and to assert more national control over the future of the mines. In the CIPEC forum, they discussed tactics with other CIPEC ministers. For Zambia, the results were changes in the taxation codes and in utilization of mining licences. Eventually the politicians launched the first (1969) and second (1973) takeover of the mines themselves and establishment of MEMACO. Other CIPEC members followed similar paths, so that by 1974 the CIPEC "Big Four" controlled (at least in ownership terms) their own copper mines.

In early discussions within CIPEC concerning the establishment of a cartel, the technocrats and civil servants of Zambia took a moderate and conciliatory line for dealing with the international copper market.[49] They knew the full extent of Zambia's incorporation in the Western market system and that the CIPEC nations controlled only about 40 percent of the export market. Although willing to bargain for better terms with international and locally based capital, they were reluctant to antagonize foreign investors either by aggressive economic nationalism or by militant stances of the Organization of Petroleum Exporting Countries (OPEC) variety. In the technical meetings of CIPEC, the Zambian representatives tended to support what one analyst has called the "position of the copper companies."[50] This meant Zambian backing for technical price adjustments rather than direct intervention in the market through monopoly pricing. Potential conflict within the Zambian governing class over CIPEC's role was postponed by divisions within the organization itself and papered over by the high prices for copper from 1969 to mid-1974.

The Fall of 1974 (referring to the plummet of the copper price beginning in April on the LME and August on the New York Commodities Exchange) was connected to a major recession in the West. CIPEC representatives began to discuss intervening in the market through controlling prices and production. These talks forced to the fore some incipient struggles within Zambia. Shortages of state revenues, combined with escalating costs of sales for Zambia, due largely to regional transport difficulties, meant a fiscal crisis for the GRZ and those fractions most dependent on it. Now the technocrats and civil servants were willing to discuss price ceilings and floors and even possible export adjustments at the CIPEC meetings. Yet few politicians were willing to entertain plans for actual reduction of production, knowing the implications of unemployment on the Copperbelt at a time of internal economic stress.

At the CIPEC meeting in Lusaka in April 1974, experts projected a long term of low copper prices, yet the Big Four came to no agreement on active intervention in the market. By September, as the price and revenues continued to slide, they agreed to reduce exports by 10 percent but not to cut production. Unfortunately, the copper buyers interpreted this policy as likely to produce large stockpiles of copper. This led to further reductions in the price on the LME and New York Exchange when the spot quotation on the London Metal Exchange slipped from £1,267.7 per long ton in April 1974 to £630.1 in September and the bottom had not yet been reached. By November 1974 the GRZ representatives had received cabinet permission to talk of an export quota system and even to discuss a cutback in production. At the November meeting the CIPEC delegates agreed to a 15 percent reduction in *production* to begin in April of 1975 *if* the price situation had not improved. The Zambian representative at that meeting was the minister of mines and industry, Andrew Kashita, a technocrat with a background in engineering and considerable experience in the parastatal network. Although unhappy with the political ramifications of unemployment and deferred projects, Kashita agreed to the 15 percent cutback in view of the fact that this was the only immediate action available to CIPEC that might halt the slide of the copper price.[51] Several national politicians, including the previous minister of mines and future secretary general of UNIP, Humphrey Mulemba, took issue with this decision and maneuvered to have Kashita removed on the grounds of having overstepped his mandate.[52] Such a battle is unlikely to have surfaced had the decision to cut production been a less politicized issue. In the end, Kashita was fired in January 1975. For a period it was unclear whether Zambia would honor the promise of a 15 percent cutback scheduled to begin in April. Eventually the continued doldrums of the copper price forced the national politicians who took over both the ministry and the CIPEC delegation to bow to pressures to cut back production. Mindolo Open Pit was closed and the development of Kansanshi and Kalulushi East mines was postponed.[53]

In 1974–1975, then, as the GRZ was beginning to assert effective control over the mines and determine key aspects of Zambia's foreign economic strategy, domestic class fragmentation had led to inconsistent or delayed policy. After 1975 the effect of prolonged negative terms of trade, combined with the different economic problems facing the Big Four and their divergent political philosophies, conspired to prevent the fulfillment of CIPEC's original task. Gains through monopoly pricing were out of the question. CIPEC still existed as an organization in the mid-1980s but in general has proven to be ineffectual. The CIPEC experience demonstrates the general weakness of most raw material exporters in trying to influence market forces that in turn directly affect their national fate. It also showed how internal class divisions intervene in the delicate and important areas of international economic policy.

ZAMBIA AND THE SUPERPOWERS: NONALIGNMENT

In recognition of Zambia's global irrelevance and the nature of cold war politics, Kaunda and his aides constructed a rather successful international strategy based on playing off East and West. An abiding fear of Kaunda's, one shared by many other African leaders, is that a continental crisis of significant proportions could draw in the great powers, as has happened in the Horn of Africa. At independence, Zambia joined the Nonaligned Movement, thus taking a position of basic neutrality toward both East and West. Although most of Zambia's political and economic policies are interpreted as being pro-West,[54] official nonalignment has permitted the GRZ to extract benefits from both superpower blocs. From time to time, relations have cooled toward the United States or the USSR, but Kaunda has managed to walk that tightrope to Zambia's economic advantage.

Since independence, Zambian diplomats have refined a basic neutrality in the cold war into a policy called "positive nonalignment," with particular reference to southern Africa. Zambian unwillingness to join military pacts with either the East or West was complemented by a positive commitment to the emancipation of the continent and its people. Thus Zambia has condemned equally the U.S. military involvement in Vietnam and invasion of Grenada as well as the Soviet intervention in Czechoslovakia and Angola. Belonging to the Nonaligned Movement also gave KK allies in his calls for racial and economic equity. Kaunda had established a working relationship with President Tito of Yugoslavia and various Indian leaders.

Despite a basic pro-Western stance, Zambia's relations with capitalist states have not been smooth. Tensions surfaced first toward the former colonial power, the United Kingdom, over the issue of Rhodesia in 1965. Later in 1975 Zambia criticized the United States for its unwillingness to support southern African liberation. Kaunda's disappointment was based on his dual belief that moral causes should be backed and that the great powers have historical responsibilities toward former colonies. When Britain and the United States refused to follow Kaunda's advice, the nonaligned card was sometimes played. In March 1978, for example, Kaunda said that "if the West continued to arm Rhodesia, I would have no alternative but to seek military assistance from the East."[55] Similar statements followed the October and November 1979 raids on Zambia. The British did in fact respond to this appeal-cum-threat from Zambia and sent antiaircraft weapons to Lusaka. Unwilling to accept military dependence on one source, in 1980 the GRZ concluded an arms deal with the USSR, which displeased Washington.

Despite some periodic public feints toward the Soviet bloc and some actual military arrangements, Zambia's leaders fear too heavy a reliance on the USSR. In 1976 for instance, when Zambia was under great strain over the Angolan civil war and the USSR and Cuba became involved on the side of the MPLA, Kaunda called them "the plundering bear and her cub,"[56]

TABLE 6.2
Zambia's Creditors as of December 31, 1984 (K thousands)[a]

Source of Credit	DEBT OUTSTANDING	PRINCIPAL
Bilateral Aid	2,065,705	69,173
OECD	1,006,490	25,689
Non-OECD	1,059,215	43,484
Financial	535,450	15,848
OECD	467,404	1,771
Non-OECD	68,046	14,077
Supplier	624,455	31,255
OECD	487,567	312
Non-OECD	136,888	30,943
Multilateral	2,069,853	47,255
GRAND TOTAL	5,295,463	163,531
OECD plus Multilateral	4,031,314	75,027
Non-OECD	1,264,149	88,504

[a] These figures were for the external medium- and long-term debt outstanding as of Dec. 31, 1984, and excluded the rescheduled debt, so these are low estimates.

Source: Bank of Zambia, <u>Report and Statement of Accounts for the Year Ended 31st December 1984</u>, Table 10.1 (a), p. 55 (Lusaka: Bank of Zambia, 1985).

hardly pro-Soviet sentiments. Also, economic deals with the Eastern bloc have not always worked out to Zambia's advantage. In an barter agreement with Romania, Zambia received Aro vehicles for the police. The construction and performance of these vehicles have been so bad as to have proven an object of mockery by the public and a source of embarrassment to the police! In many ways, the Zambians are more in sympathy with the Chinese for their generous railway aid. In addition to the large initial loans to build the TAZARA in 1975, the Chinese willingly rolled over the loans and used their technical personnel to refurbish the line in the early 1980s. Despite warm relations with the PRC, however, the historical dependence of Zambia upon major Western economic institutions remains entrenched.

The latitude for the GRZ to act in opposition to the wishes of the capitalist powers diminishes daily as aid and trade statistics reveal a deepening of Zambia's involvement. Foreign aid to Zambia increased 400 percent between 1975 and 1980, according to researchers A. Wood and W. Smith.[57] As Table 6.2 shows, overall financial involvement by the Western nations and Japan in 1984 was much greater than that of the socialist bloc or the OPEC countries. Bilateral loans by the Organization for Economic Cooperation and Development (OECD) countries (the major Western countries

TABLE 6.3
Zambia's Trade with Selected Countries, 1982 (K'000)

Country	Exports	Imports	Total
Japan	202,635	57,733	260,368
United Kingdom	62,992	120,381	137,386
West Germany	75,414	48,911	124,325
USA	27,786	92,702	120,488
China	34,228	3,061	37,289
East African countries	3,981	6,431	10,412

Source: Republic of Zambia, Central Statistical Office, Monthly Digest of Statistics 21, nos. 2-3 (February/March 1985), Table 23, p. 22.

plus Japan) almost matched aid from the non-OECD nations, primarily the socialist bloc countries and the Arab donor nations. Of the debt to the non-OECD countries, the funds outstanding to the Chinese accounted for a large portion. When amounts are measured, however, bank lending from the Western commercial institutions far outstripped the non-OECD sources. Suppliers' credits from OECD countries were almost four times as great as funds from outside the OECD. Finally, multilateral funds came primarily from the African Development Bank and the African Development Fund, the International Bank for Reconstruction and Development (IBRD) and other World Bank affiliates as well as the sister agency, the IMF. All of these agencies are identified most closely with the capitalist world. These funds represent a growing portion of Zambia's annual capital budget.

In some areas, such as agriculture, aid gives the donors considerable power over the direction and priorities of rural development. A. Wood and W. Smith detected a neocolonial pattern in agriculture aid. The Dutch control most of agricultural development programs and projects in Western Province, the Germans are in North-Western, the Swedes are in Northern and Eastern provinces, and the EEC in general is influential in programs along the line of rail.[58] In 1985 Western aid donors offered to increase their official aid to Zambia to $400 million from $360 million in 1984/85. This additional amount plugged the foreign payments' gap exactly.[59] Aid from the capitalist states is not only the major source of foreign funds but has given the donor agencies access into the making of sectoral policies, a certain intrusion by external bodies.

In 1982 Zambia's major trading partners were, in descending order of importance: Japan, the United Kingdom, South Africa, West Germany, the United States, China, and other East African countries (see Table 6.3). Three interesting patterns have occurred in Zambia's trade and aid relations outside the region in the 1980s. First is the growing prominence of Japan in many aid and trade projects. In addition to being the major purchaser of Zambia's exports, the Japanese also send a substantial amount of manufactured goods to Zambia annually.[60] Two Japanese corporations, Mitsui and Mitsubishi, made substantial suppliers' loans to ZCCM for the copper facilities in the early 1980s. In 1984 they rescheduled K 27 million of that debt for Zambia.[61] Japanese construction companies have completed a pediatric wing for the University of Zambia's Teaching Hospital in Lusaka and the new school of veterinary science at UNZA. Japanese technical personnel are also involved in the major overhaul of Nitrogen Chemicals of Zambia. This new economic partnership is based on Zambia's copper and cobalt reserves and Japan's global strategy to gain access to vital raw materials.

The second pattern is growing EEC involvement, specifically German trade, and Scandinavian aid connections. Because Zambian direction of trade figures separate the sterling area from the EEC and European Free Trade Association (EFTA) zones, it is possible to see how trade with the major continental European powers by 1979 had begun to approach the level of Zambia-U.K. commerce. Trade figures of 1982 show West German trade alone valued at K 124 million relative to the U.K.'s K 183 million.[62] These new trading patterns seem connected to Zambia's participation in Lomé I (1975) and Lomé II (1979) conventions. Under various Lomé agreements, selected commodities from participating countries have a slight advantage in access to the European market; there are also clauses concerning lessening European trade barriers to more processed or fabricated products from the less developed partners. Benefits to ZCCM from participation in the Lomé trade arrangements were few by 1985, primarily because copper has not been included on the select list of commodities,[63] which guarantees the relative stability of export earnings by compensating for shortfalls in exports earnings due to price fluctuations. In the mid-1980s discussions were under way to include copper and cobalt as well as to encourage Zambia to export agricultural commodities such as cotton (or unprinted cotton cloth), sugar, and coffee to Europe.

The Scandinavian countries have been important in Zambia's overall aid program, especially in the area of technical cooperation where they contribute over 50 percent to Zambia's technical cooperation schemes.[64] Their trade with Zambia is far more limited and their capital assistance programs (loans) are much smaller than those of Canada, West Germany, Japan, and the United Kingdom. Still, through the Lomé system, several European countries have deepened their economic and political commitment to an area that had previously been considered an exclusive British preserve. As an example of this new involvement, the EEC, together with the World Bank and the African Development Bank, are funding the major rehabilitation of the mines in the 1980s.

Finally, trade between Zambia and the United States grew from a mere K 34 million in 1970 to K 128 million in 1982.[65] Although exports of raw minerals to the United States have varied, U.S. imports have steadily increased, from K 33 million in 1970 to K 93 million in 1982.[66] This growing commercial relationship is matched by increasing U.S. aid to Zambia. U.S. power within the IMF, and that institution's crucial role in Zambia (see

Chapter 5), has meant that the U.S. hand is becoming stronger in both domestic and foreign policy.

Taken as a whole, the new trade and aid with Japan, the EEC, and the United States, have meant that the exclusivity of the economic relationships of the colonial days has given way to a more multilateralized dependency. Now Zambia has ties with a wider number of nations, primarily in the Western arena, however. Those relations are still unequal, as Zambia remains an exporter of raw materials, agricultural now overtaking minerals, and an importer of manufactured goods from the West.

CONCLUSION

Zambia's international relations have not changed dramatically in the first twenty years of independence despite vast changes in the region. Zambia's major economic links remain with the West and South Africa, although there are now new partners in trade and aid. Zambia's leaders support organizations such as SADCC and PTA in hopes that these institutions will offer more economic alternatives and some mutual defense against South Africa, but to date Zambia continues to be embroiled and vulnerable. Nonalignment effectively has meant being able to take aid and military hardware from both East and West without having to pay the price of belonging to either camp. President Kaunda has used a balancing technique globally, similar to the one he so skillfully employs domestically, to gain the best from both worlds. So far he has managed to keep the United States and the Soviet Union out of Zambia's domestic affairs, except insofar as their aid has become increasingly important to the financial survival of the state. Whether Kaunda or any successors will be able to walk this tightrope as the liberation war over South Africa heats up is unclear at this time. If such a major crisis exploded, however, it is likely that the basic cultural, economic, and political ties to the West will prevail.

7
Zambia's Future, Zambia's Choices

Where is Zambia bound? Of course, none of us can predict the future with any degree of accuracy. Yet by 1985 some trends were constant enough to allow insight into options for the country as well as knowledge of the likely pressures to move in one or another direction. After more than twenty years of independence, the dead hand of the colonial past still lies on Zambia. The unevenly developed colonial economy, lopsided in its dependence on mining and inequitable in its distribution of skills, education, and wealth, has proven a trap out of which a modern, well-integrated and (relatively) autonomous Zambia has not emerged.

Watching Zambia since independence is rather like watching a friend who is a social drinker becoming an alcoholic. Policies and practices ostensibly directed to self-reliance have, after twenty years, left the country no less externally oriented, more deeply in debt, and because of the international environment, with fewer options than in 1964. The wars on and near the borders that plagued the early years have largely ended. The relatively new phenomenon of fiscal deficit and negative international balance of payments has meant a new, but equally powerful, subordination to the West of the Zambian people and their governing class.

What does the social and economic face of Zambia look like in the late 1980s? Can we speculate as to the future? And are there some alternatives to the bleak vision of this book? The social and cultural fabric of the nation, so complex and multifaceted, has been stretched by the economic recession of the past decade. Yet Kaunda and the UNIP leadership have avoided the violent potential in such an ethnically and class-divided society, mostly through the pragmatic tactics of reshuffling and ethnic balancing. The bloodshed and brutality in Zimbabwe in the early 1980s between Shona and Ndebele is a lesson that other alternatives lie open to the leadership of such fissiparous states. Since 1973 no powerful opposition party or movement has emerged with ethnolinguistic affinities. UNIP remains a national party, although there are pockets of resistance. "Tribalism" still flourishes in the press and in popular perceptions, however. As the number of jobs and favors shrinks and the population increases, claims of nepotism and tribal favoritism are likely to grow as well. UNIP's technique of coopting potentially antagonistic leaders of various ethnic groups may be less successful in the next twenty years because of fewer resources for patronge than were available from 1964 to 1977.

The one-party system has not aged well in Zambia. With the removal of contenders for the presidency and with the shortage of funds for local projects and cadres, UNIP began to lose its purpose and its way. Below the district level, the party had no real presence in the countryside in the 1980s. Lack of registered, paid-up members and sometimes even candidates to run for office in the 1983 election indicates that the system is in danger of collapse. In the absence of leadership from the party, more and more the focus of politics is on Kaunda and to a lesser degree on the bureaucracy. Presidentialism has flourished partly because the strong executive is filling a vacuum left by the atrophy of UNIP at the base; it is not only because of the manipulations by the central leadership. The national assembly is a vocal but comparatively powerless representative of some sections of the Zambian governing class; the central committee has become an old politicians' club. The semiautonomy of the judiciary is still being contested. When Edward Shamwana, the former High Court commissioner jailed for treason, was brought to court in April 1985 to hear the Supreme Court rule against his appeal to overturn the death sentence, he shouted "the independence of the judiciary is gone and so has the freedom of this country."[1] Twenty years of KK's rule have left the system dependent on one man's guidance. If Kaunda were removed suddenly, the likelihood of chaos is high, as no clear successor has been designated and the other institutions of power have atrophied greatly.

A review of the processes of the economy offers a bleak picture as well. Following the advice of development experts from the United Nations, the Food and Agriculture Organization, and Commonwealth countries, in the late 1960s Zambian planners and civil servants used the nation's plentiful moneys to develop the country's infrastructure and social services as well as create import-substitution industries in the manufacturing sector. Little consideration was then given to ensuring local inputs and no actions were taken to expand or develop key capital goods industries. The weaker of the state firms in this overdiversified and import-dependent manufacturing sector are "going to the wall" in the brutal conditions of the 1980s.

With the decline of the mines and a large section of manufacturing, a process of *deindustrialization* has begun. Some optimists hope for a return to the golden years of the First Republic, when there was a buoyant national economy based on high returns from copper and a new tax regime. Most observers, however, do not see such a recovery for the copper industry. Instead, the survival of mining in Zambia is linked to commercial possibilities for other minerals: zinc, lead, coal, amethyst, emerald, gold, oil, and uranium.

The first three base metals suffer from the same problems as copper—generally, poor international terms of trade, given domestic costs of production and the costs of sales internationally. High-quality emeralds are found in Zambia. In October 1982 a Saudi Arabian company entered a joint venture with Zambia's Reserve Minerals Corporation to prospect for and market these gems.[2] Unfortunately, 90 percent of the emeralds are located and smuggled out of Zambia by illegal prospectors in alliance with some West African entrepreneurs and presumably with the connivance of some Zambian officials.[3] Gains the GRZ might obtain from these precious stones are nullified by this burgeoning illicit trade. The mining of amethyst is more controlled, but this semiprecious stone is far less valuable than the emerald. Gold and uranium have either not been found in commercially viable deposits or remain elusive to prospectors. There is no latter-day Copperbelt on Zambia's horizon, although rumors circulate about considerable deposits of oil in the Luangwa Valley and uranium in the Gwembe Valley.

Most foreign experts argue, and Zambian senior politicians echo this opinion, that Zambia's long-term future lies in agriculture. For Zambia to reach the goal of an efficient agricultural economy, the IMF, World Bank, and several bilateral donors suggest strongly that the country dismantle its parastatal system, allowing all but the most efficient, government-owned manufacturing industries to die a natural death. The mines are supposed to close their less profitable enterprises, renovate their stronger mines, and prepare to wrap up operations early in the twenty-first century. Most new investment should go into commercial agriculture or infrastructural support for agriculture. The state should get out of certain enterprises, under the term *privatization*. What foreign donors really mean is *denationalization*. This is likely to involve handing many parastatal firms back to foreign companies or resident expatriates because most local entrepreneurs are unable to raise sufficient capital to buy these large, capital-intensive companies or pay for the managerial expertise to turn them around. In 1986 the U.S. multinational Heinz was rumored to be considering a takeover of parts of ROP, while the Dutch company, Heineken, would absorb the National Brewery. Signs of such direct foreign corporate involvement so far are few perhaps because of the parlous state of the Zambian economy. Yet options are also limited, given the domestic and international conditions.

When copper was king, many serious social, political, and economic problems could be pasted over. In the 1980s when the moneys have dried up, the effects of the copper collapse on social programs and consequent problems are easy to see. State intervention in the economy, especially in manufacturing and mining, was meant to enhance local control and provide revenues for populist programs of social welfare. In the boom years of the First Republic, many people came to the towns and cities seeking employment and stayed to offer their children a better future than the hard life of the peasant farmer. By the mid-1970s the cities could barely absorb and service the growing population and funds were directed toward some imaginative housing programs.

When the state began to enter a long period of fiscal crisis after 1975, social services so proudly launched in the 1960s began coming apart at the seams. In 1985 only some roads were being repaired. Schools lack vital materials and sometimes even teachers. The reintroduction of boarding school fees at the primary and secondary schools in 1986 narrows education to those with some funds. The main hospitals are desperately short of doctors, staff, and often of basic medicines. Water services to some of the cities often lack chemicals and electrical blackouts occur in Lusaka, the capital city. Basic sanitary services such as sewage and garbage collection are inefficient or nonexistent. None of this should be a surprise. In the budgets from 1978 onward, the amounts committed to infrastructure were held down to help lessen the budget deficits. Steady paring of wages, lack of FOREX for spare parts, as well as reduced capital expenditures when the population continues to grow, means an inevitable decline and possibly even a collapse of some vital services.

Politicians and civil servants are sitting on a population time bomb made worse by the many secondary school graduates expecting a job in the urban areas. Many of the young, urban, disappointed men are turning to shady activities to survive—petty vending, begging, and theft. Others are joining well-organized, violent gangs for burglaries and auto thefts. Distinct classes have emerged from within the previously less differentiated African colonial population. The new upper class, the *apamwamba*, aggrandized itself eagerly, especially during the prosperous conditions of the First Republic. The Mulungushi reforms of 1968-1972 filled the pockets of some new businesspeople and offered jobs to a growing technocratic elite, adding numbers to these fractions within the governing class. In the 1980s conspicuous consumption by the *apamwamba* makes the advantages of wealth visible to the have-nots, unconsciously encouraging crime. There seems to be little tradition of noblesse oblige within the governing class. There are few charities or job-training schemes for young men and women other than some run by the churches or funded by domestic and foreign nongovernmental agencies. The unions are struggling just to keep wages at the survival level for their members and to maintain some autonomy from UNIP. IMF pressures to take unpopular actions, such as the removal of subsidies on maize meal and cooking oil, face the leaders with possibilities of serious social unrest.[4] One way to keep the lid on such a potentially dangerous situation is to increase the level of surveillance and actual repression of this poor urban population. This seems to be in the cards with the presence of offices of defense and security in all districts of Zambia, with special agents in the towns. When the benevolent one-party rule does not prevail, the iron fist of the state intervenes.

By 1985 government and people faced a serious dilemma. The economy was still dependent on international forces and held hostage to copper markets abroad. After ten years of depression, social divisions and contradictions that had been muted by copper revenues are appearing or reappearing. Public acquiescence to the imposition of one-party rule and belt-tightening measures announced by the central government may lessen as more and more families drop below subsistence level. Cutbacks in state employment and the shriveling of social welfare programs, under strong external pressures, may lead to either a collapse of the economy (as in Ghana) or a major outbreak of resistance or random violence (as in Uganda).

* * *

Zambians could begin to redirect their economy toward agriculture and related industries. But to develop these options requires a plan and the insightful and consistent political choices by a committed leadership. The result would be continued dependency as a raw materials exporter, agricultural this time rather than mineral. External aid agencies are unlikely to back radical alternatives that could lead to greater autonomy for Zambia, if past practices are any indicator. Current policies of the west and South Africa push Zambia elsewhere. Significantly, when a Third World country has pursued self-reliance under a socialist rubric (even as lukewarm as Zambia's), it has been ruthlessly attacked by the West, as the examples of Chile, Grenada, Nicaragua, not to mention Mozambique and Angola, show us. Given the nature of the Zambian leadership, such aggressive policies are unlikely; instead they are eagerly searching for some reforms that would permit the country to survive and its *apamwamba* to continue to live a comfortable life-style.

Deindustrialization and denationalization are not good strategies for Zambia to undertake for social, economic, and political reasons. Zambia is an urban country; many of its citizens have lived all of their lives in and around the towns. Deindustrialization, the way it is currently being implemented, means the loss of jobs in the mines and manufacturing enterprises without replacement by other jobs. The service and government sectors cannot absorb these workers; mechanized agriculture implies machinery and not people. Finally, the residual base of UNIP is in the towns and cities, and the party has much more limited presence in the rural areas.

Although Zambia is often portrayed as an economy without enough skilled and trained workers, such conclusions derive from a narrow focus on a particular kind of worker, specifically management. The wealth of submanagerial skills, especially those at artisan and technician levels, is overlooked. Forty years of industrial mining have left Zambia with some distinct benefits that should not be jettisoned in the desire to whittle down parts of the economy that do not function well.

Although the maintenance of inefficient and unprofitable mines is not desirable, especially in the light of international oversupply and growing alternatives to copper in industrial usage, mine closures could take place in stages and with a plan for the careful redeployment (and possible reeducation) of many miners. For example, Zambia currently imports phosphates, a vital element in its fertilizer industry. At the same time, Zambia has known deposits of phosphates in the Luangwa Valley of Eastern Province and around Kaluwe and Nkombwa Hill. Certainly some of the redundant Copperbelt miners could be relocated near these phosphate deposits, whose mining should go on for many years. Resistance might come from the fact that the Copperbelt miners are mostly urbanites and would find such a geographical relocation difficult indeed. If it is the difference between no job and a job in the Luangwa Valley, however, many would opt for the latter. There they could use basic skills of mining and contribute to the true import substitution of raw materials for fertilizers, which in turn are vital to agriculture. This strategy, moreover, would require the regime to cooperate with the powerful MUZ, which could hold out political payoffs as well.

Equally, it would be shortsighted to cut off all unprofitable and inefficient state-owned companies, without regard to what they make or how integrated they are now or could be. Possibly Livingstone Motor Assemblers should be allowed to die a quiet death, if Zambians could then import cars without too heavy a duty when they have the FOREX. Otherwise, the ready availability of bicycles from the Chipata bicycle plant or even the investment in public transport would ease the local transport problems without the government's having to keep an inefficient car manufacturer in business through state subsidies. A firm like Kapiri Glass, however, whose glass containers are integral to most of the bottling and food processing industry in Zambia and whose major inputs (silica, soda ash) are available locally, should be maintained under better management. It is not likely to survive otherwise. Without this company, processors of agricultural commodities would again be dependent on Zimbabwe or South Africa for their containers.[5] Equally, Kafue Textiles should be protected, so that the company can continue to encourage small- and medium-scale cotton farming, supply the local market with cloth, and perhaps even begin to move into the important area of bags for agricultural products. These are examples of industries that offer considerable forward and backward linkages to the economy and require only limited amounts of FOREX. This would mean that they would help the rest of the economy be more self-sufficient and provide jobs in manufacturing for the urban population.

As it stood in late 1985 when auctioning had been in progress only for three months, this system seems likely to prove disastrous for many parastatals, because they must bid, along with all other holders of kwacha accounts, for the necessary FOREX to buy equipment, spare parts, and raw materials. Driving these firms out of business does not mean that competitors will spring up in the extremely difficult conditions that manufacturers face today. Rather, initial experience suggests that the lucky bidders are more likely to use their FOREX to import luxury goods, make a quick profit in kwacha, and then externalize it through the auctioning system. Instead of the open market promoted by the Western aid donors, the Zambian politicians and planners could consider a more internally directed plan.[6] Such a plan would require the maintenance of a reduced but logically connected manufacturing sector, the trimming of the mines, and the development of key agricultural-input industries, such as agricultural hand tools, to help Zambia's farmers produce. If manufacturing and agriculture could be reoriented toward people's basic needs (food/clothing/shelter) the regime would reap political and social rewards. This would require Zambia's leaders to fight for a careful, well-integrated economic plan and not simply adhere to doctrines that would denationalize and deindustrialize.

Sadly, the pressures of the IMF and World Bank and several other bilateral donors such as the U.S. Agency for International Development (AID) are for a blanket removal of parastatals on the grounds that they interfere with the free market. Indeed they do, but a free market would flood Zambia with Zimbabwean and South African goods, ending employment for nearly 300,000 people and making the country dependent, all over again, on external supplies of finished and raw materials. In the 1980s Zambia would be without the traditional means—copper—to pay for them.

Of the three main sectors—agriculture, mining, and manufacturing—agriculture has the best prospects for rapid expansion under current domestic and international conditions. An upsurge in production is possible using either of two very different strategies. One would be for the state to encourage capital-intensive farming that would include the steady consolidation of land, mechanization of farming, and heavy application of pesticides and fertilizers. As most of these steps imply import dependency and as the availability of FOREX is problematic, this route could stall unless the governing class decides to open the doors completely to foreign multinational corporations specializing in agribusiness[7] or unless a major donor such as AID decides to underwrite the Zambian economy with heavy flows of aid.

Fortunately, agriculture does not have to be approached in this fashion in order to increase production. Peasant farmers have produced for the market since the 1940s under very discouraging conditions. Data in the 1980s showed peasant farmers responding to producer price incentives. A good percentage of un- and underutilized land could be put into production by small- or medium-scale producers, family farmers, or cooperatives. In 1985 the peasant farmers of Zambia produced what was called a "bumper maize crop," responding to the higher producer prices and not discouraged by the higher prices of seed, fertilizer, and pesticides. Unfortunately, much of the 1985 maize crop was lost when the transport shortage, lack of tires and diesel fuel, and chronic bureaucratic snafus left the maize to be spoiled by early and heavy rains.[8] What the Zambian peasant farmer needs is reliable marketing, agricultural extension services, and water conservation programs, all possible without a heavy reliance on FOREX.

An agrarian policy based on offering decent producer prices for a wide range of food crops plus reasonably priced agriculture inputs would inspire small- and medium-sized farmers as well as the large commercial farmers. Food self-sufficiency would pay some political rewards to the national politicians as well. Increased food production would allow them to maintain low prices for staples for the urban population, to improve rural incomes and thus stem the rural to urban flow, to provide local inputs for industries, and to lessen the national import bill. Yet this route has some hidden political disadvantages in that it would give more power to the rural classes, and in particular to the neglected rural farmers, which could threaten the urban-based governing class currently in power. Approaching agriculture in this fashion also requires that national politicians trust the peasants and vice versa. A conscious tipping of the balance of social rewards and terms of trade to the rural population would require a commitment and consistency not visible so far in the behavior of the governing class. Equally, a strategy based on the smaller rural producers runs contrary to the goals of many of the foreign aid donors, especially the United States and West Germany.

Realistic alternatives rely on the foresight and courage of the GRZ to redesign and implement some difficult options. This in turn would require a change in the nature of the governing class or at least their perceptions of self-interest. The corruption and malaise that now characterize government and local businesses are symptoms of the decadence and weakness of the class that holds power. This class is not a revolutionary bourgeoisie on the order of the European industrialists and merchants in the eighteenth and nineteenth centuries, who overthrew the feudal order and using technology and accumulated capital, introduced modern industrial capitalism. The years of living off the "copper goose" has made many *apamwamba* complacent. Now they resort with little compunction to illegal activities such as poaching and Mandrax dealing to obtain the ready cash for their expensive life-styles. Such a decadent class is not likely to tighten its own belt and begin the hard work of transforming the economy. The president personally is admirable, but in the past decade he has tended to surround himself more and more with yes-men or national politicians who have been around for a long time and have no new ideas except loyalty to the president. With people of this kind at the helm, the governing class is likely to rely more and more upon foreign aid whose donors both have a clear ideological program and the money to back it.

Nor are there other likely sources of alternative policies. The working class in Zambia was fatally weakened as a political force by the tactics of the regime, the narrow economistic goals of the leaders, and the overall economic troubles since 1975. The actual number of jobs in the formal sector shrinks yearly. The lucrative jobs in mining are being pared away, and those salaries, which often supported an extended family of ten, are gone. The informal sector is too small to absorb the surplus job seekers[9] and terribly vulnerable to alterations in policy.[10] Although such leaders as Frederick Chiluba of the MUZ are an important voice in Zambian politics, the constituency for a new government does not seem to reside with him. The large bulk of Zambia's population is now the urban and rural poor and no one currently speaks for them.

The disposition of the military is an unknown in Zambian politics. Little information is publicly available. The military men have also been carefully reshuffled and the rules of tribal balancing adhered to, which tends to divide their ranks. Individuals such as General Kingsley Chinkuli have held ministerial posts in the civilian government and may give the rest of the military some idea of the frustrations of government as well as its rewards. In the 1980 Treason Trial, several military men were implicated but none were found guilty of treason. A coup from within the middle ranks of the military in some alliance with technocrats and civil servants is possible, but Kaunda and Grey Zulu's careful management of military affairs and the pervasive intelligence gathering tends to discourage such maneuvers.

Without any significant internally generated social or political reform on the horizon, what then follows? First there will be more foreign involvement in Zambia's internal and regional policies. Second, the social problems of Zambia are likely to worsen rapidly. This connects to the first point, as the regime is likely to open itself further to infusions of foreign funds, with the donors calling the shots. Third, there is likely to be a shift in foreign policy, notably toward South Africa.

Zambia's nonaligned status as well as its backing for socialist neighbors and the remaining freedom fighters are likely to come under increasing pressure from both the West and South Africa. In December 1985, Lusaka was one of the few places from which the ANC, SWAPO guerrillas, and head officials had not been expelled. Kaunda continues to back Mozambique and Angola, but the U.S. revival of UNITA means more activity on Zambia's western borders. Will KK turn a blind eye? Does he have any real choice? Whatever the Soviet Union's rhetorical position, the actual amounts of aid, military and economic, are quite small. If the ideological war between East and West heats up and if the South African regime hangs onto power using an anticommunist line, Kaunda will be pushed hard to make the pro-Western tendency within Zambia's foreign policy into a clear commitment.

If KK and other nationalists resist too strongly, Zambia could experience a campaign of destabilization, directed from South Africa and taking an economic and military form. Many allegations were made during the Treason Trial that the South Africans had backed the coup attempt, although these charges were never substantiated. Yet it would be more comfortable for Pretoria if Lusaka became another Malawi, a compliant neighbor totally incorporated in the South African "constellation of states." Whether the United States would cooperate with such a change of regime seems to lie with Washington's assessment of the benefits of KK's pragmatic leadership in the region balanced against his moral commitments to the ANC and SWAPO. If South Africa gains its independence in the near future, then a different scenario presents itself, with Zambia gaining more space for its balancing act between East and West.

Zambia is now truly at a watershed. The generation of politicians who brought the country to independence and guided it, sometimes well and sometimes poorly, is about to pass. The inherited copper-based economy is changing in a fundamental way that affects the fiscal basis of the state and the social fabric of the nation. The inheritors, whatever their ideological dispositions, will have far fewer choices than the freedom fighters of the 1960s, because the weak economy does not offer many alternatives and the debt situation is a very powerful undertow. Future Zambian politicians and civil servants simply cannot afford to default on their international debts; the *apamwamba* would be unwilling to give up the privileges attached to the infusion of foreign funds, and the reliance on foreign funds to prop up the state means that they cannot take such a radical step even if they were so inclined. In the future the regime will probably continue to be more and more dependent on foreign aid and grants and less and less able or willing to break away, kick the habit, and start afresh. Signs of hope glimmer here and there, but the overall picture for the majority of the people is bleak indeed.

Appendix A: Glossary

apamwamba	Nyanja word for "those at the top" referring to the upper class
boma	Kiswahili word to describe provincial or district headquarters in colonial times; used today for administrative offices
chibuku	opaque beer made from maize, sorghum or millet, very potent
chitemene	Bemba word for slash-and-burn cultivation
chitenge	a locally printed cotton cloth
Coloureds	people of mixed parentage, usually European and African
kabalala	thieves
Kuomboka	Lozi ceremony of migration to higher ground when the floodplains were inundated
kwacha	Zambian currency; name means "dawn"
litunga	centralized kingship of the Lozi
lobola	bridewealth
mbanje	local marijuana
mfecane	the great civil wars that took place in the 1800s in the southern tip of Africa, driving people northward
ng'anga	traditional herbalist and folk healer (pl. bang'anga)
nshima	local maize porridge, staple in the Zambian diet
rondavels	Afrikaans word for the round huts made of brick with grass-thatched roofs
sunka mulamu	"push me, my brother-in-law," Nyanja phrase for an unreliable car
ujamaa	Kiswahili word for "familyhood," or the unit of family extended to the nation; used to describe Tanzanian socialism

Appendix B: Abbreviations and Acronyms

AAC or Anglo	The Anglo American Corporation of South Africa, Ltd.
AID	Agency for International Development (U.S.)
ANC (NR)	African National Congress (Zambia—Nkumbula)
ANC (SA)	African National Congress (South Africa)
ANC (Z)	African National Congress (Zimbabwe—Bishop Muzorewa)
ARC	African Representative Council
BSAC	The British South Africa Company
c.i.f.	Cost-insurance-freight charges
CAPCO	The Central African Power Corporation
Chartered	The British South Africa Company
CIPEC	Intergovernmental Council of Copper Exporting Countries
DSM	Dar es Salaam, the capital of Tanzania
EEC	European Economic Community
f.o.r.	Free-on-rail charges, costs to produce up to the rail head
FINDECO	Financial Development Corporation (of Zambia)
FLS	Frontline States
FNDP	First National Development Plan (1966–1971)
FNLA	National Front for the Liberation of Angola (Holden Roberto)
FOREX	Foreign exchange; especially the currencies of the Western industrial countries
FRELIMO	Front for the Liberation of Mozambique
FROLIZI	Front for the Liberation of Zimbabwe
GDP	Gross domestic product
GRZ	Government of the Republic of Zambia
IBRD	International Bank for Reconstruction and Development, also known as the World Bank
ILO	International Labour Organization
IMF	International Monetary Fund
INDECO	Industrial Development Corporation (of Zambia)
KK	President Kenneth Kaunda
LME	London Metal Exchange
MCC	Member of the Central Committee of UNIP
MEMACO	Metal Marketing Corporation of Zambia Ltd.

APPENDIX B

MINDECO	Mining Development Corporation (of Zambia)
MNC	Multinational corporation
MP	Member of Parliament
MPLA	Popular Movement for the Liberation of Angola
MUZ	Mineworkers' Union of Zimbabwe
NCCM	Nchanga Consolidated Copper Mines Ltd.
NCZ	Nitrogen Chemicals of Zambia Ltd.
NPP	National Progress Party (formerly the UFP)
NRAMWU	Northern Rhodesian African Mineworkers' Union
NRANC	Northern Rhodesian African National Congress (Nkumbula)
OAU	Organization of African Unity
OECD	Organization for Economic Cooperation and Development
OPEC	Organization of Petroleum Exporting Countries
PM	Prime Minister
PRC	Peoples' Republic of China
PTA	Preferential Trade Agreement
RCM	Roan Consolidated Mines Ltd.
Rhoanglo	Rhodesian Anglo American Corporation Ltd.
ROP	Refined Oil Products (1975)
RST	Roan (originally Rhodesian) Selection Trust Ltd.
SACTU	South African Congress of Trade Unions
SADCC	Southern African Development Coordination Conference
SDR	Special Drawing Rights, unit of exchange for the International Monetary Fund
SG	Secretary General of UNIP
SNDP	Second National Development Plan (1972–1976)
SWAPO	South West African Peoples' Organization (Namibia)
TAZARA	Tanzania-Zambia Railway Authority
TNDP	Third National Development Plan (1979–1983)
TUC	Trades Union Congress
UDI	Unilateral Declaration of Independence by Rhodesia in 1965
UFP	United Federal Party
UNIP	United National Independence Party (Zambia)
UNITA	National Union for the Total Independence of Angola (Savimbi)
UNZA	University of Zambia
UP	United Party (mostly Lozi)
UPP	United Progressive Party (Kapwepwe)
ZAMEFA	Metal Fabricators of Zambia Ltd. (INDECO subsidiary)
ZANC	Zambia African National Congress
ZANLA	Zimbabwe African National Liberation Army (ZANU)
ZANU	Zimbabwe African National Union
ZAPU	Zimbabwe African Peoples' Union
ZCCM	Zambia Consolidated Copper Mines Ltd.
ZCTU	Zambia Congress of Trade Unions
ZIMCO	Zambia Industrial and Mining Corporation Ltd.
ZIPRA	Zimbabwe People's Revolutionary Army (ZAPU)

Notes

Notes to Chapter 1

1. ILO/JASPA, *Zambia: Basic Needs in an Economy Under Pressure: Findings and Recommendations of an ILO/JASPA Basic Needs Mission to Zambia* (Addis Ababa: ILO/JASPA, 1981), p. xxv.
2. From 1976 to 1983, the contribution of the copper industry to government revenue fluctuated between K 42 million and nil. This represented only 6 percent or less of the government's revenues versus 53 percent in 1974. *Zambia Mining Yearbook,* 1980, and Central Statistical Office, *Monthly Digest of Statistics* 20, 12 (December 1984), Table 21, p. 20.
3. ILO/JASPA, *Zambia: Basic Needs*, Table 0.1, p. xxi, for 1976 figure; and Dr. Neva Makgetla, "The IMF in Zambia." Paper presented to the Business and Economics Department Seminar, University of Zambia, 1985, p. 10.
4. Ralph Jeker, "Assessment of the Risks from a Developing Country's Point of View: Zambia," *Aussenwirtschaft* 33, 1–2 (1978): 109–127.
5. A. Wood, "An Economy Under Pressure: Some Consequences of the Recession in Zambia." Paper read at Annual Conference of Institute of British Geographers, Durham, U.K., January 1984, p. 12.
6. The choice of the term to call any new governing group in an African state is difficult as there are many contending views of the nature of these new rulers. Generally, I have avoided the use of the terms *bourgeoisie* and *petite bourgeoisie* (and the long debate about whether Zambia has its own national bourgeoisie) because it seems that the degree of control over the productive forces in Zambia is largely mediated through the state and still heavily influenced by the international minerals market. Thus the term *governing class* has been employed in this manuscript in order to highlight the position of this class that governs and also to make the reader aware of the overwhelming power of external classes and forces.

Notes to Chapter 2

1. Movement of peoples across regional boundaries persisted in colonial and postcolonial central Africa despite bureaucratic impediments such as passports, citizenship papers, and border posts. See S. H. Phiri, "Some Aspects of Spatial Interaction and Reaction to Government Policies in a Border Area" (Ph.D. dissertation, University of Liverpool, 1981). Modern Zambia has been the recipient of considerable immigration over the past twenty years; the United Nations High Commission for Refugees estimates 103,000 refugees have settled in Zambia by 1984 and most intend

NOTES TO CHAPTER 2

to stay. Adian R. Wood, "Agricultural Needs and Food Security in Refugee Affected Areas of Senanga-West, Zambia," mimeo, 1984, p. 4.

2. B. M. Fagan, "Early Farmers and Ironworkers (100 B.C. to A.D. 1500)", *A Short History of Zambia*, ed. B. M. Fagan (Nairobi: Oxford University Press, 1966).

3. Andrew D. Roberts, *A History of Zambia* (London: Heinemann, 1976), D. W. Phillipson, "Iron Age History and Archaeology in Zambia," *Journal of African History* 15, 1 (1974): 1–25, and Fagan's works are the best sources on Zambia's prehistory. The discussion that follows is drawn from their writings and general ideas.

4. Roberts, p. 43.

5. Andrew D. Roberts, "The Age of Tradition (A.D. 1500 to 1850)," ed. Fagan, *A Short History*, p. 103.

6. Traditionally the paramount chiefs of these kingdoms took the ritual name of the founder, so one has Kazembe II Kanyembo Mpemba, and the paramount of the Bemba has the title of Chitimukulu today.

7. Andrew D. Roberts, *A History of the Bemba: Political Growth and Change in Northeastern Zambia Before 1900* (London: Longman, 1973).

8. I. G. Cunnison, "Kazembe and the Portuguese," *Journal of African History* 2, 1 (1961): 61–76.

9. This information is culled from Richard Gray and David Birmingham, *Pre-Colonial African Trade* (London: Oxford University Press, 1970).

10. For this information on the Lozi, see M. Mainga, "The Lozi Kingdom," *A Short History*, ed. Fagan, p. 123. A more complete study on the early period of the kingdom to be found in M. Mainga, *Bulozi Under the Luyanga Kings: Political Evolution and State Formation in Pre-Colonial Zambia* (London: Longman, 1973); Max Gluckman's many studies, especially *Economy of the Central Barotse Plain* (Lusaka: Rhodes-Livingstone Institute Paper, No. 7, 1941), and Gerald Caplan, *The Elites of Barotseland 1878–1969* (London: C. Hurst and Co., 1970), are standard texts on the Lozi. A controversial reinterpretation of the Lozi sociopolitical system and its interactions with colonialism is made by Gwyn Prins, *The Hidden Hippopotamus* (Cambridge: Cambridge University Press, 1980).

11. *The Plateau Tonga of Northern Rhodesia: Social and Religious Studies* (Manchester: Published on behalf of the Rhodes-Livingstone Institute of Northern Rhodesia by Manchester University Press, 1962), pp. 66–68.

12. Although Southern Rhodesia is the focus in I. T. Phimister, "Rhodes, Rhodesia and the Rand: Mining in Southern Rhodesia 1890–1902," *Journal of Southern African Studies* 1, 1 (October 1974): 74–90, the author surveys Rhodes's complex investment strategies for the whole region. Also see John Marlowe, *Cecil Rhodes* (London: Paul Elek, 1972), chapters 6–10, pp. 90–173.

13. L. H. Gann, *A History of Northern Rhodesia: Early Days to 1953* (London: Chatto and Windus, 1964), p. 64.

14. Roberts, *A History of Zambia*, pp. 174–175.

15. F. L. Coleman, *The Northern Rhodesian Copperbelt, 1899–1962: Technological Development up to the End of the Central African Federation* (Manchester: Manchester University Press, 1971) and J. A. Bancroft, *Mining in Northern Rhodesia: A Chronicle of Mineral Exploration and Mining Development* (Bedford, U.K.: The Sidney Press Ltd., for the British South Africa Company, 1961).

16. Peter Slinn, "The Legacy of the British South Africa Company: The Historical Background," *Economic Independence and Zambian Copper: A Case Study of Foreign Investment*, ed. Mark Bostock and Charles Harvey (New York: Praeger, 1972), pp. 26–34.

17. Patrick Ohadike and Habtemariam Tesfaghiorghis, *The Population of Zambia* (New York: CIRCRED, UN, 1975), Table 5.1, p. 114.

18. Gann thoroughly reviews European politics in Northern Rhodesia up to 1953, in his *A History of Northern Rhodesia*, especially chapters 8–13.

19. Ohadike and Tesfaghiorghis, p. 114.

20. J. W. Davidson, *The Northern Rhodesian Legislative Council* (London: Faber and Faber Ltd., 1948) offers a concise description of those administrative arrangements.

21. Although the deposits in Northern Rhodesia averaged around 3.5 percent copper (which was more than double the world average) it was not until the system of extraction of the metal from the sulphide ore concentrates had been developed by the London firms of Minerals' Separation Ltd. that the ores could be profitably mined. Coleman, pp. 29 and 131, n. 103.

22. An authorized but very thorough history of the original Oppenheimer companies, especially the Anglo American Corporation, is Sir Theodore Gregory, *Ernest Oppenheimer and the Economic Development of Southern Africa* (Capetown, S. A.: Oxford University Press, 1962). A more critical assessment is made by Duncan Innes, *Anglo American and The Rise of Modern South Africa* (New York: Monthly Review Press, 1984). For more details on the early history of the mining companies in Northern Rhodesia see Marcia M. Burdette, "The Dynamics of Nationalization between AMAX, Inc., the Anglo American Corporation of South Africa Ltd., and the Government of the Republic of Zambia." (Ph.D. dissertation, Columbia University, 1979).

23. Gann, p. 206.

24. Roberts, *A History of Zambia*, p. 186.

25. Between 1945 and 1953 copper was responsible for 86.5 percent of the value of all exports; it was roughly the same proportion during the federation years, according to Robert Baldwin, *Economic Development and Export Growth: A Study of Northern Rhodesia, 1920–1960* (Berkeley: University of California Press, 1966), p. 36.

26. Roberts, *A History of Zambia*, p. 193.

27. Ibid.

28. Gann, p. 392.

29. Ohadike and Tesfaghiorghis, p. 114.

30. Roberts, *A History of Zambia*, p. 186.

31. The particular character of this working class is well delineated by Michael Burawoy, *The Colour of Class on the Copper Mines: From African Advancement to Zambianization*. Zambian Papers, no. 7 (Manchester: Manchester University Press, 1972); and by Jane Parpart, *Labor and Capital on the African Copperbelt* (Philadelphia: Temple University Press, 1983), chapters 3 and 4, pp. 54–95.

32. Roberts, *A History of Zambia*, p. 191.

33. *Land, Labour and Diet in Northern Rhodesia* (London: Oxford University Press, 1939), as cited in Lionel Cliffe, "Labour Migration and Peasant Differentiation: Zambian Experiences," *Development in Zambia: A Reader*, ed. Ben Turok (London: ZED Press, 1980), p. 154.

34. Robin Palmer traces the main outlines of the land question in Zambia in "Land in Zambia," *Zambian Land and Labour Studies*, 1, ed. Robin Palmer, National Archives Occasional Paper, no. 2, 1973, pp. 56–66.

35. Thirty thousand Africans were employed in 1931; by January 1932 their number had been reduced to 11,636; by December 1982 they had dwindled to 6,677 only to swell again in 1933 with the reopening of the Mufulira Mine. As a result, "large numbers of unemployed workers drifted around the Copperbelt in search of work, and the government reported a floating population of at least 5,000 unemployed moving between Ndola and the mines as late as 1935." Parpart, p. 47.

NOTES TO CHAPTER 3

36. William J. Barber, *The Economy of British Central Africa: A Case Study of Economic Development in an Dualistic Society* (London: Oxford University Press, 1961), Table VI, p. 110.

37. A thorough biography of Gore-Browne was written by Robert I. Rotberg, *Black Heart: Gore-Browne and the Politics of Multiracial Zambia* (Berkeley: University of California Press, 1977).

38. Roy Welensky described his own life in *Welensky's 4000 Days: The Life and Death of the Federation of Rhodesia and Nyasaland* (London: Collins, 1964).

39. Roberts, *A History of Zambia*, p. 207.

40. Ibid., p. 209.

41. Figures derived from Baldwin, Table 8.2, "Contribution of the Mining Industry to Government Revenue Originating in Northern Rhodesia since Federation, 1954–1960," p. 190.

42. Arthur Hazlewood, "The Economics of Federation and Dissolution in Central Africa," *African Integration and Disintegration: Case Studies in Economic and Political Union*, ed. Arthur Hazlewood (London: Oxford University Press, 1967), p. 185.

43. David Mulford, *Zambia: The Politics of Independence 1957–1964* (London: Oxford University Press, 1967), pp. 5–6.

44. Hazlewood, p. 199.

45. Baldwin, Table 2.2, p. 33, and Table 2.6, p. 43.

46. Jan Pettman, *Zambia: Security and Conflict* (Devizes, Wiltshire, U.K.: Davison Publishing Ltd., 1974), p. 82, citing G. Kay, *A Social Geography of Zambia* (London: University of London Press, 1967), pp. 68–73.

47. Hazlewood, pp. 203–204.

48. Roberts, *A History of Zambia*, p. 215.

49. Ibid., p. 214.

50. See Harry Franklin, *Unholy Wedlock: The Failure of the Central African Federation* (London: Allen and Unwin, 1963), for the internal politics surrounding the choice of dam sites.

51. Parpart, Table 11, p. 181.

52. Robert Bates, *Unions, Parties and Political Development: A Study of Mineworkers in Zambia* (New Haven: Yale University Press, 1971), p. 21. Also see Elena Berger, *Labour, Race and Colonial Rule: The Copperbelt from 1924 to Independence* (Oxford: Clarendon Press, 1974), pp. 138–140.

53. Mulford, pp. 35–44.

54. Nicos Poulantzas distinguished between the traditional petite bourgeoisie—shopkeepers, artisans, and small peasants—and the "new" petite bourgeoisie of clerical workers, supervisors, and salaried personnel in modern industry and commerce. He used the term in the European context. See Part 3, "The Petty Bourgeoisie: Traditional and New" in *Classes in Contemporary Capitalism*, trans. David Ferback (London: New Left Books), pp. 193–336.

Notes to Chapter 3

1. *Peri-urban* is a term used for residential areas outlying the formal city center and sometimes even municipal boundaries but incorporated in and vital to urban life.

2. Zambia, *1980 Census of Population and Housing: Preliminary Report* (Lusaka: Central Statistical Office, 1981), p. 3.

3. Brothers to All Men (BAM), "Female Headed Households in Chungu," Report prepared by Rural Development Studies Bureau for BAM (1980–1982).

4. Information based on local farmers' assessments of crop yields, 1979, 1980, 1981, 1982, and projected for 1983. Interviews, April 1983, Chief Chungu's area, Northern Province, Zambia.

5. A. Marter and D. Honeybone, *The Economic Resources of Rural Households and the Distribution of Agricultural Development in Zambia* (Lusaka: Rural Development Studies Bureau, 1976).

6. For a study of these village and ward development committees, see Michael Bratton, "The Social Context of Political Penetration: Village and Ward Committees in Kasama District," *Administration in Zambia*, ed. W. Tordoff (Manchester: Manchester University Press, 1980), pp. 213–239.

7. This calculation is based on the "Law of 70" described by James L. Newman and Gordon E. Matzke in *Population: Patterns, Dynamics, and Prospects* (Englewood Cliffs, N.J.: Prentice-Hall, Inc., 1984), pp. 56–57.

8. Positions in this debate are staked out by Carolyn Baylies and Morris Szeftel, "The Rise of a Zambian Capitalist Class in the 1970s," *Journal of Southern African Studies* 8, 2 (April 1982): 187–213; Tony Southall, "Zambia: Class Formation and Government Policy in the 1970s," *Journal of Southern African Studies* 7, 1 (October 1980): 91–108; and Marcia Burdette, "The Mines, Class Power and Foreign Policy in Zambia," *Journal of Southern African Studies* 10, 2 (April 1984): 198–218.

9. For the 1981 and 1982 figures see Zambia, *Country Profile, Zambia 1984* (Lusaka: Cantral Statistical Office, 1984), Table 39, p. 38. The 1984 figure is based on the consumer prices for high-income and low-income groups in urban Zambia found in the *Monthly Digest of Statistsics* 20, 4 and 6 (April/June 1984), Tables 43 and 44, pp. 40–41. Informed estimates place inflation between 20 and 30 percent per year in 1983–1984 and close to 100 percent in 1985.

10. Of the 127,359 students enrolled in Grade 1 in 1970, by 1977 only 23,237 had been enrolled in Form 1 (the first year of secondary education), and of these, only 797 were accepted into the University of Zambia in 1982. Statistics drawn from "The Educational Progression of the 1970 Grade 1 Cohort," (Department of Education, University of Zambia, 1983), p. 6A (mimeographed).

11. According to the *World Development Report 1981*, Zambia ranked sixth in terms of GNP per capita on the African continent in 1980, excluding South Africa. (New York: Oxford University Press, 1981), Table 1, p. 134.

12. ILO/JASPA, *Zambia: Basic Needs in an Economy under Pressure: Findings and Recommendations of an ILO/JASPA Basic Needs Mission to Zambia* (Addis Ababa: ILO/JASPA, 1981), Table 0.1, p. xxi.

13. Dr. Neva Makgetla, "The IMF in Zambia," Paper presented to the Business and Economics Department Seminar, University of Zambia, 1985, p. 10.

14. Mubanga E. Kashoki, "The Language Situation in Zambia," *Language in Zambia*, ed. Sirarpi Ohannessian and Mubanga E. Kashoki (London: International African Institute, 1978), pp. 26–31.

15. According to Graham Mytton, the average urban Zambian spoke 2.8 different languages and rural respondents average 1.9 languages. *Multilingualism in Zambia*, Zambia Broadcasting Services Research Project and Papers, no. 7, February 1973, Table 2, p. 3.

16. From discussion with Dr. John Chileshe, assistant dean of education and lecturer in languages and literature, University of Zambia, Feb. 1985. To support this point, Chileshe cites reviews in Western literary magazines of novels and short stories of Joseph Muyuni and Grieve Sibale. *Voices of Zambia*, a collection of short stories edited by Mufalo Liswaniso and published by NECZAM in 1971, offers the reader the opportunity to examine this judgement.

17. John Chileshe, "Literacy, Literature and Ideological Formation: The Zambian Case" (D. Phil., 1983, University of Sussex).

18. From conversations with the Zambian ethnomusicologist, Dr. Mwese Mapoma, April 1983.

19. Mention should be made of the mass adoption of football (soccer) and boxing with such enthusiasm that now Zambians are producing world-class athletes in these sports, especially boxing.

20. Karen Tranberg Hansen, "Urbanization Policy in Zambia: Uncertain Priorities," in R. A. Obudho, Saleh El-Skakhs, Joseph Sarfoh, and Hoo sang Amirahmadi, eds., *Contemporary Issues on African Urbanization and Planning* (Albany: State University of New York, forthcoming).

21. Leo van den Berg, ed., *Hard Times in the City*, Studies in Zambian Society, Vol. 3, (Lusaka: University of Zambia, 1978).

22. A 1974 survey showed that of the K 43 million spent on housing that year (the government contributed about 78 percent of this total figure), a full K 31 million (or 73.6 percent) went to high- and medium-cost houses. Squatter houses, which accounted for 61 percent of all new urban dwellings that year, were financed by less than 5 percent of the money and all of this came from nonpublic funds. Stefanie Knauder, *Shacks and Mansions: An Analysis of the Integrated Housing Policy of Zambia* (Lusaka: Multimedia Publications, 1982), p. 16.

23. Van den Berg.

24. Karen Tranberg Hensen, "'Bachelor Town' and the 'Immorality Issue': Economic Consequences of Colonial Ideologies for Women's Wage Labor in Post-Colonial Lusaka, Zambia," paper presented for the Symposium on Culture, Economy and Policy in the Colonial Situation, May 14–15, 1981, organized by the Department of Anthropology, University of Minnesota.

25. Lionel Cliffe, "Labour Migration and Peasant Differentiation: Zambian Experiences" in *Development in Zambia: A Reader*, ed. Ben Turok (London: ZED Press, 1979), pp. 149–169.

26. Ilsa Schuster, *New Women of Lusaka*, Exploration of World Ethnography Series, (Palo Alto, California: Mayfield Publishing Co., 1979).

27. ILO/JASPA, Technical Paper No. 6 and esp. Chapter 2.

28. A fascinating study of religion, medicine, and art in the Lusaka township of Marrapodi is available in Benetta Jules-Rosette, *Symbols of Change: Urban Transition in a Zambian Community* (Norwood, N.J.: Ablex Publishing Co., 1981).

29. The pages and editorial columns of the *Times of Zambia* and the *Zambia Daily Mail* have been filled with references to and comments upon the "Milingo affair" since it began in 1982.

30. Jules-Rosette, passim.

31. Ibid., esp. Chapter 6, "The Urban Bang'anga—Folk Healers as Psychological Entrepreneurs," pp. 129–163.

32. Bonnie Keller, "Marriage and Medicine: Women's Search for Love and Luck," *African Social Research* 26 (December 1978): 489–505.

33. Zambia, *Country Profile, Zambia 1984*, Section 2.1 "Population Size," p. 3.

Notes to Chapter 4

1. The term *governing class* is used to distinguish between the class that effectively controls the state and party apparatus and a foreign bourgeoisie (the *ruling class*) that owns directly (shares) or indirectly (massive loans) the means of production.

NOTES TO CHAPTER 4

2. The Zambian kwacha was created in January 1968 and set equal to 0.5 Zambian pounds (from 1964–1968 1 Zambian pound = U.S. $2.80). Coins are designated in ngwee of which 100 = 1 kwacha. The exchange rate vis-à-vis the dollar has changed over time but was 1 K = $1.40 from January 1968 to February 1973.

3. David Mulford details the events from 1962–1964 in *Zambia: The Politics of Independence, 1957–1964* (London: Oxford University Press, 1967).

4. The reserved seats were for non-Africans only and abolished in 1968.

5. William Tordoff and Robert Molteno, "Government and Administration," *Politics in Zambia*, ed. W. Tordoff (Berkeley: University of California Press, 1974), pp. 253–254.

6. Robert Molteno, "Cleavage and Conflict in Zambia Politics: A Study in Sectionalism," *Politics in Zambia*, p. 81.

7. Ben Turok, "The State and Society," The Open University, D 209, December 1983, p. 27, mimeographed.

8. Tordoff and Molteno, p. 243.

9. W. Tordoff and R. Molteno, "Introduction," *Politics in Zambia*, p. 11.

10. For a fuller exposition on the colonial situation and the postcolonial policies of the GRZ, see the book by the first minister of education, John Mwanakatwe, *The Growth of Education in Zambia Since Independence* (Lusaka: Oxford University Press, 1968), and the study by John Saxby "The Politics of Education in Zambia" (Ph.D. dissertation, University of Toronto, 1980).

11. Zambia, *Manpower Report: A Report and Statistical Handbook on Manpower, Education, Training and Zambianization, 1965–1966* (Lusaka: Government Printer, 1966).

12. Irving Kaplan, ed., *Zambia: A Country Study*, Foreign Area Studies, American University (Washington: Government Printing Office, 1979), p. 114.

13. Central and specialist hospitals were still primarily an urban phenomenon with the University Teaching Hospital (UTH) in Lusaka; Ndola Central Hospital in Ndola, Kitwe Central Hospital in Kitwe; Arthur Davidson's Hospital for Children in Ndola; and Chainama Hills Hospital for Mental Care in Lusaka. Only Liteta Hospital was located outside a town (Kabwe). Zambia, *Country Profile, Zambia 1984* (Lusaka: Central Statistical Office, 1984), p. 63.

14. In this period, constitutional and statutory expenditures covered the party expenses as well as debt servicing; later, defense was included.

15. Tordoff and Molteno, "Government and Administration," pp. 252–287.

16. Ibid., p. 266.

17. Ibid., p. 267.

18. Jan Pettman, *Zambia—Security and Conflict* (Lewes, Sussex, U.K.: Julian Friedmann Publishers Ltd., 1974), Appendix B., "List of Ministers in the Government of the Republic of Zambia, 1964–71," pp. 247–257.

19. Tordoff and Molteno, "Government and Administration," pp. 274–287.

20. Ibid., p. 247.

21. Personal information from former ministers who were reshuffled, 1976.

22. Robert I. Rotberg, *The Rise of Nationalism in Central Africa: The Making of Malawi and Zambia, 1873–1964* (Cambridge: Harvard University Press, 1965), Robert I. Rotberg, "Tribalism and Politics in Zambia," *Africa Report* 12, 9 (December 1967): 29–39; Richard Hall, *Zambia* (London: Pall Mall Press, 1965); Thomas Rasmussen, "Political Competition and One-Party Dominance in Zambia," *Journal of Modern African Studies* 7, 3 (October 1969): 407–424.

23. Archie Mafeje, "The Ideology of Tribalism," *Journal of Modern African Studies* 9, 2 (August 1971): 253–261.

NOTES TO CHAPTER 4

24. Dr. Jotham C. Momba makes this argument based on the colonial period in "Peasant Differentiation and Rural Party in Colonial Zambia," *Journal of Southern African Studies* 11, 2 (April 1985): 281-294, and extends the argument into the early independence period in other works forthcoming.

25. Sikota Wina took his post as minister of local government in the second cabinet, formed January 22, 1965.

26. Pettman, p. 247.

27. William Tordoff and Ian Scott, "Political Parties: Structures and Policies," *Politics in Zambia*, ed. W. Tordoff, p. 115.

28. Tordoff and Molteno, "Government and Administration," p. 247.

29. Molteno, "Cleavage and Conflict," and Tordoff and Scott, "Political Parties," pp. 62-106 and 107-154.

30. On February 25, 1972, President Kaunda gave a speech in which he referred to the party demands to end the multiparty system. "You know that since independence there has been a constant demand for the establishment of a One-Party State in Zambia. The demands have increasingly become more and more widespread in all corners of Zambia. In recent months I have received hundreds of messages and letters from organizations and individuals appealing to me to take concrete steps to bring about a One-Party system of Government. In the resolutions passed by almost every conference, whether political or non-political, unequivocal demands have been made for government to introduce a One-Party system of government."

31. Tordoff and Scott, "Political Parties," p. 139.

32. Included in these so-called entrenched clauses in the Independence Constitution were provisions protecting the rights of existing property owners (i.e., the mines owners and the expatriate farmers), protecting the independence of the judiciary, and requiring a referendum to change any of these conditions or to amend the constitution.

33. For a longer explanation of these events, see Patrick Ollawa, *Participatory Democracy in Zambia: The Political Economy of National Development* (Elms Court, Ilfracombe, Devon: Arthur H. Stockwell Ltd., 1979), pp. 254-260.

34. Ibid.

35. Tordoff and Molteno, "Government and Administration," p. 244.

36. Dennis Dresang, *The Zambian Civil Service* (Nairobi: East African Publishing House, 1975), p. 142.

37. Richard Hall, *The High Price of Principles: Kaunda and the White South* (Harmondsworth, U.K.: Penguin Books Ltd., 1973); the earlier Tordoff, *Politics*, and Fergus MacPherson's biography of Kaunda.

38. From the address by President Kaunda to the Ninth National Council of UNIP, September 20, 1976 in *Communocracy (A Strategy for Constructing a People's Economy Under Humanism)*—Address by His Excellency the President, Dr. K. D. Kaunda (1976).

39. For a sympathetic assessment of Humanism, see Tordoff's "Introduction to *Administration in Zambia*, (Manchester: Manchester University Press, 1980), pp. 24-30.

40. Turok, p. 24.

41. Anthony Martin, *Minding Their Own Business: Zambia's Struggle Against Western Control* (Harmondsworth, U.K.: Penguin Books, 1975), p. 39.

42. There was an Emergency National Development Plan in place at independence that served to 1966.

43. Zambia, Central Planning Office, *An Outline of the Transitional Development Plan* (Lusaka: Government Printer, 1965), pp. 41-48.

44. M.L.O. Faber, "A Future for Zambia's Copper Industry?," *Towards Economic Independence: Papers on the Nationalisation of the Copper Industry in Zambia*, ed. M.L.O. Faber and J. C. Potter (Cambridge: Cambridge University Press, 1972), p. 61.

45. Ann Seidman, "The Distorted Growth of Import Substitution: The Zambian Case," *Development in Zambia: A Reader*, ed. Ben Turok (London: Zed Press, 1979), pp. 101–102.

46. Taffere Tesfachew, "The Development, Growth Potential and Constraints of the Capital-Goods Industry in Zambia," Paper presented to the University of Zambia, Humanities and Social Science Seminar, Lusaka, March 28, 1985.

47. Alistair Young, *Industrial Diversification in Zambia* (New York: Praeger Publishers, 1973), p. 27.

48. Ibid., p. 149.

49. Ibid., p. 195

50. Robert Klepper, "Zambian Agricultural Structural and Performance," *Development in Zambia*, ed. Turok, p. 139.

51. Kenneth D. Kaunda, *Towards Complete Independence*, Address to UNIP National Council, Matero, August 11, 1969 (Lusaka: Government Printers, 1969), pp. 29.

52. Andrew A. Beveridge and Anthony R. Oberschall, *African Businessmen and Development in Zambia* (Princeton: Princeton University Press, 1979), review many of these early capitalist endeavors around Lusaka.

53. Young, p. 134.

54. Tordoff and Molteno, "Government and Administration," p. 274.

55. KK appointed Sardanis as full-time chairman and chief executive of INDECO in June 1965. After Mulungushi II, Sardanis was also appointed as the permanent secretary in trade, industry and mines and then took up the permanent secretary position in the new Ministry of State Participation with KK as minister.

56. The complex history of INDECO is outlined by Sheridan Johns, "The Parastatal Sector," *Administration in Zambia*, ed. Tordoff, pp. 104–129 and Ben Turok, "Control in the Parastatal Sector of Zambia," *Journal of Modern African Studies* 19, 3 (1981): 421–445.

57. Sheridan Johns offers a succinct definition for parastatal: the quasiautonomous governmental body outside the regular civil service structure and generally with wide latitude to conduct its own internal affairs. "The Parastatal Sector," p. 104.

58. Young, p. 195.

59. Kenneth Kaunda, Address to the National Council of UNIP, Mulungushi, November 9, 1968 (Lusaka: Government Printer, 1968), pp. iii–v.

60. Kaunda, *Towards Complete Independence*, p. 2.

61. Kaunda, *Zambia: Towards Economic Independence*, p. 49.

62. Martin, *Minding Their Own Business*, p. 170.

63. See Marcia M. Burdette, "The Dynamics of Nationalization between Multinational Companies and Peripheral States: Negotiations Between AMAX, Inc., the Anglo American Corporation of South Africa Ltd., and the Government of the Republic of Zambia" (Ph.D. dissertation, Columbia University, 1979), pp. 96–101 and pp. 226–290.

64. Ibid., Table 5, "Estimate of Service Contract Fees from RCM to AMAX, Corporate Years, 1970–1973" and Table 6, "Estimate of "Service Contract Fees from NCCM to Anglo, Corporate Years, 1970–1973," pp. 311 and 312.

65. Young, p. 199.

66. Although the phrase originated with Lenin, its exponent for Africa has been Ann Seidman to describe basic industries, imports, exports, internal wholesale trade, and financial institutions. See *Planning for Development in Sub-Saharan Africa* (Dar es Salaam: Tanzania Publishing House, 1974), p. 86.

67. Ben Turok, "The Penalties of Zambia's Mixed Economy," *Development in Zambia*, ed. Turok, p. 74.

68. This is the key phrase on the compensation of international companies under U.S. law in cases of confiscation, expropriation, and nationalization according to David Newsom, former undersecretary of state for African affairs, interview on September 2, 1977, Washington, D.C.

69. Kenneth D. Kaunda, *Take Up the Challenge . . . Speeches Made by His Excellency, the President, to the United National Independence Party National Council at Mulungushi Hall, November 7–10, 1970, Lusaka* (Lusaka: Government Printers, 1971), pp. 40 and 49–51.

70. For more background to Zambian state capitalism, see Peter Meyns, "The Political Economy of Zambia," *Beyond Political Independence: Zambia's Development Predicament in the 1980s*, ed. Klaas Woldring (Berlin: Mouton Publishers, 1984), pp. 15–17, and B. Turok, "Zambia's System of State Capitalism," *Development and Change* 11 (1980): 455–478.

71. Ministry of Development Planning and National Guidance, *Second National Development Plan: January 1972–December 1976* (Lusaka: Government Printers, 1971), p. 21.

72. Ibid., pp. 21–23.

73. Ibid.

74. Ibid., p. 23.

75. Zambia, Central Statistical Office, *Monthly Digest of Statistics* 2, 4 (April 1966) Table 3, p. 2, and *Monthly Digest of Statistics* 13, 4 and 5 (May 1977), Table 6(a), p. 5.

76. *Second National Development Plan*, p. 18.

77. Doris Jansen Dodge, *Agricultural Policy and Performance in Zambia: History, Prospects and Proposals for Change*, Institute of International Studies Research Series, no. 32 (Berkeley: University of California Press, 1977), p. 65.

78. *Second National Development Plan*, p. 1.

79. Seidman, p. 101.

80. Young, pp. 127–135.

81. Carolyn L. Baylies and Morris Szeftel, "The Rise of a Zambian Capitalist Class in the 1970s," *Journal of Southern African Studies* 8, 2 (April 1982): 191.

Notes to Chapter 5

1. ILO/JASPA, *Zambia: Basic Needs in an Economy Under Pressure: Findings and Recommendations of an ILO/JASPA Basic Needs Mission to Zambia* (Addis Ababa: ILO/JASPA, 1981), Table 0.1, p. xxi. Ralph Van der Hoeven in "Zambia's Economic Dependence and the Satisfaction of Basic Needs," *International Labour Review* 121, 2 (March/April 1982): 217–231, counted Zambia among the groups of countries with the highest income inequalities in the world.

2. President Kaunda's Address to the Third National Convention of the United National Independence party, July 24, 1984, p. 1.

3. National Debt Office quoted in Bank of Zambia, *1984 Annual Report*, p. 54.

4. The Zambian kwacha is now valued in terms of a basket of currencies for which the U.S. dollar is the intervention currency. Since July 1983 the GRZ has followed a flexible exchange rate policy, making periodic adjustments in the official

value of the kwacha. In October 1985 the country began to auction its foreign exchange, driving the value of the kwacha down to U.S. $0.16.

5. World Bank, *Zambia: Country Economic Memorandum: Issues and Options for Economic Diversification* (Washington, D.C., April 16, 1984), Table 3.03, p. 80.

6. Some of this decrease stemmed from a drop in copper production. The amount of blister and electrolytic copper produced declined from 702.1 thousand metric tons in 1974 to 640.3 thousand metric tons in 1975.

7. Ian Scott, "Party and Administration Under the One-Party State," *Administration in Zambia*, ed. William Tordoff (Manchester: Manchester University Press, 1980), pp. 146-157.

8. Zambia, *Constitution of Zambia and Chapter 1 of the Laws of Zambia* (Lusaka: Government Printer, n.d.), p. 12.

9. Scott, pp. 151-157.

10. The president and the national assembly form the parliament in Zambia. William Tordoff, "Residual Legislatures: The Cases of Tanzania and Zambia," *Journal of Commonwealth and Comparative Politics* 15, 3 (November 1977): 243.

11. For more details on the backgrounds of these new MPs see Tordoff, "Residual Legislatures," pp. 236-237 and 242.

12. Ibid., p. 240.

13. Ibid., pp. 243-247.

14. Rodger M. Chongwe, chairman of the Law Association of Zambia, "Foreword" to *Civil Liberties Cases in Zambia*, ed. Muna Ndulo and Kaye Turner (The African Law Reports: Oxford, 1984), pp. ix-xiii.

15. For example in July 1984 President Kaunda publicly exonerated a member of the central committee of UNIP for wrongdoings attributed to him by the wider public. TV Zambia, July 1984.

16. *Times of Zambia*, April 21, 1980, p. 1.

17. World Bank, *Zambia*, Table 8.04, p. 106.

18. Commodity Research Unit of New York, *1976 Report on Zambia*, p. 3.

19. For more details on the technical reasons for these cost increases, see Marcia Burdette, "Were the Copper Nationalizations Worthwhile?," *Beyond Political Independence: Zambia's Development Predicament in the 1980s*, ed. Klaas Woldring (Berlin: Mouton Publishers, 1984), pp. 23-71.

20. Information from RCM and NCCM marketing managers, interviewed in 1981.

21. Zambia, Central Statistical Office, *Monthly Digest of Statistics* 20, 12 (December 1984), Table 51, p. 48.

22. Zambia, Central Statistical Office, *Annual Agricultural Statistical Bulletin 1981* (November 1982), quoted in World Bank, *Zambia*, Table 7.01, p. 102.

23. World Bank, *Zambia*, Table 4.02, p. 87.

24. M. S. Nyirongo, general manager of ROP (1975) Ltd., "Industry in Zambia—Intentions versus Performance," *UNZA Business and Economics Journal* 1, 3 (June 1979): 9.

25. Patu Simoko, "What the Budget Means to Us All," *Times of Zambia*, Times Review, February 6, 1983, p. 3.

26. This phrase was originally used by A. C. Mills in "Dependent Industrialization and Income Distribution in Ghana," *Industrialization and Income Distribution in Africa*, ed. J. Rweyemamu (Senegal: Codesria, 1980), but the situation described pertains to Zambia as well.

27. The general conference of UNIP, September 1978, adopted amendments to the party constitution whose effect was to ban Kapwepwe, Nkumbula, and Robert

NOTES TO CHAPTER 5

Chiluwe from contesting the nomination within the party on the grounds that they had not been UNIP members for a sufficient length of time. Tordoff, *Administration in Zambia*, p. 263. Kapwepwe and Nkumbula petitioned the Supreme Court on the constitutionality of this matter, but in August 1979 their case was dismissed.

28. Tordoff, *Administration in Zambia*, p. 263.

29. For an overview of the corruption of the late 1970s and early 1980s, see Klaas Woldring, "Survey of Recent Inquiries and Their Results," *Beyond Political Independence*, ed. Woldring, pp. 183-207.

30. Morris Szeftel, "Political Graft and the Spoils System in Zambia—The State as a Resource in Itself," *Review of African Political Economy* 24 (May/August 1982): 4-21.

31. *African Research Bulletin*, Political Series 16, 3 (April 15, 1979): 5191.

32. Woldring, pp. 188-197, and Szeftel, pp. 4-21.

33. *African Contemporary Record* 13 (1980-1981), ed. Colin Legum, (New York: Africana Publishing Company, 1981), p. B902.

34. Ibid., p. B909.

35. Scott, p. 155.

36. Ibid., p. 156.

37. *Times of Zambia*, November 26, 1982, p. 1.

38. *Africa Contemporary Record*, 13, p. B909.

39. Zambia, Central Statistical Office, *Monthly Digest of Statistics* 20, 11 (December 1984), Table 1, p. 1.

40. Mining operations ceased in February 1984, but the concentrator was not shut until April. ZCCM Ltd., *1984 Annual Report*, Chairman's Statement, p. 5.

41. *Zambia Daily Mail*, February 5, 1984, p. 1, and *Times of Zambia*, Business Review, October 3, 1983, p. 4.

42. *Times of Zambia*, January 31, 1986, p. 1.

43. Mrs. H. C. Chilupe, Corporate and Economic Planning Department, INDECO Ltd., "The Manufacturing Industry in Zambia: Indeco's Experiences," A Paper presented to the University of Zambia workshop on "How to Increase the Share of Local Inputs for the Manufacturing Industry in Zambia," June 4-7, 1985, Mulungushi Hall, Lusaka, Zambia, p. 3.

44. *Sunday Times of Zambia*, July 22, 1984, p. 7.

45. *Times of Zambia*, March 23, 1983, p. 2.

46. According to the *Zambia Daily Mail* (June 13, 1985, p. 3) inflation was 23.6 percent in December 1984, and by March 1985 it had reached 31.9 percent. This was before auctioning, after which estimates have been that inflation increased from 100 to 150 percent.

47. World Bank, *Zambia*, Table 5.02, p. 91.

48. Bank of Zambia, *1984 Annual Report*, p. 54.

49. *Times of Zambia*, November 7, 1984, p. 1.

50. It could be argued that tensions appeared earlier when the U.S. $400 million drawing in 1978 was tied to reopening the border with Rhodesia in order to purchase fertilizer in October of that year.

51. Adrian P. Wood, "An Economy Under Pressure: Some Consequences of the Recession in Zambia," Paper presented to the Annual Conference of Institute of British Geographers, Durham, U.K., January 1984, p. 7.

52. Former minister of finance, Kebby Musokotwane, quoted in *Financial Review of Zambia* 1, 1 (June 1981): 12.

53. Interviews with ZCCM officials, confirmed by World Bank, *Zambia*, p. 29.

54. World Bank, *Zambia*, p. viii.

55. Ibid., Table 4.01, p. 86.

56. Bank of Zambia, *1984 Annual Report*, p. 10.

57. *Africa Research Bulletin*, Economic Series 22, 10 (November 30, 1985), p. 7970 B-C.

58. From conversations with members of the Ministry of Agriculture and Water Development, Planning Unit, 1984-1985. Also see Fred Roos, "External Aid Agencies," *Beyond Political Independence*, ed. K. Woldring, pp. 230-231, and Adrian Wood and W. Smith, "Zambia Up For Grabs? The Regionalisation of Agricultural Aid," unpublished paper, University of Zambia, Special Collections Library, 1984.

59. Of the U.S. $1.7 billion in bilateral loans through December 1983, approximately $1.1 billion came from the capitalist states and $619 million from the socialist ones. World Bank, *Zambia*, Table 4.01, p. 86.

60. In July 1985 foreign banks loaned Zambia K 243 million to cover the fuel bill.

61. World Bank, *Zambia*, p. 24.

62. Ibid., p. 29.

63. In March 1984, ZCCM was given these special privileges; later the 35 percent was cut to 25 percent or less. *Sunday Times of Zambia*, August 4, 1985, p. 5.

64. Representative of these opposing opinions are the ideas found in *The Guidelines for Formulation of the Fourth National Development Plan* (NCDP, Lusaka: March 1985).

65. J. Van Donge, "Planning for Chaos or Chaos in Planning?" Social Sciences Foundation Course, Correspondence Readings, 1975.

66. *Zambia Daily Mail*, January 21, 1983, p. 1.

67. Ibid., November 23, 1982, p. 1.

68. Woldring, pp. 200-204; *Africa Contemporary Record* 13 (1980-1981) pp. B898-899.

69. *Times of Zambia*, January 24, 1983, p. 2.

70. The leadership code was first outlined in general terms in August 1969 and in more concrete form in November 1970, but its implementation was postponed several times because of lack of cooperation within the governing class that would be most affected. The basic idea of the code was to outlaw leaders from having private business interests, other than small-scale enterprises or smallholding of land. The code has generally been violated, as the research by Carolyn Baylies and Morris Szeftel illustrates; see "The Rise of a Zambian Capitalist Class in the 1970s," *Journal of Southern African Studies* 8, 2 (April 1982): 187-213.

71. According to Woldring (pp. 200-201), Kaunda declared in April 1980 that "dissidents led by former Cabinet Ministers are behind a plot to incite the army into overthrowing the Government and assassinating me." He named Chipimo, Musakanya, Andrew Kashita (a former minister of mines and industry), and later implicated a manager of Barclays Bank, Zambia, Francis Nkhoma, and former minister of education and of finance, John Mwanakatwe. In October 1980 Chipimo, Musakanya, Patrick Chisanga, Shamwana, and others were arrested, although Chisanga and Chipimo were later released uncharged.

72. Ibid., p. 201. For a further analysis of the labor movement in Zambia today, see Michael Burawoy, "The Hidden Abode of Underdevelopment: Labour Process and the State in Zambia," *Politics and Society* 11, 2 (1982): 123-166.

73. *Africa Contemporary Record* 14 (1981-1982), p. B841.

74. *Zambia Daily Mail*, January 25, 1983, p. 1.

75. *Times of Zambia*, July 17, 1985, p. 2.

76. Ibid., June 11, 1985, p. 1.

77. Former Chiwala MP M. Banda, serving as a Zambian diplomat, was arrested in West Germany in connection with heroin smuggling in May 1983; former central committee member and cabinet minister Sikota Wina, along with Zambia Airways Marketing director Sam Kongwa, were picked up in 1983 in India for Mandrax smuggling; and Susan Chakulya, the wife of former minister of defense and member of central committee Wilson Chakulya, was jailed for two years in England for drug smuggling. *Times of Zambia*, March 8, 1984, p. 1.

78. *Sunday Times of Zambia*, January 6, 1984, p. 1.

79. According to evidence presented to a tribunal sitting in Lusaka and dealing with these drug cases (the Mandrax tribunal), "Mwaanga sent his assistant to London to deposit 114,980 South African rand in his account with the Bank of Credit and Commerce, International." *Zambia Daily Mail*, November 6, 1985, p. 1. In 1986 Mwaanga and twenty-three other Mandrax defendants were released from detention but had their passports confiscated. Mwaanga's side of the story is available in Vernon J. Mwaanga, *The Other Society: A Detainee's Diary* (Lusaka: Fleetfoot Publishing Co., 1986).

80. Frantz Fanon, *The Wretched of the Earth* (London: Penguin Books, 1980) pp. 122-123, and cited on Zambia by Gilbert Mudenda, "The Process of Class Formation in Contemporary Zambia," *Beyond Political Independence*, ed. Woldring, p. 147.

Notes to Chapter 6

1. The northern border with Zaire has also been troubled with repeated land disputes and even small incursions into Zambia, mostly over invasions in Shaba Province. A recent M.A. thesis by B. H. Zimba ("Zambian Policy towards Zaire, 1974-1978," Carleton University, Canada, 1979) traces some of these developments. Also territorial disputes with Malawi have cropped up from time to time. However, relations with the south have had an immediacy in Zambian foreign policy dictated by the fact that by 1965 almost 40 percent of Zambia's imports came from Rhodesia and another 22 percent from South Africa. Lionel Cliffe, "Zambia in the Context of Southern Africa," *The Evolving Structure of Zambian Society*, ed. Robin Fincham and John Markakis (Edinburgh: Centre of African Studies, University of Edinburgh, 1980), p. 243.

2. Richard Sklar, "Zambia's Response to the Rhodesian Unilateral Declaration of Independence," *Politics in Zambia*, ed. William Tordoff (Berkeley: University of California Press, 1974), p. 327.

3. Richard Sklar, *Corporate Power in an African State: The Political Impact of Multinational Mining Companies in Zambia* (Berkeley: University of California Press, 1975), p. 136.

4. Carol B. Thompson, *Challenge to Imperialism: The Frontline States in the Liberation of Zimbabwe* (Harare: Zimbabwe Publishing House, 1985), pp. 44-53 and pp. 63-65.

5. Sklar, "Zambia's Response," p. 327.

6. Sklar, *Corporate Power*, p. 152.

7. Sklar, "Zambia's Response," p. 340.

8. Sklar, *Corporate Power*, pp. 162-163.

9. W. Tordoff and Robert Molteno, "Introduction," *Politics in Zambia*, p. 30.

10. Backing for this assertion can be found in K. Eriksen, "Zambia: Class Formation and Détente," *Review of African Political Economy* 9 (May/August 1978): 10-11. John Stockwell, *In Search of Enemies* (New York: W. W. Norton, 1978),

offhandedly discusses how CIA policies towards Angola were based on friendly relations between KK, Savimbi, and Mobutu.

11. Eriksen, p. 10. The GRZ also supported Daniel Chipenda, a rival to Neto for the leadership of MPLA.

12. In 1971 the GRZ had deported 129 ZAPU guerrillas to Rhodesia, which, according to Eriksen, had the effect of bolstering the existing leadership (Nkomo) within ZAPU. Ibid., p. 9.

13. David Martin and Phyllis Johnson offer an account of these events in *The Chitepo Assassination* (Harare: Zimbabwe Publishing House, 1985). These two journalists drew on interviews with former Rhodesian security officers. Lionel Cliffe offers an academic assessment in "Zambia in the Context of Southern Africa," *The Evolving Structure*, pp. 240-261.

14. Martin and Johnson, passim.

15. "[I]n late 1974 and early 1975 in the Détente exercise, ... Zambia vigorously espoused a negotiated settlement of the Rhodesian issue, and indeed forced the Zimbabweans into a united body to negotiate and unilaterally forced a ceasefire, ahead of negotiations, by physical restraint of all the cadres of ZANU, which had been escalating the guerrilla war dramatically at that time." Cliffe, p. 245, and further comments on pp. 256-257.

16. Reuben Kamanga, then a member of the central committee of UNIP, said that the opening of the border had been discussed at several cabinet and central committee meetings and that "[d]uring all these meetings, we agreed that the only way we could save our agricultural industry [sic] was through the reopening of the southern route. *Times of Zambia*, October 12, 1978, cited in Thompson, pp. 62-63.

17. Thompson, p. 87, n. 16.

18. Cliffe, p. 247.

19. Ibid.

20. Thompson, pp. 62-64.

21. *Zambia Daily Mail*, October 20, 1982, p. 1.

22. Sklar, *Corporate Power*, p. 27.

23. Colin Legum, *Southern Africa: The Secret Diplomacy of Détente* (New York: Africana Publishing Company, 1975), passim.

24. Douglas Anglin, "Zambia and Southern African Détente," in *Zambia's Foreign Policy: Studies in Diplomacy and Dependence*, Douglas Anglin and Timothy Shaw (Boulder, Colo.: Westview Press, Special Series on Africa, 1979), pp. 272-309.

25. Zambia, *Dear Mr. Vorster . . . Details of Exchange Between President Kaunda of Zambia and Prime Minister Vorster of South Africa* (Lusaka: Information Services, 1971).

26. For example, in 1977 Kaunda (along with Nkomo) promoted independence for Rhodesia, *before elections*, which was violently opposed by the other Frontline presidents as well as ZANU. See Thompson, p. 60.

27. Marcia Burdette, "The Mines, Class Power and Foreign Policy in Zambia," *Journal of Southern African Studies*, 10, 2 (April 1984): 215.

28. Joseph Hanlon, *Beggar Your Neighbours: Apartheid Power in Southern Africa* (London: Catholic Institute for International Relations in collaboration with James Currey and Indiana University Press, 1986), p. 252.

29. Ibid., p. 246.

30. Thompson, p. 16.

31. Peter Meyns, "Non-Alignment and Regional Cooperation in Southern Africa," Paper read before the Fourth Biannual Conference on Liberation and Development of the African Association of Political Science, Harare, Zimbabwe, May 23-27, 1981, p. 23.

32. Thompson, p. 258–293.
33. "The Business of Liberation," *South Magazine* (December 1984), p. 69.
34. Information about SADCC to be found in Thompson, pp. 274–280.
35. See Reginald Green's annual summary on SADCC (1980–1984) in the *Africa Contemporary Record* and Arne Tostensen, *Dependence and Collective Self-Reliance in Southern Africa: The Case of SADCC*, Research Report, No. 62 (Uppsala: The Scandinavian Institute of African Studies, 1982).
36. Thompson, pp. 284–289, and Cliffe, pp. 257–259.
37. Syd Ullyett, deputy general manager of the Reserve Bank of Zimbabwe, "Hard Cash Realities on the PTA," *CZI Industrial Review* (October 1984), p. 5.
38. "The Remaking of Africa," *South Magazine* (December 1984), p. 68.
39. ZAMEFA has suffered from serious production and manpower problems bringing its capacity utilization rate in 1982 down to 20 percent of rated capacity, according to Patu Simoko, *Sunday Times of Zambia*, February 6, 1983, p. 3. There was marked improvement by 1985 when, according to a Dutch study, ZAMEFA was producing 5,000 tons per year out of total installation capacity of 6,000 tons. Jan W. Vingerhoets and Ad M. Sannen, *Fabrication of Copper Semi-Manufactures in Zambia: A Preliminary Assessment*. Technical University, Eindhoven and Tilburg University, the Netherlands, February 1985, p. 48.
40. Zambia, "Economic Memorandum," prepared by the Bank of Zambia with the assistance of Meridian International Bank Ltd., n.d. (c. 1983) p. 18.
41. Anglin and Shaw, "Introduction," *Zambia's Foreign Policy*, p. 11.
42. Ibid.
43. Meyns, p. 18.
44. "Zambia and the Recognition of Biafra," *African Review* 1, 2 (September 1971): 102–136.
45. Anglin and Shaw, p. 26.
46. *Africa Contemporary Record*, Political Series, 15 (1982–83) p. B876.
47. For further information on how the international banks have operated in Zambia, see Dr. Neva S. Makgetla, "Transnational Corporations and Banks in Zambia: The Changing Forms of Dependence," Paper presented to an Economics Seminar, October 1985, Lusaka, Zambia.
48. Karen A. Mingst, "Cooperation or Illusion? An Examination of the Intergovernmental Council of Copper Exporting Countries," *International Organization* 30, 2 (Spring 1976): 276–287.
49. Interview with former permanent secretary in Ministry of Finance, E. G. Kasonde, December 16, 1975.
50. Mingst, p. 282.
51. Interview with A. Kashita, November 21, 1975, Lusaka. At the Lusaka meeting, CIPEC representatives also discussed the possibility of a buffer stock of copper to be funded by the IMF. This came to naught, however, according to Simon Cunningham, *The Copper Industry in Zambia: Foreign Mining Companies in a Developing Country* (New York: Praeger, 1981), p. 216.
52. Interview with A. Kashita, December 4, 1975, in Lusaka.
53. E.I.U., *Quarterly Economic Review: Zambia*, no. 2 (1976): 13.
54. See Anglin and Shaw, pp. 23–25; Eriksen, p. 7, and Cliffe, p. 253.
55. Cliffe, p. 254.
56. Ibid., p. 253.
57. Adrian Wood and W. Smith, "Zambia Up For Grabs? The Regionalisation of Agricultural Aid," unpublished paper, 1984, p. 6. In the University of Zambia's Special Collections Library.

58. Wood and Smith, passim.
59. *Africa Research Bulletin*, Economic Series 22, 6 (July 31, 1985): 7814A.
60. Zambia, Central Statistical Office, *Monthly Digest of Statistics*, 21, 2 (February/March 1985), Table 23, p. 22.
61. Bank of Zambia, *Report and Statement of Accounts for the Year Ended 31st December 1984*, p. 58.
62. Zambia, *Monthly Digest*, 21, p. 22.
63. Lynn K. Mytelka, "The Lomé Convention and a New International Division of Labour," *Review of European Integration*, no. 1 (1977), Canada, p. 73.
64. UNDP, *Report on Development Cooperation in Zambia, 1984* (Lusaka: UNDP, Table III, p. 20.
65. Zambia, *Monthly Digest* 21, p. 22.
66. Ibid.

Notes to Chapter 7

1. *Africa Research Bulletin*, Political Series 22, 4 (May 15, 1985), p. 7622A.
2. *Africa Research Bulletin*, Economic, Financial and Technical Series, 20, 10, (October 15–November 14, 1983) p. 7048ABC.
3. Ibid.
4. This was borne out in riots on the Copperbelt and in Lusaka in December 1986 that claimed fifteen lives and left many private and state shops as well as several UNIP and government offices looted and burned. *Herald* (Zimbabwe), December 22, 1986.
5. In 1985 Zambia Breweries imported ten million beer bottles from Zimbabwe, worth more than K 1,300,000, to meet the shortfall created by a stoppage of production at Kapiri Glass Factory. *Zambia Daily Mail*, August 8, 1985, p. 5.
6. Clive Thomas, *Dependence and Transformation: The Economics of the Transition to Socialism* (New York: Monthly Review Press, 1974).
7. One of the more successful agricultural projects in Zambia is the Nakambala Suger Estates, which is run by the multinational giant Tate and Lyle.
8. Ken Good, "Systematic Agricultural Mismanagement: The 1985 'Bumper' Harvest in Zambia," unpublished paper, 1986, UNZA collection.
9. For a good review of the potentials and limitations of Zambia's informal sector see *African Social Research* 33, June 1982 (Gweru, Zimbabwe: published for the Institute for African Studies, Zambia, by Mambo Press).
10. One small-scale entrepreneur in Lusaka's townships began making shoes. He had initial success, given the high price of manufactured shoes in Zambia and high demand. Then in 1984 BATA shoes began to import the plastic "jelly bean" shoes, which were very cheap and durable and quickly drove the small man out of business.

Selected Bibliography

The bibliography is limited to the more pertinent documents cited in the text and a few additions.

Anglin, Douglas, and Shaw, Timothy. *Zambia's Foreign Policy: Studies in Diplomacy and Dependence.* Boulder, Colo.: Westview Press, Special Studies on Africa, 1979.

Baldwin, Robert. *Economic Development and Export Growth: A Study of Northern Rhodesia, 1920–1960.* Berkeley: University of California Press, 1966.

Bancroft, J. A. *Mining in Northern Rhodesia: A Chronicle of Mineral Exploration and Mining Development.* Bedford, U.K.: The Sidney Press Ltd., for the British South Africa Company, 1961.

Bank of Zambia, *Report and Statement of Accounts for the Years,* 1971–1985.

Bates, Robert. *Rural Response to Industrialization: A Study of Village Zambia.* New Haven: Yale University Press, 1976.

———. *Unions, Parties and Political Development: A Study of Mineworkers in Zambia.* New Haven: Yale University Press, 1971.

Baylies, Carolyn. "The State and the Growth of Indigenous Capital: Zambia's Economic Reforms and Their Aftermath." In *The Evolving Structure of Zambian Society,* ed. Robin Fincham and John Markakis. Edinburgh: Centre of African Studies, University of Edinburgh, May 30 and 31, 1980, pp. 198–227.

Baylies, Carolyn, and Szeftel, Morris. "The Rise of a Zambian Capitalist Class in the 1970s." *Journal of Southern African Studies* 8, 2 (April 1982): 187–213.

Berg, Leo van den (ed.). *Hard Times in the City.* "Studies in Zambian Society," no. 3. Lusaka: University of Zambia Publications, 1978.

Berger, Elena L. *Labour, Race and Colonial Rule: The Copperbelt from 1924 to Independence.* "Oxford Series in African Affairs." Oxford: Clarendon Press, 1974.

Beveridge, Andrew A., and Oberschall, Anthony R. *African Businessmen and Development in Zambia.* Princeton: Princeton University Press, 1979.

Bhagavan, M. R. *Zambia: Impact of Industrial Strategy on Regional Imbalance and Social Inequality.* Research Report, no. 44, to Scandinavian Institute of African Studies. Uppsala, Sweden, 1978.

Bodemeyer, Reinhard. "Administration for Development: The Effects of Decentralization on District Development in Zambia." *Materialien* 5 (Zentrum fur regionale Entwicklungsforschung der Justus-Liebig-Universitat, Giessen, West Germany, February 1984).

Bostock, Mark, and Harvey, Charles (eds.). *Economic Development and Zambian Copper: A Case Study of Foreign Investment*. New York: Praeger, 1972.

Bratton, Michael. "The Social Context of Political Penetration: Village and Ward Committees in Kasama District." In *Administration in Zambia*, ed. W. Tordoff. (Manchester: Manchester University Press, 1980): 213–239.

Burawoy, Michael. *The Colour of Class in the Copper Mines: From African Advancement to Zambianization*. Zambian Papers no. 7. Manchester: Manchester University Press, 1972.

———. "The Hidden Abode of Underdevelopment: Labour Process and the State in Zambia." *Politics and Society* 11, 2 (1982): 123–166.

Burdette, Marcia. "The Dynamics of Nationalization Between Multinational Companies and Peripheral States: Negotiations Between AMAX, Inc., the Anglo American Corporation of South Africa Ltd., and the Government of the Republic of Zambia." Ph.D. dissertation, Columbia University, 1979.

———. "The Mines, Class Power and Foreign Policy in Zambia." *Journal of Southern African Studies* 10, 2 (April 1984): 198–218.

———. "Were the Copper Nationalizations Worthwhile?" In *Beyond Political Independence: Zambia's Development Predicament in the 1980s*, ed. Klaas Woldring. (Berlin: Mouton Publishers, 1984): 23–71.

———. "Zambia." In *The Political Economy of African Foreign Policy: A Comparative Analysis*, ed. Timothy Shaw and Okajide Aluko (Aldershot, U.K.: Gower Press, 1984): 319–347.

Cliffe, Lionel. "Zambia in the Context of Southern Africa." In *The Evolving Structure of Zambian Society*, ed. R. Fincham and J. Markakis. Edinburgh: Centre of African Studies, University of Edinburgh, 1980, pp. 240–261.

Coleman, F. L. *The Northern Rhodesian Copperbelt, 1899–1962: Technological Development up to the End of the Central African Federation*. Manchester: for the Manchester University Press by Augustus M. Kelley Publishers, 1971.

Daniel, Philip. *Africanisation, Nationalisation and Inequality: Mining Labour and the Copperbelt in Zambian Development*. "Papers in Industrial Relations and Labour," no. 4. Cambridge: Cambridge University Press, 1979.

Davies, D. Hywel. *Zambia in Maps*. Sevenoaks, Kent, U.K.: Hodder and Stoughton Ltd., 1975.

Dodge, Doris Jansen. *Agricultural Policy and Performance in Zambia: History, Prospects and Proposals for Change*. Institute of International Studies Research Series, no. 32. Berkeley: University of California, 1978.

Dresang, Dennis. *The Zambian Civil Service*. Nairobi: East African Publishing House, 1975.

Dumont, René, and Mottin, Marie France. *Towards Another Development in Rural Zambia*. Report to the Government of the Republic of Zambia, 1980.

Eriksen, Karen. "Zambia: Class Formation and Détente." *Review of African Political Economy* 9 (May/August 1978): 4–26.

Faber, M.L.O., and Potter, J. C. *Towards Economic Independence: Papers on the Nationalisation of the Copper Industry in Zambia*. Cambridge: Cambridge University Press, 1972.

Fagan, B. M. "Early Farmers and Ironworkers (100 B.C. to A.D. 1500)." In *A Short History of Zambia*, ed. B. M. Fagan. Nairobi: Oxford University Press, 1966.

Franklin, Harry. *Unholy Wedlock: The Failure of the Central African Federation*. London: Allen and Unwin, 1963.

Fry, James. "An Analysis of Employment and Incomes Distribution in Zambia." Ph.D. dissertation, Nuffield College, University of Oxford, 1974.

SELECTED BIBLIOGRAPHY

Gertzel, Cherry. "Dissent and Authority in the One-Party State: Parliament, Party and President in the Second Republic, 1974-1976." University of Zambia, Special Collections Library. (Mimeographed.)

Gregory, Sir Theodore. *Ernest Oppenheimer and the Economic Development of Southern Africa*. Capetown, S.A.: Oxford University Press, 1962.

Hall, Richard. *The High Price of Principles: Kaunda and the White South*. Harmondsworth, U.K.: Penguin Books Ltd., 1973.

Hanlon, Joseph. *Beggar Your Neighbours: Apartheid Power in Southern Africa*. London: Catholic Institute for International Relations in collaboration with James Currey and Indiana University Press, 1986.

Hansen, Karen Tranberg. "'Bachelor Town' and the 'Immorality Issue': Economic Consequences of Colonial Ideologies for Women's Wage Labor in Post Colonial Lusaka, Zambia." Paper presented to symposium on Culture, Economy and Polity in the Colonial Situation, May 14-15, 1981. Department of Anthropology, University of Minnesota.

_____. "Negotiating Sex and Gender in Urban Zambia." *Journal of Southern African Studies* 10, 2 (April 1984): 219-238.

_____. "Urbanization Policy in Zambia? Uncertain Priorities." In *Contemporary Issues in African Urbanization and Planning*, ed. R. A. Obudho, Saleh El-Skakhs, Joseph Sarfoh, and Huosang Amirahmadi. Albany: State University of New York, forthcoming.

Harvey, Charles. "The Structure of Zambian Development." In *Development Paths in Africa and China*, ed. Ukandi Damachi, Guy Routh, and Abdel-Rahman E. Ali Taha. London: Macmillan, 1978, pp. 136-151.

Hazelwood, Arthur. "The Economics of Federation and Dissolution in Central Africa." In *African Integration and Disintegration: Case Studies in Economic and Political Union*, ed. A. Hazelwood. London: Oxford University Press, 1967.

Henderson, Ian. "Early African Leadership: The Copperbelt Disturbances of 1935 and 1940." *Journal of Southern African Studies* 11 (1975): 83-97.

_____. "The Origins of Nationalism in East and Central Africa: The Zambian Case." *Journal of African History* 11 (1970): 591-603.

ILO/JASPA. *Zambia: Basic Needs in an Economy Under Pressure: Findings and Recommendations of an ILO/JASPA Basic Needs Mission to Zambia*. Addis Ababa: ILO/JASPA, 1981.

Innes, Duncan. *Anglo American and the Rise of Modern South Africa*. New York: Monthly Review Press, 1984.

Jeker, Ralph. "Assessment of the Risks from a Developing Country's Point of View: Zambia." *Aussenwirtschaft* 33, 1-2 (1978): 109-127.

_____. "Commodity Price Stabilisation and the Compensatory Financing Facility in the International Monetary Fund: The Case of Zambia." *Aussenwirtschaft* 2, 32 (June 1977): 121-145.

Jules-Rosette, Bennetta. *Symbols of Change: Urban Transition in a Zambian Community*. Norwood, N.J.: Ablex Publishing Corporation, 1981.

Kandeke, Timothy. *Fundamentals of Zambian Humanism*. Lusaka: NECZAM, 1981.

Kashoki, Mubanga. "The Factor of Language in Zambia." Unpublished manuscript, University of Zambia, Institute for African Studies, 1982.

Kaunda, Kenneth D. *Humanism Part I* (1967) and *Humanism Part II* (1974). Lusaka: Government Printer.

_____. *Take Up the Challenge* (1971).

_____. *Towards Complete Independence* (1969).

_____. *The Watershed Speech* (June 30, 1975).

———. *Zambia: Towards Economic Independence* (1968).
Kay, George. *A Social Geography of Zambia*. London: University of London Press, 1967.
Keet, Dot. "The African Representative Council, 1946–1958: A Focus on African Political Leadership and the Politics of Northern Rhodesia." Master's thesis, University of Zambia, 1975.
Keller, Bonnie. "Marriage and Medicine: Women's Search for Love and Luck." *African Social Research* 26 (December 1978): 489–505.
Kessell, Norman. "The Mineral Industry and Its Effects on the Development of the Zambian Economy, 1945–70." Ph.D. dissertation, Leeds, 1971.
Knauder, Stephanie. *Shacks and Mansions: An Analysis of the Integrated Housing Policy of Zambia*. Lusaka: Multimedia Publications, 1982.
Legum, Colin. *Southern Africa: The Secret Diplomacy of Détente*. New York: Africana Publishing Company, 1975.
Mafeje, Archie. "The Ideology of Tribalism." *Journal of Modern African Studies* 9, 2 (1971): 253–261.
Markakis, John, and Curry, Robert L., Jr. "The Global Economy's Impact on Recent Budgetary Politics in Zambia." *Journal of African Studies* 3, 4 (Winter, 1976/77): 403–427.
Marter, Alan, and Honeybone, D. *The Economic Resources of Rural Households and the Distribution of Agricultural Development in Zambia*. Rural Development Studies Bureau Paper, University of Zambia, 1976.
Martin, Anthony. *Minding Their Own Business: Zambia's Struggle Against Western Control*. London: Hutchinson 1972; reprinted Penguin Books, 1975.
Martin, David, and Johnson, Phyllis. *The Chitepo Assassination*. Harare: Zimbabwe Publishing House, 1985.
———. *The Struggle for Zimbabwe: The Chimurenga War*. London and Boston: Faber and Faber, 1981.
Mezger, Dorothea. *Copper in the World Economy*. Translated by Pete Burgess. New York: Monthly Review Press, 1980.
Mingst, Karen. "Cooperation or Illusion? An Examination of the Intergovernmental Council of Copper Exporting Countries." *International Organization* 30, 2 (Spring 1976): 263–287
Mlenga, Kelvin. *Who's Who in Zambia, 1979*. Zambia: Roan Consolidated Mines Ltd., August 1979.
Momba, Jotham. "Peasant Differentiation and Rural Party Politics in Colonial Zambia." *Journal of Southern African Studies* 11, 2 (April 1984): 281–294.
Mudenda, Gilbert. "Class in Zambia—A Marxist Analysis." In *Beyond Political Independence: Zambia's Development Predicament in the 1980s*, ed. Klaas Woldring. (Berlin: Mouton Publishers, 1984): 129–160.
Mulford, David. *Zambia: The Politics of Independence, 1957–1964*. London: Oxford University Press, 1967.
Muntemba, M. S. "Thwarted Development: A Case Study of Economic Change in the Kabwe Rural District of Zambia, 1902–70." In *Roots of Rural Poverty in Central and Southern Africa*, ed. Robin Palmer and Neil Parsons. Berkeley: University of California Press, 1977.
———. "Women as Food Producers and Suppliers in the Twentieth Century: The Case of Zambia." *Development Dialogue* 1–2 (1982): 29–50.
Mytton, Graham. *Multilingualism in Zambia*. Zambia Broadcasting Services Research Project and Papers, no. 7. February 1973.

SELECTED BIBLIOGRAPHY

Ncube, Patrick D. "Notes on the Zambian Economy: Patterns of Investments and the Problem of Diversifying the National Economy." Paper read to the Local Government Association of Zambia, Annual Conference, june 23-26, 1980.
Nolutshungu, Sam. *South Africa in Africa: A Study in Ideology and Foreign Policy.* Manchester: Manchester University Press, 1975.
Ollawa, Patrick. *Participatory Democracy in Zambia: The Political Economy of National Development.* Elms Court, Ilfracombe, Devon, U.K.: Arthur H. Stockwell Ltd., 1979.
Parpart, Jane. *Labor and Capital on the African Copperbelt.* Philadelphia: Temple University Press, 1983.
Petras, James. "State Capitalism and the Third World." *Development and Change* 8 (January 1977): 1-17.
Pettman, Jan. *Zambia—Security and Conflict.* Lewes, Sussex, U.K.: Julian Friedmann Publishers Ltd., 1974.
Prins, Gwyn. *The Hidden Hippopotamus: Reappraisal in African History: The Early Colonial Experience in Western Zambia.* Cambridge: Cambridge University Press, 1980.
Quick, Stephen. *Humanism or Technocracy? Zambia's Farming Co-Operatives, 1965-1972.* Zambian Papers, no. 12. Published for the University of Zambia by Manchester University Press, 1978.
Roberts, Andrew. *A History of Zambia.* London: Heinemann, 1976.
Rural Development Bureau. "Female Headed Households in Chungu." Report prepared for BAM (Brothers to All Men), n.d., c. 1980-1981, Lusaka: UNZA. (Mimeographed.)
Saxby, John. "The Politics of Education in Zambia." Ph.D. dissertation, University of Toronto, 1980.
Schuster, Ilsa. *New Women in Lusaka.* Exploration in World Ethnography Series. Palo Alto: Mayfield Publishing Company, 1979.
Serpell, Robert. *Culture's Influence on Behavior.* London: Methuen, 1976.
Shaw, Timothy. *Dependence and Underdevelopment: The Development and Foreign Policies of Zambia.* Athens: Ohio University Press, 1976.
_____. "The Political Economy of Zambia." *Current History* (March 1982): 125-128 and 144.
Sklar, Richard. *Corporate Power in an African State: The Political Impact of Multinational Mining Companies in Zambia.* Berkeley: University of California Press, 1975.
Southall, Tony. "Zambia: Class Formation and Government Policy in the 1970s." *Journal of Southern African Studies* 7, 1 (October 1980): 91-108.
Stockwell, John. *In Search of Enemies.* New York: W. W. Norton, 1978.
Szeftel, Morris. "Conflict, Spoils and Class Formation in Zambia." Ph.D. thesis, Manchester University, 1978.
Thompson, Carol B. *Challenge to Imperialism: The Frontline States in the Liberation of Zimbabwe.* Harare: Zimbabwe Publishing House, 1985.
Tordoff, William (ed.). *Administration in Zambia.* Manchester: Manchester University Press, 1980.
_____. *Politics in Zambia.* Berkeley: University of California Press, 1974.
_____. "Residual Legislatures: The Cases of Tanzania and Zambia." *Journal of Commonwealth and Comparative Politics* 15, 3 (November 1977): 235-249.
Turok, Ben (ed.). *Development In Zambia: A Reader.* London: ZED Press, 1979.
_____. "The Penalties of Zambia's Mixed Economy," in *Development in Zambia*, ed. Ben Turok, pp. 71-86.
_____. "The State and Society," D209 Open University, December 1983 (mimeographed).

———. "Zambia's System of State Capitalism." *Development and Change* 11 (1980); 455-478.
Valentine, Theodore. "Income Distribution Issues in a Structurally Dependent Economy: An Analysis of Growing Income Inequality in Zambia." In *The Zambian Economy: Problems and Prospects*. Ottawa: IDRC, 1985.
Vingerhoets, Jan W., and Sannen, Ad M. *Fabrication of Copper Semi-Manufactures in Zambia: A Preliminary Assessment*. Technical University, Eindhoven and Tilburg University, the Netherlands, February 1985, pp. 1-100.
Woldring, Klaas (ed.). *Beyond Political Independence: Zambia's Development Predicament in the 1980s*. Berlin: Mouton Publishers, 1984.
World Bank. *Zambia: Country Economic Memorandum: Issues and Options for Economic Diversification*. Washington, D.C.: World Bank, April 16, 1984.
Wood, Adrian. "An Economy Under Pressure: Some Consequences of the Recession in Zambia." Paper Presented to the Annual Conference of Institute of British Geographers, Durham, U.K. 1984.
Wood, Adrian, and Smith, W. "Zambia Up For Grabs? The Regionalisation of Agricultural Aid." Unpublished paper, University of Zambia, Special Collections Library, 1984.
Young, Alistair. *Industrial Diversification in Zambia*. New York: Praeger Publishers, 1973.
Zambia. *Constitution of Zambia and Chapter 1 of the Laws of Zambia*, n.d.
———. *Mining Yearbook*, 1971-1982.
———. *National Assembly Debates*, 1977-1985.
———. *Operation Food Production*, 1980.
———. *Report of the Special Parliamentary Select Committee*, 1977.
Zambia. Bank of Zambia. "Economic Memorandum." Prepared with the assistance of Meridian International Bank Ltd., n.d. (c. 1983).
Zambia. Central Statistical Office. *Census of Population and Housing: Final Report, Vol. 1: Total Zambia*, 1973.
———. *1980 Census of Population and Housing: Preliminary Report*, 1981.
———. *1980 Census of Population and Housing: Analytical Report, Vol. 11, Demographic and Socio-Economic Characteristics of Zambian Population*, 1986.
Zambia. Ministry of Development and Planning. *Annual Review: Performance of the Zambian Economy*, 1975.
Zambia. Ministry of Development Planning and National Guidance. *Second National Development Plan, January 1972-December 1976*. Lusaka: Government Printer, 1971.
Zambia. National Commission for Development Planning, Office of the President. *Economic Review 1986 and Annual Plan 1987*. Lusaka: Government Printer, January 1987.
———. *Guidelines for Formulation of the Fourth National Development Plan*, March 1985.
———. *Third National Development Plan, 1979-1983*. October 1979.

Index

AAC. *See* Anglo American Corporation of South Africa Ltd.
African democratic socialism, 77
African Development Bank, 126, 157, 158
African Development Fund, 157
African Education, Ministry of, 65, 72
African National Congress (ANC) (1951) (N. Rhodesia/Zambia), 29, 30, 31, 32, 33, 65, 71, 73, 74, 97-98(table), 104
  split (1959), 31
  /UNIP coalition, 32
  See also Zambia African National Congress
African National Congress (ANC [SA]) (South Africa), 143, 144, 145, 168
African National Congress (ANC [Z]) (Zimbabwe), 141
African nationality, 39-40
African Representative Council (ARC), 28
African trade, 3, 35, 37, 82, 133-134, 143-145, 147-149
  and colonialism, 13
  early, 7, 9, 10
  See also Transport, links
Afrikaners, 3, 24, 144
Agency for International Development (AID), U.S., 166
Agricultural implements factory, 87
Agriculture, 1, 110
  black capitalist, 94
  cash, 23, 34, 82, 85
  chitemene, 21, 56
  commercial, 3, 78, 83, 85, 92, 93, 96, 117, 119, 120, 124
  crops, 21, 83, 85, 119
  development, 3, 23, 27, 36, 82-83, 84, 85, 91, 103, 114, 120, 157, 159, 162, 164, 166
  early, 7, 10
  floodplain, 14
  industry, 165
  inputs, 117, 120, 166
  labor force, 20, 21, 37
  land, 14, 22, 83, 94, 166
  peasant, 3, 23, 27, 35, 56, 71, 83, 93, 119, 120, 166-167

prices, 166
production, 21, 83, 93, 113, 117, 119, 120, 166
white settler, 14, 15, 20, 22, 23, 93-94
Agriculture, Ministry of, 72
Agriculture and Water Development, Ministry of, 114
AID. *See* Agency for International Development
Airlines, 134
Airport, 84, 90, 136
AMAX, Inc., 86(table), 87, 103, 152
American Metals Company, 18. *See also* AMAX, Inc.
Amethysts, 161, 162
Amin, Idi, 150
ANC. *See* African National Congress (N. Rhodesia/Zambia)
ANC (SA). *See* African National Congress (South Africa)
ANC (Z). *See* African National Congress (Zimbabwe)
Anglicans, 59
Anglin, Douglas, 150
Anglo American Corporation of South Africa Ltd. (AAC), 17, 18(table), 19, 82, 86, 87, 103, 144, 152
Anglo-German accord (1890), 12
Anglo-Portuguese Convention (1891), 13
Angola, 6, 10, 130, 133, 135, 139, 145, 146, 150
  colonial, 11, 13, 134, 138
  and Cuba, 138, 155
  and PRC, 138
  and South Africa, 138, 144
  and Soviet Union, 138, 139
  and U.S., 138, 139
  and Zambia, 110, 136, 137, 138, 139, 144, 155, 168
Annfield, A. Pierce, 127
Anode casting plant, 88
Anthrax, 14
Antiracism, 77, 133, 151
Apamwamba. See Wealthy class

197

INDEX

Apartheid, 3, 133, 151
Arabs, 5, 8(fig.), 9
ARC. See African Representative Council
Archaeology, 6-7
Army, 115, 127
Art, 48, 49, 62
Asian nationality, 39, 40, 89
Attorney general, 72
Auctioning. See under Foreign exchange
Austerity budget (1978), 97-98(table), 113, 142, 163-164
Automobiles, 41, 42, 53, 165
Azania, 150

"Back to the land" policy, 3, 95, 119
Balance of payments, 2, 160
Balance-of-trade accounts, 92, 95-96, 113, 122
Baluba mine, 18
Bancroft mine, 17, 18(table)
Banda, Dingiswayo, 71
Banda, Hastings, 29
Bang'anga, 62
Bangladeshis, 40
Bangweulu, Lake, 35
Bank of Zambia, 113, 115, 122, 124
Banks, 17, 86(table), 88-89
Bantu (language), 46
Baptists, 59
Barclays Bank, 17, 86(table)
Barotseland, 11, 13, 14, 15, 22, 30, 56, 71, 83
Barotse people, 38
Basic needs, 43, 165
Basketry, 49, 51(illus.)
Baylies, Carolyn L., 94
Beads, 9
Beatty, Alfred Chester, 17, 18
Beer, 59, 162, 190(n5)
  surtax, 121
Beira (Mozambique), 134, 135(fig.), 136, 140
Belgium, 6, 11, 12
Bemba (language), 46
Bemba people, 8(fig.), 9, 13, 20, 35, 38, 56
  crafts, 49, 50(illus.)
  and Federation, 25
  in government, 73
Bemba plateau, 35
Benguela Railway, 135, 136, 138, 139, 140
Benson Constitution. See Federation of Rhodesia and Nyasaland, Constitution
Berlin, Conference of (1884-1885), 11
Biafra (Nigeria), 150
Bicycles, 36
Big game hunters, 11
Bisa people, 8(fig.), 9, 35
Blacksmiths, 49
Boer republics. See Orange Free State; Transvaal
Boers, 9
Bomas, 38
Bordering countries, 6
Botha, P. W., 144
Botswana, 6, 135(fig.), 143, 145, 146
  and Zambia, 140, 142, 146
Bridewealth. See Lobola

Bridges, 120, 146
British South Africa Company (BSAC), 12, 13, 14, 15, 16, 17, 19, 24, 81
  landholdings, 22
Broken Hill. See Kabwe
Broken Hill Man, 6-7
Brown Commission Report (1966), 83
BSAC. See British South Africa Company
Building societies, 54, 86(table), 88, 89
Bulozi floodplain, 10
Burlap plant, 84
Bwana Mkubwa Mine, 16, 17, 18(table), 117

Cabinet, 69-70, 71-72. See also under Kaunda, Kenneth David
Cabora Bassa Dam (Mozambique), 148
Canada, 158
Canals, 56
Capacity utilization rates, 118, 119
CAPCO. See Central African Power Corporation
"Cape to Cairo Railroad," 12
Capital (Zambia). See Lusaka
Capital goods, 82, 114, 161
Capitalism, 71, 90, 93
Caprivi Strip, 12
Cassava, 21, 83
Catholicism, 59, 60
Cattle, 7, 9, 13, 22
  diseases, 3, 7, 14, 23
Cement, 91
Central Africa, 6, 7, 9, 11
Central African Airways Corporation, 134
Central African Federation. See Federation of Rhodesia and Nyasaland
Central African plateau, 5, 11
Central African Power Corporation (CAPCO), 134, 136
Central Cigarette Manufacturers, 89
Central Intelligence Agency (CIA), 138
Centralized kingship (*litunga*), 10
Central Province, 22, 38
Chad, 151
Chambishi mine, 18, 118
Changufu, Lewis, 31
Chawinga, Christopher, 127
Chewa speakers, 8(fig.), 9, 16
Chibuku, 59
Chibuluma mine, 18
Chieftainship, 9, 10-11, 15, 175(n6)
Chikerema, James, 141
Chilanga Cement Ltd., 91
Children, 44
Chile, 87, 152
Chilelabombwe, 17
Chiluba, Frederick, 129, 167
Chimba, Justin, 30, 66(table), 71, 75
China, People's Republic of (PRC), 112, 138
  and Zambia, 136, 140, 147, 156, 157
Chinkuli, Kingsley, 167
Chinsali, 30
Chinsali District (Northern Province), 61
Chipata, 22, 46, 136
Chipimo, Elias, 97-98(table), 110, 186(n71)

INDEX

Chirwa, Dennis, 127
Chisanga, Patrick, 186(n71)
Chisata, John, 31, 66(table)
Chitenge, 37, 46, 49
Chitepo, Herbert, 141
Chitimukulu (Bemba chief), 9
Choma, 94
Chona, Mainza, 31, 66(table), 72, 74, 128
Christianity, 34, 44, 59, 71, 77
Chungu (chief), 35
CIA. *See* Central Intelligence Agency
c.i.f. *See* Cost-insurance-freight
CIPEC. *See* Intergovernmental Council of Copper Exporting Countries
Civil rights, 77
Civil service, 66, 69, 71, 76, 78, 94, 104, 106, 116, 121, 126, 168
  personal accumulation, 93
  politicized, 69, 93
  reshuffling, 69–70, 75
  wages, 83, 97–98(table), 121
  whites in, 66
Class, 34, 40–42, 43, 48, 52, 63, 84, 94, 160, 163
  alliances, 64
  friction, 95
  See also Governing class; Peasants; Petite bourgeoisie; Wealthy class; Working class
"Click sound," 51
Cliffe, Lionel, 56, 142
Cloth, 9, 165. *See also Chitenge*
Clothes, 37, 41, 42, 46, 49
Coal, 14, 27, 78, 134, 161
Cobalt, 1, 6, 81, 101, 102(table), 111, 118, 158
  prices, 99–100(table), 111
Coffee, 158
Coke, 14, 134
Colonial rule, 5, 6, 11, 12, 13–14, 15–24, 28, 34, 43, 47
Color bar, 20, 27, 28
Coloureds, 39, 40
Colson, Elizabeth, 11
Commerce and Health, Ministry of, 71
Commodity Research Unit, 111
Commonwealth countries, 161
Commonwealth Group of Experts (1975–1976), 149
Comprador, 128
"Comrade Bonzo," 46
Comrie, William, 28
Congo. *See* Zaire
Congo Free State, 11
Consolidated Tyre Services (CTS), 118
Constitution
  1964, 74, 75, 76, 181(n32)
  1973, 97–98(table), 104
Constitutional and Statutory expenditure, 68, 180(n14), 121
Construction firms, 91
Consumer goods, 2, 41, 43, 82, 91, 96, 98
  pricing, 42, 120, 125
Consumer price index, 91, 120
Consumption, 2
Cooperative farms, 85

Cooperatives, Ministry of, 114
Copper, 1, 6, 13, 15, 17, 20, 23, 26, 110, 151–152, 158, 161
  artifacts, 7
  cartel, 111, 133, 151, 152–154
  fabricating project, 84
  flotation process, 17, 19
  and GDP, 80(table), 101, 102(table), 110
  mine, first, 16
  mines, 6, 13, 16, 17, 18, 19, 28, 91, 97–98(table), 117, 118, 154
  mining, 9, 13, 14, 16, 17
  nationalization, 87, 88
  operating costs, 124
  prices, 1, 64, 78, 79(fig.), 85, 91, 96, 98, 99–100(table), 101, 103, 110, 113, 117, 152, 153, 154
  processed, 147
  production, 19, 26, 31, 64, 91, 96, 111, 117, 154
  production costs, 111, 112–113, 118, 126, 161
  profits, 23, 81, 86, 87, 91, 112, 137
  slump, 86(table), 92, 94, 95, 103, 110, 117, 162
  substitutions for, 118, 164
  See also Copperbelt; Exports
Copperbelt, 14, 15, 16–19, 23, 26, 30, 31, 81, 82, 116, 134
  energy supply, 136
  lingua franca, 46
  mechanization in, 126
  population, 26, 165
  riots, 129
  taxes, 19
  wages, 26, 28
  working conditions, 20, 28
  world supply percentage of, 26
  See also Mining towns; Trade unions
Copperbelt Province, 38, 74
Corruption, 95, 96, 97–98(table), 110, 115–116, 130–131, 167
Corrupt Practices Act (1980), 97–98(table), 115
Cost-insurance-freight (c.i.f.), 111, 112, 117
Cotton, 119, 158, 165
Coup attempt (1980), 2, 97(table)
Crafts, 48–49, 50–51, 59, 62
Credit, 94
Crime, 26, 34, 42, 163
Crocodile Clan, 9
Crown lands, 22
CTS. *See* Consolidated Tyre Services
Cuba. *See under* Angola
Cultural transformation, 34, 44, 45–46, 48, 52, 62
Currency. *See* Kwacha
Customary law, 22

Dams, 148. *See also* Kafue Dam; Kariba Dam
Dance, 49, 51
Dar es Salaam (Tanzania), 112, 135(fig.), 136, 140
Davis, Edmund, 16, 17
Death, 44

De Beers (company), 12, 17
Debt, 2, 96, 97–98(table), 110, 113, 124, 160, 169
  servicing, 121
Decentralization program (1980), 129
Decolonization, 40, 149
Defense, 71, 76, 106, 163
Deindustrialization, 161, 164
Denationalization, 162, 164
Destabilization, 168
Detribalization, 37
Development Planning and National Guidance, Ministry of, 69
Development Planning Division, 69
Diamond mines (S. Africa), 12
Diet, 41
District council areas, 53
Dos Santos, Eduardo, 145
Drought, 113, 117, 119
Drugs and nutritional foods plant, 84
Drug trade, 2, 97–98(table), 130
Dry season, 7, 42
Duly Motors, 116
Duncan, Gilbey & Matheson (company), 89
Dunlop Zambia Ltd., 91
Durban (S. Africa), 143
Dutch. *See* Netherlands

East African Common Market, 146
Eastern Bloc, 136, 156, 157
Eastern Province, 22, 38(table), 137, 164
East London (S. Africa), 143, 145
Economic Crusade (1984), 97–98(table)
Economic nationalism, 148
Economic pricing, 120, 126
Economism, 129
Economy, 40, 62, 133, 160, 168–169
  colonial, 5, 19–20, 23–24, 32
  of First Republic, 64, 65, 77, 78–94, 95
  foreign domination of, 5, 64. *See also* Foreign investment
  1960s, 78, 151, 153
  1970s, 1, 2, 95, 96, 97–98(table), 98–104, 110–114, 116, 142, 149
  1980s, 1–2, 96, 117–127, 132, 139, 163–164
  recommendations for, 162, 164–166
  rural, 35, 37. *See also* Agriculture, development
  urban, 91
Education, 27, 41, 42, 43, 62, 64, 65–66, 68, 163, 178(n10)
  abroad, 28, 30, 41, 93
  colonial, 47, 66
  enrollments, 67
  expenditure on, 68, 121
  official language of, 46, 47
  primary and secondary, 67
  See also Hone, Evelyn, College; University of Zambia; Zambia Institute of Technology
EEC. *See* European Economic Community
EFTA. *See* European Free Trade Association
Egalitarianism, 77
Elections, 1
  boycotts, 31
  1962, 32, 65, 66(table)
  1964, 65, 66(table)
  1967, 73
  1968, 73
  1971, 74
  1973, 97–98(table), 104
  1978, 97–98(table)
  1979, 115
  1983, 97–98(table), 161
Electoral system, 2, 32, 65
Electricity, 42, 54, 78, 84, 89, 90, 134, 136, 163
  export of, 148
Elite, 1, 2, 40, 163. *See also* Governing class; Wealthy class
Elizabethville. *See* Lubumbashi
Emeralds, 161, 162
Emergency airlifts, 140
Emergent farmers, 85
Energy sources, 134, 135–136. *See also* Electricity
English (language), 37, 46, 47–48, 55
Ethiopia, 148
Ethnic groups, 5, 6, 7–9, 10, 11, 35, 38
Ethnicity, 34, 38–40, 43. *See also* Tribalism
Ethnoregionalism, 64, 65, 70–73, 75, 95, 160
Europe, 9, 11, 23
European Economic Community (EEC), 126, 157, 158, 159
European Education, Ministry of, 66
European Free Trade Association (EFTA), 158
European nationality, 39, 40
Expatriate farmers, 3
Explorers, 11
Exports, 1, 19, 23, 64, 78, 80(table), 81, 96, 98, 99–100(table), 101, 102(table), 110, 117, 121, 126, 143, 145, 147, 148, 154, 158, 159, 164. *See also* African trade; International trade; Western trade
Extension services, 94

Faber, Michael L.O., 81, 82
Fabian socialism, 28, 77
Fagan, Brian M., 7
Faith healing, 59, 62
Family, 44–45, 55–56, 63, 95. *See also* Women
Famine relief, 26
Fanon, Frantz, 131
Favoritism, 161
Federation of African Societies, 29
Federation of Rhodesia and Nyasaland (1953–1963), 24–27, 30–32
  Constitution (1959), 26, 31
Fertilizer, 84, 117, 120, 164, 165
Finance, Ministry of, 69, 71, 122
Finance and Development Corporation (FINDECO), 86(table), 89
FINDECO. *See* Finance and Development Corporation
First National Development Plan (FNDP) (1966–1971), 84–85, 89, 90, 91, 92, 93, 136
Flood, 97–98(table), 115

INDEX

FLS. *See* Frontline States
FNDP. *See* First National Development Plan
FNLA. *See* National Front for the Liberation of Angola
Food and Agriculture Organization, 161
Food processing, 84, 91, 165
Food shortages, 83
Food subsidies, 113
F.o.r. *See* Free on rail
Foreign Affairs, Ministry of, 76
Foreign aid, 36, 96, 118, 122, 125–126, 156–158, 159, 164, 169
Foreign exchange (FOREX), 86, 90, 92, 95, 96, 98, 103, 112, 113, 114, 115, 117, 118, 119, 126, 147, 163, 165, 166
  auctioning, 97–98(table), 124–125, 165
  restrictions, 123, 124
Foreign investment, 85, 88, 89, 91, 148, 162
Foreign policy, 164, 168
  regional, 3, 110, 133–149, 150–151, 157, 168
  and Third World, 3, 133, 149–154
  See also individual countries, and Zambia; *under* Kaunda, Kenneth David
Forests, 7
FOREX. *See* Foreign exchange
Forward purchasing system, 152
Freedom House, 76, 106
Freehold tenure, 107
Free market, 166
Free on rail (f.o.r.), 111, 112
Frei, Eduardo, 152
FRELIMO. *See* Front for the Liberation of Mozambique
FROLIZI. *See* Front for the Liberation of Zimbabwe
Front for the Liberation of Mozambique (FRELIMO), 137, 138, 140, 141
Front for the Liberation of Zimbabwe (FROLIZI), 141
Frontline States (FLS), 139, 142, 144, 145–146, 149, 151
Fuel shortage, 97–98(table), 124, 145

Gaberone (Botswana), 143
Gandhian passive resistance, 28, 30
GDP. *See* Gross domestic product
Geography, 5–6
Germany, 11, 12, 19. *See also* West Germany
Ghana, 164
Gladstone, William E., 12
Glass, 87, 165
GNP. *See* Gross national product
Gold, 7, 9, 12, 13, 17, 161, 162
Gore-Browne, Stewart, 20, 24
Governing class, 3, 64, 65, 76, 83, 84, 92, 93, 94, 95, 116, 121, 126, 127, 130, 149, 161, 163, 167
  defined, 174(n6), 179(n1)
Government, 1, 2, 167–168
  African-led (1962), 32, 33
  assets, 89
  budget deficits, 120, 121, 126
  colonial, 15–16, 19–20, 22, 25, 29
  expenditures, 68, 96, 113, 120–121, 126, 163

Federation, 25–26
First Republic (1964–1972), 64, 65–70, 75–77, 94, 95
  headquarters. *See* State House
  inefficiency, 95. *See also* Corruption
  levels of, 104
  revenues, 78, 80(table), 81, 92, 96, 98, 101, 102(table), 103, 110, 113, 114, 120, 137
  scandals, 115
Second Republic (1973), 93, 97–98(table), 106–107
  See also Debt; Governing class; One-party rule; Political opposition
Great Britain, 5, 6, 11–12, 13, 15–24, 28, 134, 135
  and Zambia, 41, 133, 151, 155, 157, 158
Great Depression (1929), 19, 52
Great East Road, 84, 90, 136
Great North Road, 84, 90, 136
Grindlays (bank), 86(table), 88
Grocery stores, 42
Gross domestic product (GDP), 2, 26, 80(table), 81, 90, 91, 101, 102(table), 103, 113, 117
Gross national product (GNP), 178(n11)
Groundnuts, 119(table)
Group of 77 (UNCTAD), 149
GRZ (Government of the Republic of Zambia). *See* Government
Guns, 9, 13
Gwembe Valley, 162

Haamaundu, G., 127, 128
Hansen, Karen Tranberg, 52
Harare (Zimbabwe), 27, 142
Hazlewood, Arthur, 26
Headman, 15
Health, Ministry of, 62, 71
Health care, 26, 62, 64, 66, 67–68, 163
  expenditure on, 68, 121
Heineken (Dutch company), 162
Heinz (U.S. company), 162
Herbalists, 62
"Highlife" music, 51
Home Affairs, Ministry of, 72
Hone, Evelyn, College, 129
Housing, 1. *See also under* Rural areas; Urban areas
Housing and Social Development, Ministry of, 72
Hove, Richard, 147
Humanism, 77, 90, 93, 95, 107, 126, 127
Humanism Parts I and II (Kaunda), 77
Hunting, 35
Hut tax, 14
Hydroelectric power, 84, 90, 134, 136, 148
Hygiene, 26

IBRD (International Bank for Reconstruction and Development). *See* World Bank
IDA. *See* International Development Association
IFC. *See* International Finance Corporation
Ila people, 7, 8(fig.), 29, 71

ILO. *See* International Labour Organisation
IMF. *See* International Monetary Fund
Imperialists, 11, 12
Import licensing, 92, 113, 125, 126
Imports, 49, 82, 92, 96, 98, 101, 103, 110, 112, 113, 114, 117, 123, 124, 125, 143, 147, 159, 164, 165
 food, 3, 82, 119, 143
Import-substitution strategy, 2, 84, 92, 126, 161, 165
Income gap, 27, 43, 62
INDECO. *See* Industrial Development Corporation
Indeni, 90
Independence (1964), 1, 28, 65
India, 130
Indians, 40
Indirect rule, 15
Industrial Development Act (1977), 97–98(table)
Industrial Development Corporation (INDECO), 82, 85, 86(table), 89, 118, 119
 Milling Company, 91
Industrialization, 2, 26, 48, 103
Industry, 78, 91, 92, 101, 113, 120, 161
Inflation, 95, 96, 97–98(table), 103, 110
Informal sector, 59, 163, 167
Information and broadcasting, 121
Infrastructure, 84, 85, 90, 92, 120, 121(table), 126, 161. *See also* Railroads; Roads
Ingombe Ilede, 7, 8(fig.)
Insurance companies, 86(table), 88, 89
Intergovernmental Council of Copper Exporting Countries (CIPEC), 151, 152–154
Intermediate goods, 2, 82, 114
International Bank for Reconstruction and Development (IBRD). *See* World Bank
International Development Association (IDA), 97–98(table)
International Finance Corporation (IFC), 126
International Labour Organisation (ILO), 2, 42, 43
International lenders. *See* International Monetary Fund; Paris Club; World Bank
International Monetary Fund (IMF), 2, 96, 97–98(table), 122–124, 126, 132, 142, 157, 158, 162, 166
International trade, 1, 2, 95, 136, 152–154, 157–158, 159
 early, 9
 See also African trade; Western trade
Investment, 78, 84, 85, 116, 121, 126, 162. *See also* Foreign investment
Iron, 7, 9
Iron Age, 7
Iron and steel industry, 27, 87
Ivory, 7, 9, 13

Japan, 1, 147, 157–158, 159
Jazz, 51
Jehovah's Witnesses, 60
Johnston, Harry, 13
Joint ventures, 78, 85, 86(table), 116, 162

Judicial Service Commission, 107
Judiciary, 107, 161
Justice, Ministry of, 72

K. *See* Kwacha
Kabalala, 42
Kabulonga (Lusaka suburb), 41–42, 52
Kabwata Cultural Village (Lusaka), 49–50
Kabwe, 6, 13, 16, 17, 19, 46, 90
Kabwe Industrial Fabrics Ltd., 91
Kafironda Explosives (company), 91
Kafue Dam (1972), 90, 136, 148
Kafue "Hook," 16
Kafue River, 13, 16, 27
Kafue Textiles of Zambia, 46, 91, 119, 165
Kalambo Falls, 6, 8(fig.)
Kalengwa mine, 18
Kalingalinga (Lusaka slum), 42, 52
Kalomo District, 94
Kalulu, Solomon, 72
Kalulushi East mine, 154
Kalundu, 42
Kaluwa, George, 29
Kaluwe, 164
Kamanga, Reuben, 30, 71, 72
Kansanshi mine, 14, 18(table), 118, 154
Kanyama flood (1978), 97–98(table), 115
Kaonde (language), 46
Kaonde speakers, 8(fig.), 38
Kapiri Glass (company), 165
Kapwepwe, Simon, 30, 31, 32, 66(table), 71, 72, 73, 74, 75, 93, 97(table), 104, 105(table), 114, 115, 144
Kariba, Lake, 5, 6
Kariba Dam, 7(illus.), 27, 84, 134
Kashita, Andrew, 154, 186(n71)
Kasonde, Emmanuel, 128
Katanga Pedicle, 6, 12
Katanga Province. *See* Shaba Province
Katilungu, Lawrence, 28, 30, 31
Kaunda, David, 29, 109(table)
Kaunda, Kenneth David (KK), 1, 35, 59, 97–98(table), 109(table), 127, 128, 130, 160, 167, 186(n71)
 agricultural policy, 3, 119
 and ANC, 29, 30
 cabinet, 71–72, 75, 104, 106
 and CIPEC, 152
 and civil service, 69, 70
 doctrine. *See* Humanism
 and economy, 84, 85, 86, 87, 88, 89, 90, 103, 110, 117, 122, 142, 149
 father. *See* Kaunda, David
 and FLS, 145, 151
 and foreign policy, 3, 133, 136, 137, 138, 139, 142, 144, 145, 149, 150, 151, 155, 159, 168
 life-style, 107
 and military, 168
 as minister, 32
 mother, 109(table)
 and OAU, 149–150
 opposition to, 108, 110, 114, 115
 popularity, 107

INDEX

portrait, 108
power, 75, 76, 106, 107, 110, 115, 161
as president of First Republic, 66(table), 75–77
as president of Second Republic, 97–98(table), 104, 106, 107, 108–110, 184(n10)
and PTA, 147
and successor, 2, 161
and UNIP, 32, 71, 72, 73, 74, 75, 76
and ZANC, 31, 32
Kazangula road, 146
Kazembe, Mwata (Lunda chief), 9
Kazembe people, 35
Khama, Seretse, 145
Kimberley diamond mines (S. Africa), 12
Kingdoms, 9, 13
Kissinger, Henry, 141
Kiswahili (language), 77
Kitwe, 26
KK. See Kaunda, Kenneth David
Klepper, Robert, 82
Kololo people, 8(fig.), 10
Konkola, Dixon, 31
Konkola III shaft, 118
Korean War (1950–1953), 26
Kuomboka ceremony, 10
Kwacha (K), 98, 180(n2), 183–184(n4)
devaluation, 96, 97–98(table), 122–123, 124
floated, 124

Lakes, 5, 6, 35
Lamba people, 8(fig.), 16
Lancaster House Constitutional Conference on Zimbabwe (1979), 151
Land
alienation, 20, 22
availability, 63
categories, 22
conflicts, 9, 16
fertility, 22
holdings, 94
productive capacity, 22
tenure, 107
See also under Agriculture
Lands and Natural Resources, Ministry of, 72
Language, 46–48
official, 46
Lead, 13, 16, 19, 81, 161
Leadership Code (1973), 93, 128, 186(n70)
Legum, Colin, 151
Lenje speakers, 71
Lenshina, Alice, 61
Leopold II (king of Belgium), 11, 12
Lesotho, 146
Lever Brothers (company), 82, 89
Lewanika (Lozi king), 10, 13
Liberalism, 77
Limpopo River, 12
Literacy campaigns, 46
Literature, 47, 48, 49
Litunga. See Centralized kingship
Livestock, 85
Livingstone, 14, 20, 46, 52

Livingstone, David, 11
Livingstone Motor Assemblers (LMA), 118, 165
LMA. See Livingstone Motor Assemblers
LME. See London Metal Exchange
Lobengula (Ndebele paramount chief), 12
Lobito (Angola), 135
Lobola, 44
Local Government and Housing, Ministry of, 32, 71
Lochner treaty, 12
Locusts, 23
Lomé I (1975) and Lomé II (1979) conventions, 158
London Metal Exchange (LME), 78, 81, 92, 98, 152, 153, 154
Lourenço Marques. See Maputo
Lozi (language), 46
Lozi people, 8(fig.), 9–10, 14, 31
crafts, 49, 51(illus.)
in government, 71
Luangwa Industries, 118
Luangwa River, 8(fig.), 9
Valley, 9, 162, 164
Luanshya, 91
Luanshya mine, 18, 88, 118
Luapula Province, 37, 38, 73, 74, 83
Luapula River, 5
Luapula Valley, 9
Luba people, 7, 38
Lubumbashi (Zaire), 14
Lumpa Church, 61
Lunda Empire (18th century), 8(fig.), 9
Lunda/Luvale (language), 46
Lunda people, 7, 8(fig.), 9, 38, 56
Lungu people, 8(fig.), 9
Lusaka, 1, 49, 52, 136, 163
archdiocese, 60
International Airport, 90, 136
lingua franca, 46
population, 26
suburbs, 41–42, 52
Lusaka Brewery, 91
Lusaka Manifesto (1969), 137
Lusaka Province, 38
Luvale. See Luba people; Lunda people

Machel, Samora, 138, 145
Machine tool industry, 27
Mafeje, Archie, 70
Maize, 3, 21, 36, 41, 83, 113, 119, 120, 143
Makololo. See Kololo people
Malawi, 6, 9, 13, 84, 135(fig.), 136, 146, 168
president. See Banda, Hastings
and Zambia, 187(n1)
Malnutrition, 21
Managerial skills, 164
Mandrax, 130, 167
Manufacturing sector, 2, 77, 81–82, 83, 84, 85, 87, 89, 91, 92–93, 96, 103, 110, 114, 117, 118–119, 120, 124, 161, 162, 165
GDP share, 90, 113
Maputo (Mozambique), 134, 135(fig.), 140
Marijuana, 130

Marketing centers, 38
Market mamas, 59
Marriage, 44–45
Mashonaland (Zimbabwe), 13
Matabeleland (Zimbabwe), 12
Matero Reforms (1969), 66(table), 87
Matoka, Peter, 72
Matrilineal family, 44
Mbala, 22
Mbanje, 130
MCC (member of central committee). *See* United National Independence Party, central committee
Medical care. *See* Health care
MEMACO. *See* Metal Marketing Corporation of Zambia Services Ltd.
Members of Parliament (MPs), 73, 97(table), 104, 106, 107, 144
Mestizo merchants, 9, 10
Metal Fabricators of Zambia Ltd. (ZAMEFA), 147, 189(n39)
Metal Marketing Corporation of Zambia (MEMACO) Services Ltd., 152
Metal products, 82
Metal tools, 7, 82
Methodists, 59
Mfecane. *See* Southern Africa, civil wars
Middle Easterners, 40
Migrations, 6, 7–9, 10, 11, 43–44, 174–175(n1)
  and copper industry, 20
  forced, 20
Milingo (archbishop), 60
Military, 115, 127, 167–168
Millenarian sects, 60–61
Millet, 21, 83
Mindolo Open Pit, 154
MINEDECO. *See* Mining Development Corporation
Mineral prices, 95, 99–100(table). *See also* Cobalt, prices; Copper, prices
Miners' strike (1985), 97–98(table)
Mines, Ministry of, 152
Mineworkers' Union of Zambia (MUZ), 128, 129, 165, 167
Mining, 1, 2, 13, 16, 19–20, 33, 64, 77, 81, 84, 86–87, 96, 101, 103, 117–118, 120, 126, 158, 161–162, 164, 167
  early, 9
  licenses, 153
  mechanization, 91, 126
  wages, 27, 30
  work force, 20, 21, 23, 26, 111, 118
  See also Coal; Cobalt; Copper; Lead; Zinc; *under* South Africa
Mining Development Corporation (MINEDECO), 88, 89
Mining Mirror (Ndola), 46
Mining towns, 1, 53
Missionaries, 11, 15, 60
Mitsubishi (Japanese company), 158
Mitsui (Japanese company), 158
Miyanda, Godfrey, 127
MNCs. *See* Multinational corporations
Mobility, 34, 40

Mobutu Sese Seko, 138
Mogadishu Accord (1970), 137
Molteno, Robert, 69
Monarch (company), 118
Moore, Leopold, 24
Morocco, 151
Mozambique, 6, 133, 136, 139, 141, 145, 146, 150
  colonial, 11, 134, 137
  dam, 148
  independence (1975), 138
  ports, 134, 135(fig.)
  refugees in Zambia, 137
  and Zambia, 97–98(table), 110, 137, 140, 142, 168
MPLA. *See* Popular Movement for the Liberation of Angola
Mporokoso, Anderson, 127
MPs. *See* Members of Parliament
Mramba, Basil, 146
Mudenda, Elijah, 72
Mufulira mine, 18, 19, 91
Mufulira welfare society, 30
Mugabe, Robert, 142
Mulaisho, Dominic, 88
Mulemba, Humphrey, 154
Mulikita, Fwanyanga, 128
Multinational corporations (MNCs), 77, 82, 89, 91, 103, 152, 162
Multiparty system. *See* Political parties
Mulungushi Club, 150
Mulungushi I and II Reforms (1968, 1970), 66(table), 86, 89, 90, 93, 163
Mumba, Goodwin Voram, 127
Mundia, Nalumino, 71, 73, 74, 104
Musakanya, Valentine, 127, 128, 186(n71)
Music, 48, 49, 51–52, 62
Musonda, Kapelwa, 46
Mutendere township, 42
Mutondo, 35–37, 57
MUZ. *See* Mineworkers' Union of Zambia
Muzorewa, Abel, 141
Mwaanga, Vernon, 131, 149
Mwanakatwe, John, 72, 186(n71)
Mwanakatwe Report (1977), 97–98(table)
Mwanza, Jacob, 125
Mweru, Lake, 5, 8(fig.), 9
Mwinilunga Fruit Canning Factory, 91

NAMBOARD. *See* National Marketing Board
Namibia, 6, 11, 130, 133, 134, 135(fig.), 144, 145, 150
Natal (S. Africa), 9
National assembly, 75, 97–98(table), 106–107, 144, 161, 184(n10)
National Brewery, 162
National Building Society, 54
National Commercial Bank, 89
National Dance Troupe, 49
National development planning, 78, 84–85, 93, 113, 114
National dress competition, 46
National Educational Corporation of Zambia Ltd. (NECZAM), 48

INDEX

National Front for the Liberation of Angola (FNLA), 138
National identity, 47
Nationalist alliance, 4, 128
Nationalist movement, 24, 27-33, 63, 65, 93
Nationalist party (S. Africa), 24
Nationality groups, 39-40
Nationalizations, 64, 85-86, 87-89, 103
National Marketing Board (NAMBOARD), 89, 120
National Milling Company, 89
National Progress Party (NPP), 65
National Union for the Total Independence of Angola (UNITA), 138, 139, 168
National unity, 47
Native Reserves. *See* Reserves
Natural resources, 16, 19, 161, 164. *See also* Cobalt; Copper
NCCM. *See* Nchanga Consolidated Copper Mines Ltd.
NCECO. *See* North Charterland Exploration Company
Nchanga Consolidated Copper Mines Ltd. (NCCM), 86(table), 87, 88, 103, 111, 117
Nchanga mine, 17, 18(table)
NCZ. *See* Nitrogen Chemicals of Zambia Ltd.
Ndebele people, 8(fig.), 10, 12, 160
Ndola, 16, 30, 136
Ndola Copper Refinery, 118
NECZAM. *See* National Educational Corporation of Zambia Ltd.
Nepotism, 161
Netherlands, 157, 162
Neto, Agostinho, 138, 145
Newspapers, 46
New York Commodities Exchange, 153, 154
Ng'anga, 62
Ngoni people, 8(fig.), 9, 13, 14, 16, 25
Nigeria, 150
Nitrogen Chemicals of Zambia Ltd. (NCZ), 85, 91, 158
Nkana mine, 28
Nkana oxide concentrator, 118
Nkhoma, Francis, 186(n71)
Nkombwa Hill, 164
Nkomo, Joshua, 141, 142, 144, 150
Nkumbula, Harry, 29, 30, 31, 32, 71, 74, 97-98(table), 104, 114, 115, 144
Nonaligned Movement, 155
Nonalignment, 113, 159, 168
Nonviolence policy, 137
North Charterland Exploration Company (NCECO), 22
Northern Drug Company, 89
Northern Province, 22, 30, 31, 35, 37, 38, 61, 73, 74, 83, 157
Northern Rhodesia (Zambia), 12-14, 15
  capital. *See* Livingstone
  colonial rule, 15-24
  concession areas, 17, 18
  Federation period (1953-1963), 24-27, 30-32
  named (1911), 13
  white population, 15

Northern Rhodesia African Congress (1948), 29
Northern Rhodesia General Workers' Trade Union, 30
Northern Rhodesian African Mineworkers Union (NRAMWU), 28, 30, 31
Northmead, 42
North-South Dialogue (1975-1977), 149
North-West Province, 30, 38(table), 83, 139, 157
NPP. *See* National Progress Party
NRAMWU. *See* Northern Rhodesian African Mineworkers Union
Nsenga speakers, 8(fig.), 9
Nshima, 41
Nyamwezi people (Tanzania), 9
Nyanja (language), 46
Nyanja people, 38, 49
Nyasaland, 13, 20, 24, 25. *See also* Malawi
Nyerere, Julius, 77, 136, 145, 150, 151

OAU. *See* Organization of African Unity
Obasanjo, O., 150
Obote, Milton, 150
OECD. *See* Organization for Economic Cooperation and Development
Office of National Development Planning (ONDP), 69
Office of the President, 69, 76, 106
Oil, 161, 162
  pipeline, 78, 84, 87, 90, 136
  prices, 96
  refinery, 87, 90, 136
  supply, 135
Oligopoly, 19
ONDP. *See* Office of National Development Planning
One-party rule (1972), 1, 65, 66(table), 74-75, 76, 94, 95, 96, 97(table), 104-110, 161, 163. *See also* United National Independence party
"One Zambia, One Nation," 34
OPEC. *See* Organization of Petroleum Exporting Countries
Operation Food Production, 119
Oppenheimer, Ernest, 17
Oppenheimer family, 17
Orange Free State, 11
Organization for Economic Cooperation and Development (OECD), 156
Organization of African Unity (OAU), 149-150, 151
  Assembly of the Heads of States, 145
  Charter, 150
  Council of Ministers, 145
  Declaration of Support for a Government of National Unity in Angola, 138
Organization of Petroleum Exporting Countries (OPEC), 153, 156, 157
Overgrazing, 22
Oxen, 36

Pakistanis, 40
Paramount chiefs, 10, 12, 13, 25

Paramountcy of native interests, 15, 24, 25
Parastatal sector, 85, 86, 88, 89, 91–92, 97–98(table), 103, 107, 114, 118, 125, 127, 144, 147, 162, 166
  defined, 182(n57)
Paris Club, 97–98(table), 122, 124, 126
Parliament, 106, 184(n10). *See also* Members of Parliament
Participatory democracy, 75
"Partnership between the races," 25
Passfield, Lord, 24
Patrilineal family, 44
Patriotic Front (ZANU/ZAPU alliance), 141, 142
Patronage, 76, 86, 110, 121, 161
Peasants, 4, 23, 29, 71, 83, 93
Pensions, 121, 129
Peri-urban, 34, 54, 177(n1)
Peru, 152
Petauke, 137
Petite bourgeoisie, 29, 31, 40, 41, 42–43, 54, 64, 89, 93, 115, 177(n54)
Phosphates, 164
Pleuropneumonia, 14
PM. *See* Prime minister
Polisario, 151
Political opposition, 2, 96, 97(table), 104, 110, 126, 127–130, 160
Political organization (precolonial), 9, 10–11
Political parties, 1, 2, 28, 29, 31–33, 64, 65, 66(table), 71, 73–75. *See also* One-party rule; *specific parties*
Political satire, 46
Politics, 4, 24, 64, 96, 104–110, 115
  incipient class, 71–73
  and licenses, 59
  patron/client, 70
Popular Movement for the Liberation of Angola (MPLA), 138, 139, 155
Population, 7, 39(table), 40, 161
  density, 22
  and disease, 23
  provincial distribution, 38(table)
  rate, 40, 63
  white, 15, 20
Populist programs, 64, 76–77, 162
Ports, 112, 134, 135, 143
Portugal, 134, 137–138
Portuguese, 5, 9, 10, 11, 13
Posts and Information, Ministry of, 72
Pottery, 7, 49, 50(illus.)
PRC. *See* China, People's Republic of
Preferential Trade Agreement (PTA) (1970s), 3, 147, 148, 149, 159
  Rule 21(a), 148
President. *See* Kaunda, Kenneth David
Presidentialism, 65, 75–77, 110, 161
Press, freedom of the, 77
Price controls, 123
Prime minister (PM), 106
Private sector, 81, 84, 90, 93, 110, 115, 127
Privatization, 162
Protestantism, 59
Provincial cooperative unions, 120

PTA. *See* Preferential Trade Agreement
Public works, 82
Publishing, 48

Race, 34. *See also* Nationality groups; Racialism
Racialism, 150, 151
Radio, 51
Radio Zambia, 46
Railroads, 14, 20, 23, 78, 82, 84, 97–98(table), 112, 134, 135, 136–137, 138, 139, 140, 146
  provinces, 38
  strike (1980), 97–98(table)
  workshop, 90
Railway Commission, 115
RCM. *See* Roan Consolidated Mines Ltd.
Recessions (1954, 1957), 26
Referendum (1969), 74
Refined Oil Products (ROP), 89, 119, 162
Refugees, 137, 144, 150
Reggae, 51
Regional diversity, 39
Religion, 59–61
Relly, Gavin, 145
Reserve Minerals Corporation, 162
Reserves, 22
Reshuffling, 75, 160. *See also under* Civil service
Rhoanglo. *See* Rhodesian Anglo American Corporation Ltd.
Rhodes, Cecil John, 12, 13, 14, 16
Rhodesia, 12–13, 66(table), 75, 78, 133, 135(fig.)
  and South Africa, 142
  and Zambia, 84, 97(table), 134, 135, 136, 137, 139, 140, 141–142, 187(n1)
  See also Southern Rhodesia; Zimbabwe
Rhodesian Anglo American Corporation Ltd. (Rhoanglo), 17, 19
Rhodesian Front, 134
Rhodesian Selection Trust (RST), 18–19
Rhodesia Railway, 135, 139, 140, 142
Rhokana mine, 17, 18(table)
Rice, 36
Richards, Audrey, 21
Rinderpest, 23
Riots, 125, 129
Rivers, 5, 8(fig.)
Roads, 1, 23, 35, 53, 84, 120, 135(fig.), 136, 140, 146, 163
Roan Antelope mine, 18
Roan Consolidated Mines Ltd. (RCM), 86(table), 87, 88, 103, 111, 117
Roan Selection Trust (RST), 19, 86, 87, 103, 152
Roberto, Holden, 138
Roberts, Andrew D., 26
Rock music, 51
Romania, 156
Rondavels, 49, 50
ROP. *See* Refined Oil Products
Rothman-BAT. *See* Central Cigarette Manufacturers

INDEX

RST. *See* Rhodesian Selection Trust; Roan Selection Trust
Rudd, Charles, 12
Ruling class, 3
Rural areas, 1, 30, 35–37, 63, 66
  age and sex distribution, 37
  authority structure, 37
  and colonial rule, 15, 20, 23, 35
  crafts, 49
  health care, 67–68
  as homogeneous, 34
  housing, 34, 36, 49, 50
  income, 78
  migration from, 20, 21, 23, 35, 43–44, 55, 56, 82
  music, 51–52
  population, 34
  underdevelopment, 22, 23–24, 93, 94
  See also Women, rural
Rural Reconstruction program (1975), 97–98(table)
Rural-urban migration, 22, 35, 37, 55

SACTU. *See* South African Congress of Trade Unions
SADCC. *See* Southern African Development Coordination Conference
Salariat, 31, 93
Salima (Malawi), 136
Salisbury (S. Rhodesia), 25, 27. *See also* Harare
Salt, 9, 13
Sampa, Chitalu, 129
Sanitation, 54, 163
Sardanis, Andrew, 85, 87, 88
Saudi Arabia, 9, 162
Savimbi, Jonas, 138
Scandinavian aid, 158
Scott, Ian, 74, 116
SDR. *See* Special Drawing Rights
Seabed hearings, 149
Sebitwane (Kololo king), 10
Second National Development Plan (SNDP) (1972–1977), 93, 103, 104, 113
Security forces, 106, 163
Seidman, Ann, 82, 91, 92, 113
Selection Trust, 17, 18
Self-determination, 133, 139, 149, 151
Self-reliance, 146, 147, 160, 164
  collective, 148
Settlement, 7–9. *See also* White settlers
Settlement schemes, 85
Seventh-Day Adventists, 60
SG. *See* United National Independence Party, secretary-general
Shaba Province (Zaire), 6, 12, 13, 14, 23, 111
  and N. Rhodesian labor, 21
Shamwana, Edward, 127, 161, 186(n71)
Sharpe treaty, 12
Shebeens, 42
Shona people, 160
Shiwa Ng'andu (N. Rhodesian estate), 24
Sipalo, Munu, 31, 32, 71, 75
Site-and-service schemes, 54, 55

Sithole, Ndabaningi, 141
Siwale, Donald, 29
Skilled manpower, 92, 112, 164
Skinner, James, 72
Slash-and-burn. *See* Agriculture, *chitemene*
Slave trade, 9, 11, 13
  ended (1912), 14
Slinn, Peter, 13
Slums, 42, 54
Smallpox, 23
Smelting, 9
Smith, Ian, 84, 134, 135, 137, 140, 141, 142, 144, 150
Smith, W., 156, 157
Smuggling, 162
SNDP. *See* Second National Development Plan
Social dislocation, 20, 21–23, 34, 55
Socialism, 1, 2, 77, 78, 87, 90, 95, 107, 126, 127, 164. *See also* Fabian socialism
Socialist bloc, 137, 157
Social services, 27, 77, 96, 113, 121, 126, 161, 162–163, 164. *See also* Welfare services
Social status, 7, 49, 52
Social system, 29, 31
Sorghum, 83
Sotho (language), 10
South Africa, 15, 51, 146, 147, 150
  defense forces, 130
  economy, 23
  mining, 12
  19th century, 9, 10, 11, 12
  and Zambia, 3, 17, 82, 97–98(table), 133–134, 139, 143–145, 149, 157, 159, 168, 187(n1)
  See also Nationalist party; *under* Angola; Rhodesia; United States
South African Congress of Trade Unions (SACTU), 144
South African Development Bank, 146
Southern Africa, 3, 7
  civil wars, 9, 11
  See also Frontline States; Wars of liberation
Southern African Development Coordination Conference (SADCC), 3, 133, 139, 146–147, 148, 149, 159
  II (1980), 146
Southern Province, 22, 29, 38, 74
Southern Rhodesia, 13, 14, 15, 27, 134
  capital. *See* Salisbury
  and Northern Rhodesia, 21, 33, 78, 82. *See also* Zimbabwe, and Zambia
  plebecite (1922), 15
  self-rule (1923), 24
  taxes, 26
  See also Northern Rhodesia, Federation period; Rhodesia; Zimbabwe
South-West Africa. *See* Namibia
South West African People's Organization (SWAPO), 144, 145, 168
Soviet Union, 153
  and Zambia, 155, 159, 168
  See also under Angola
Spanish Sahara, 151

"Speaking in tongues," 59
Special Drawing Rights (SDR), 122
Spirit possession, 59
Sports, 179(n19)
Squatments. *See* Squatter compounds
Squatter compounds, 53–55
Sri Lankans, 40
Stabilization policies, 57, 122, 123, 126
Standard Chartered (bank), 86(table), 88
Stanley, Herbert, 16
State capitalism, 90
State House, 76, 106
State-owned companies, 2, 77, 82, 83, 84, 85, 110, 115, 127, 161, 165. *See also* Parastatal sector
State Participation, Ministry of, 76, 87
Stone Age, 6
Stratification. *See* Class
Street lights, 42
Strikes, 97–98(table), 123, 129
  ban, 93
Student opposition, 129–130, 139
Subcontracting, 90
Subsidies, 113, 120, 121, 126, 163
Sugar, 119, 158
Sulphide ores, 17
Sunday Times of Zambia (Lusaka), 46, 51
Sunflowers, 119
Sunka mulamu, 42
Supreme Action Council (1952), 30
Supreme Court, 107, 115, 161
Swahili people, 5, 8(fig.), 9
  language, *See* Kiswahili
Swamps, 35, 36
SWAPO. *See* South West African People's Organization
Swaziland, 143, 146
Sweden, 157
Syncretism, 34, 44, 59, 61
Szefdel, Morris, 94

Tabwa people, 8(fig.), 9
Tanganyika, 11, 12, 21. *See also* Tanzania
Tanganyika, Lake, 5
Tanganyika Concessions Ltd. (TANKS), 14
TANKS. *See* Tanganyika Concessions Ltd.
Tanzania, 9, 11, 74, 77, 84, 135(fig.), 137, 146, 150
  and PRC, 136
  and PTA, 148
  and Zambia, 136, 142
Tanzania-Zambia Railroad (1975), 97–98(table), 112, 136–137, 140, 156
Tanzania-Zambia Railway Authority (TAZARA), 112, 135(fig.), 136, 140, 156
Tarry, E. W. (company), 116
Taverns, 42
Taxes, 19, 25, 26–27, 78, 81, 101, 113, 121, 153, 161
  income, 24
  laws, 86
Tazama. *See* Oil, pipeline
TAZARA. *See* Tanzania-Zambia Railway Authority

Technical and trades schools, 67
Technical assistance projects, 85
Technical cooperation schemes, 158
Technocrats, 83, 94, 104, 106, 115, 126, 128, 154, 163, 168
Technology, 78, 92, 96, 112, 114, 147, 158
  capital-intensive, 91, 92, 126
Television, 41, 43
Terms of trade, 95, 96, 98, 101, 110, 114, 117, 154, 161
Textile mill, 84, 91
Theater, 49, 51
Third National Development Plan (TNDP) (1980–1983), 114, 121
Third World, 3, 122. *See also under* Foreign policy
Thomas treaty, 12
Times of Zambia (Lusaka), 46, 105(table), 116
Tire factory, 84, 91
Tito, Josip Broz, 155
TNDP. *See* Third National Development Plan
Tonga (language), 46
"Tonga Diaspora," 7
Tonga people, 7, 8(fig.), 11, 14, 16, 29, 38, 71
Torco Plant, 118
Tordoff, William, 69, 74, 77, 107
Tourism, 120
"Towards Complete Independence" (Kaunda), 87
Trades Union Congress (TUC), 28
Trade unions, 28–29, 30, 83, 93, 123, 124, 126, 128–129, 163
Traditional medicine, 59, 62
Tranches, 122, 123
Transport, 52–53, 103, 112, 124
  links, 3, 134, 135, 136, 137, 139, 140, 142
  public, 35, 52, 53, 125
  See also Railroads; Roads
Transvaal, 11, 21
Treason Trial (1980), 97–98(table), 127–128, 168
Tribalism, 70–71, 97–98(table), 115, 160–161
Truck Assembly Plant, 91
Tsetse infestation, 3, 7, 22
TUC. *See* Trades Union Congress
Tumbuka speakers, 8(fig.), 9
Turner, H. A., 93
Turok, Ben, 89

UDI. *See* Unilateral Declaration of Independence
UFP. *See* United Federal Party
Uganda, 150, 164
Ujamaa, 77
UMHK. *See* Union Minière de Haut Katanga
UNCTAD. *See* United Nations Conference on Trade and Development
Unemployment, 42, 113, 153, 163, 164, 167
Unilateral Declaration of Independence (UDI) (Rhodesia) (1965), 66(table), 75, 78, 82, 132, 134, 135, 140
Union Minière de Haut Katanga (UMHK), 14
UNIP. *See* United National Independence Party

INDEX

UNITA. *See* National Union for the Total Liberation of Angola
United Federal Party (UFP), 32. *See also* National Progress Party
United National Independence Party (UNIP) (1960), 31, 32, 33, 37, 64, 65, 66(table), 70, 71, 74, 75, 78, 83, 97–98(table), 104, 110, 126, 160, 161, 163
  and ANC, 32
  central committee, 76, 97–98(table), 104, 106, 144, 161
  conflicts, 72–73, 93, 96, 114–115
  constitution (1973), 104
  decline, 114, 116, 127, 132, 161
  elections, 72
  general conference, 104
  headquarters. *See* Freedom House
  and health care, 68
  and housing, 53–54, 55
  ideology, 77
  and Lumpa Church, 61
  membership, 116, 164
  national council, 76, 87, 97–98(table), 104
  opposition to. *See* Political opposition
  secretary-general (SG), 106, 116
  See also One-party rule; *under* Kaunda, Kenneth David
United Nations, 135, 149, 161
United Nations Conference on Trade and Development (UNCTAD), 149
United Party (UP), 66(table), 74, 104
United Progressive Party (UPP), 66(table), 73, 74, 104
United States, 153
  and South Africa, 138
  and Zambia, 119, 151, 155, 157, 158–159, 167, 168
  See also under Angola
Universal suffrage, 65, 66(table)
University of Zambia (UNZA), 54, 67, 97–98(table), 126, 129, 130, 139
  Teaching Hospital, 158
UNZA. *See* University of Zambia
UP. *See* United Party
UPP. *See* United Progressive Party
Uranium, 161, 162
Urban areas, 1, 4, 22, 23, 34, 35, 62, 63, 162, 163, 164
  and colonial planning, 52
  as decentralized, 52
  divisions, 34, 38–40, 48, 52
  and federation, 25, 26, 27
  housing, 41, 42, 50, 52–55, 162, 179(n22)
  population, 26, 35, 38
  schools, 41, 42, 43, 55
  socioeconomic strata, 41–43
  unemployment, 26
  white, 20
  See also Family; Lusaka; Women, urban
Urbanization, 23, 26, 31, 34, 37–38, 43, 44, 48, 56, 62, 71

Value-added, 113
Vanadium, 19

Vice president, 71, 76
Victoria Falls, 5, 6, 8(fig.), 14, 90
Vorster, John, 144
Voter registration campaigns, 2

Wage labor, 34, 37, 113. *See also* Mining, wages; Mining, work force
Wages, 78, 83, 91, 97–98(table)
  ceiling, 123.
  freeze, 93
  See also under Mining
Walamba, Timothy, 129
Wankie Colliery (S. Rhodesia), 14, 134
Ward Development Committee, 37
Wars of liberation, 133, 134, 137, 138, 141, 142, 144, 149, 150, 160, 168
Watchtower Bible and Tract Society, 60
Water, 42, 43, 54, 163
Waterfalls, 5, 8(fig.)
Watershed Speech (1975) (Kaunda), 107
Wealth, distribution of, 77
Wealthy class, 40, 41–42, 43, 52, 63, 93, 163, 167, 169
Webb, Sidney. *See* Passfield, Lord
Welensky, Roy, 24, 25
Welfare services, 1, 2, 65, 66–69, 77, 113, 126, 162, 164
Welfare societies, 29, 30
West Africa, 51
Westbeech, George, 11
Western capital, 26. *See also* Foreign aid
Western Province, 38(table), 74, 84, 139, 157
Western trade, 1, 23, 147, 156, 157, 158, 159
West Germany, 157, 158, 167
Westminster system, 65, 69
Wheat, 119
White collar workers, 42. *See also* Civil service
White settlers, 14, 15, 16, 20, 23, 24, 25, 27
  political party. *See* United Federal Party
  reserved land, 22
  See also European nationality
Widows, 44–45
Wiese treaty, 12
Williams, Robert, 14
Wilson, Harold, 135
Wina, Arthur, 71
Wina, Sikota, 31, 71, 130, 187(n77)
Witchcraft, 62
Women, 44–45
  rural, 35, 37, 56–57
  status of, 56, 57
  urban, 41, 42, 43, 57, 59
  working, 43, 58–59
Women's League, 116
Wood, Adrian, 156, 157, 158
Working class, 41, 42, 43, 54, 59, 64, 93, 128–129, 167
World Bank (IBRD), 2, 55, 97–98(table), 118, 122, 124, 125, 126, 157, 158, 162, 166
  Debt Reporting Service, 113
World War II, 19

Xhosa speakers, 51

Yamba, Dauti, 29
Yao people, 8(fig.), 9, 13
Yugoslavia, 116, 155

Zaire, 6, 14, 135
  and Angola, 138
  and CIPEC, 152
  music, 51
  and Zambia, 37, 111, 187(n1)
Zairean nationals in Zambia, 127
Zambezi River, 5, 8(fig.), 10, 12, 14, 27, 84
Zambia, former name. *See* Northern Rhodesia
Zambia African National Congress (ZANC) (1958), 31
  banned (1959), 32
Zambia Clay Industries, 91
Zambia Congress of Trade Unions (ZCTU), 128–129
Zambia Consolidated Copper Mines Ltd. (ZCCM), 97–98(table), 117, 118, 126, 158
Zambia Daily Mail (Lusaka), 46
Zambia Electricity Supply Corporation (ZESCO), 89
Zambia Industrial and Commercial Association (ZINCOM), 131
Zambia Industrial and Mining Corporation (ZIMCO), 86(table), 89
Zambia Institute of Technology (ZIT), 129
Zambianization, 58, 89
Zambia Oxygen (company), 89
Zambia Railways Corruption Report (1978), 97–98(table)
Zambia Steel and Building Supplies (ZSBS), 118
Zambia Sugar Company (ZAMSUGAR), 89, 119, 125
ZAMEFA. *See* Metal Fabricators of Zambia Ltd.

ZamEnglish, 48
ZAMSUGAR. *See* Zambia Sugar Company
ZANC. *See* Zambia African National Congress
ZANLA. *See* Zimbabwe African National Liberation Army
ZANU. *See* Zimbabwe African National Union
ZAPU. *See* Zimbabwe African Peoples' Union
Zanzibar, 9
ZCCM. *See* Zambia Consolidated Copper Mines Ltd.
ZCTU. *See* Zambia Congress of Trade Unions
Zecco, 116
ZESCO. *See* Zambia Electricity Supply Corporation
Zimba, Newstead, 129
Zimbabwe, 6, 12, 13, 146, 150, 160
  capital. *See* Harare
  copper, 147
  nation formed (1980), 142
  and Zambia, 41, 110, 139, 141–143, 144, 148, 151, 170(n5)
Zimbabwe African National Liberation Army (ZANLA), 141
Zimbabwe African National Union (ZANU), 141, 142
Zimbabwe African Peoples' Union (ZAPU), 141, 142
Zimbabwe People's Revolutionary Army (ZIPRA), 141, 142
ZIMCO. *See* Zambia Industrial and Mining Corporation
Zinc, 16, 19, 81, 161
ZINCOM. *See* Zambia Industrial and Commercial Association
ZIPRA. *See* Zimbabwe People's Revolutionary Army
ZIT. *See* Zambia Institute of Technology
ZSBS. *See* Zambia Steel and Building Supplies
Zulu, Grey, 31, 71, 75, 168
Zulu people, 9